THE SOARING CRANE

Stories
of Asian
Lutherans in
North America

The Soaring Crane

Edmond Yee

Augsburg Fortress, Minneapolis

The Soaring Crane
Stories of Asian Lutherans in North America

This book includes extensive material quoted from other sources. Punctuation, spelling, capitalization, and the like from the original works have been occasionally altered to provide greater clarity and maintain consistency with Augsburg Fortress style.

Cover illustration, cover and book design by Ann Rezny.

ISBN 0-8066-4274-2

Manufactured in the U.S.A.

For Renjun and Xiaojun,
my grandchildren

CONTENTS

TABLE OF ABBREVIATIONS

AAPI–ELCA	Association of Asian and Pacific Islanders–Evangelical Lutheran Church in America
ACLC	Asian Church Leadership Conference
ACTEA	Advisory Committee for Theological Education in Asia
AELC	Association of Evangelical Lutheran Churches
AIMNA	Asian Indian Ministries of North America
ALC	American Lutheran Church
ALIC	Asian Lutheran International Conference
ARCC	Asia Regional Coordinating Committee
BAM	Board of American Missions
BFM	Board of Foreign Missions
BHM	Board of Home Missions
BMS	Board for Mission Services
BS	Biblical Seminary
BSM	Board of Social Missions
CAME	Center for Asian-American Evangelism
CAN	Church of All Nations
CCMGI	Consulting Committee on Minority Group Interests
CCRR	Coordinating Committee on Race Relations
CMC	Chinese Ministry Conference
CMM	Commission for Multicultural Ministries
CMTF	Chinese Ministry Task Force
CNHD	California-Nevada-Hawaii District
CNLC	Commission for a New Lutheran Church
CPE	Clinical Pastoral Education
CS	Concordia Seminary
CTS	Concordia Theological Seminary
CW	Commission for Women
DCE	Director of Christian Education
DCM	Division for Congregational Ministries
DCS	Division for Church in Society
DGM	Division for Global Mission
DM	Division for Ministry
DMD	Department for Mission and Development
DMNA	Division for Mission in North America
DO	Division for Outreach
DPL	Division for Professional Leadership
DPS	Division for Parish Services
DSMA	Division for Service and Mission in America
DWME	Division for World Mission and Ecumenism
DWMIC	Division for World Mission and Interchurch Cooperation
ELCA	Evangelical Lutheran Church in America
ELCHK	Evangelical Lutheran Church of Hong Kong
GEM	Growth in Excellence in Ministry
GTU	Graduate Theological Union
HMC	Home Missions Committee
JACEP	Japan-America Cooperative Evangelism Program

JELC	Japan Evangelical Lutheran Church
JMA	Japanese Ministry Association
KLC	Korean Lutheran Church
KMC	Korean Ministry Conference
LCA	Lutheran Church in America
LCHKS	Lutheran Church—Hong Kong Synod
LCMS	Lutheran Church-Missouri Synod
LCP	Lutheran Church in the Philippines
LCUSA	Lutheran Council in the United States of America
LIRS	Lutheran Immigration and Refugee Service
LOGA	Lutheran Office of Governmental Affairs
LS	Luther Seminary
LSTC	Lutheran School of Theology at Chicago
LTSHK	Lutheran Theological Seminary of Hong Kong
LWF	Lutheran World Federation
LWML	Lutheran Women Missionary League
MBN	Mission Blueprint for the Nineties
NAME	North American Mission Enablers
NCCC	National Council of Churches of Christ
PLTS	Pacific Lutheran Theological Seminary
TECC	Theological Education Coordinating Committee
TLC	Taiwan Lutheran Church
UELC	United Evangelical Lutheran Church
ULCA	United Lutheran Church in America
WCC	World Council of Churches
WMC	Western Mission Cluster
WRL	Western Regional Lutheranism

PREFACE

The Soaring Crane shares stories about experiences of Asian Christians' rich religious and cultural journey over the past 60-plus years in the life of Lutheran churches in North America. They are gifts from God speaking to us, allowing us to hear, see, grow, and be transformed. These stories, our stories, reflect God's gift of Asian cultural diversity. They narrate God's unfailing faithfulness to strangers from different shores—the Asian people—and their walk of faith even in the midst of, at times, a hostile and reluctant church.

This book tells the stories of men and women who dared to believe in God. They believed God instead of the limiting social and cultural dictates imposed on them over the generations. They believed God's intention for their lives and ministry, even when others tried to keep them silent and secluded. On the way, all of God's people joined hands with the Asian community. Slowly but steadily, a strong Asian ministry is emerging. Insights from this book surely will help to shape the future of Asian Lutheran Christian witness in North America.

For Asian Lutherans, this book will help us reflect upon our history, get in touch with our traditions and community, and consider the mission before us today. Others who read these pages will learn of the sacrifices and gifts of Asians to the life and development of Lutheranism in North America. This book is a citadel of triumphant hope for Asian Lutheran Christians.

Recognizing the need to document our rich history as Asian Lutherans in the United States, leaders from the Asian community in the Evangelical Lutheran Church in America asked Edmond Yee, a veteran church leader in the Asian community to undertake this task. The request was fitting. Yee is a living human document of the Asian Lutheran story in the United States. Since the 1970s, he has been a prophetic voice, and many times a lonely voice crying in the wilderness of the American religious landscape, calling the church to pay attention to the browning of America.

A distinguished scholar, Yee has published writings in both Chinese and English. They include both arcane scholarly treatises and down-to-earth articles on ministry in the Asian American community. Since the 1970s, Yee also has played an active role in Lutheran consultations, committees, and task forces related to ethnic ministries, as well as a teaching scholar in the Evangelical Lutheran Church in America. Dr. Yee has journeyed with many of us on this long road as a friend, a brother, a mentor, a pastor, and a listener. Thus, what we read in *The Soaring Crane* is primarily an eyewitness account of what he has seen and heard.

Fred Rajan, Executive Director
Commission for Multicultural Ministries
Evangelical Lutheran Church in America

ACKNOWLEDGMENTS

This book would not and could not have been written without the help of many individuals named and unnamed. I am deeply indebted to Lily Wu, who read and edited the entire manuscript and who offered valuable suggestions on improving the text as well as support as a friend. I was humbled by William E. Wong and Frederick E. N. Rajan's request to write this book and wish to thank them both for having so much confidence in me. I am grateful to Fred Rajan, who provided me with a research grant as well as constantly gave me encouragement. To James Y. K. Moy, who indefatigably guided me in the right direction at the beginning of this project and supplied me with numerous stories of True Light Lutheran Church, I wish to say thanks. I am thankful for Paul T. Nakamura, who proofread the entire manuscript and offered valuable suggestions, as well as supplied me with endless information. I wish to thank the following individuals who generously gave me their time and supplied me with their files and other materials: Terrence Chan, David Chao, David Chen, Daniel Chu, Hwan Young Hong, Amy Hau-Mui, Ted Iverson, Daniel Lee, Simon Lee, Fern Lee Hagedorn, Stacy Kitahata, Pongsak Limthongviratn, Charles Matsumoto, Donald R. Moorman, Mabel Moy, Paul Nagano, Donald N. Rudrud, Robert J. Scudieri, S. Samuel Ujiie, Bill Wong, Wilson Wu, and Wonnor Yee.

I am grateful to Claire Buettner of the Library Resource Center, Carol Schmalenberger of the Region II Archives, Robert Shrechkrise of the Concordia Historical Institute, and Elisabeth Whitman and her staff of the Archives of the Evangelical Lutheran Church in America, who spent many of their precious hours pulling books off the shelves and unearthing information buried deep down in those dusty filing boxes for me.

I am indebted to Andrea S. L. Schieber, Augsburg Fortress editor, for her assistance in shaping the final draft of this volume. The sharpness of her editorial surgical knife is deeply appreciated.

Rhonda Goldman and Eva Ching-Nagashima tirelessly copied numerous pages from the files of the Commission for Multicultural Ministries for me. Jane Phillips graciously assisted me in various ways throughout the project. I owe them a deep gratitude.

To Guanming, Guanguang, and Naning, who often rescued me from being tortured by my computer, I wish to say you are a wonderful bunch. A special thanks to Guanming who helped me with indexing the original manuscript and other technical matters as well.

   To Guifang, thank you for your understanding and patience during the
many hours I spent typing on the computer late into the night, and to
Winchie, that little boy who keeps me human, a "humongous" hug and a gentle poke on the tummy.

   Finally, even though there were so many individuals who contributed
to this project, I alone shall assume full responsibility for any shortcoming
therein.

INTRODUCTION

CASTING A BRICK

"YOU KNOW," SAID BILL WONG ON THE OTHER END OF THE TELEPHONE LINE, "Paul Nakamura, James Moy, and you are getting old...." He paused. Old—me? I asked myself."Don't you think," he continued,"you should write a history of the Asian Lutherans in North America before the three of you..." Another pause. Before the three of us...what? I wondered. Then he told me that he and Fred Rajan had discussed the matter of a history recently and concluded that I should be the person to write it. On behalf of the community, they were requesting me to do so before the disappearance of the collective memory.

That telephone call took place in the spring of 1998. That summer I was busy writing a paper to be presented at an international conference and revising two other articles for publication, so did not start on this story gathering. Moreover, I thought such a history, insignificant and brief, would not be a very interesting subject to work on or to record. Such reasoning led to further procrastination on commencing research.

The fall of 1998 while on sabbatical, I began my research and discovered next to nothing published or systematically written on the subject. Norman J. Threinen in his book, *Like a Leaven: A History of the Alberta-British Columbia District of the Lutheran Church-Canada*, briefly mentions a Chinese ministry at Prince of Peace Lutheran Church, a white congregation in Vancouver, British Columbia. In 1986 *The Lutheran* published a series of five articles I wrote about Asian Americans and Asian Lutherans in America. Margrethe S. C. Kleiber, a student at Pacific Lutheran Theological Seminary, wrote an honors thesis on the subject of Asian ministries. The Commission for Multicultural Ministries (CMM) of the Evangelical Lutheran Church in America (ELCA) published a booklet based on the Kleiber thesis.

Suddenly I realized I could not rely much on published materials to help me to complete this project. I decided I had to do two things. First, I had to search for archival documents, papers, correspondences, minutes, and whatever there was on the subject. Second, I needed to get the word out that I would be writing this history and was in need of help from the Asian community. In the archives I discovered some valuable treasures. Those who responded from the community were enthusiastic.

As I began to examine the data and listen to the stories, I became excited about the possibility of recording such a history—a story inextricably intertwined with the histories of Western colonialism, European-American missionary movements, emigration, European-American foreign policies, apostasy and conversion, ecclesiastical policies, natural disasters, war and peace, the search for knowledge and wealth, and more. Thus, the events recorded in this book are framed within this larger historical context. Accordingly, the point of departure of this book is historical and not theological.

In the Confucian historiographical tradition the task of the historian is to record, to transmit, but not to create. The historian, however, is not without authority to render moral judgments. The subjects are "cast as either models for emulation or as unfortunate examples to be avoided."[1] In this volume, though, it is my intention if at all possible to avoid making judgments. Events and stories are simply presented as they unfolded in times past, and as I encountered or experienced them, so that the reader can be the judge.

Yet a historian is not without the freedom to select which tale to tell or to omit. Selectivity, a prerogative of any writer, involves evaluation and interpretation. Here then even the most objective Confucian historian would have a hard time escaping from being implicated on subjectivity in some ways—though the historian herself or himself may not even be aware of being consciously or unconsciously subjective. And here, too, the historian must accept the responsibility for inclusion and omission. And here I, too, must be held responsible for my own subjectivity in this volume; for I likewise have been a player, though a transitional one, in the recent Asian Lutheran history in North America. My own role in this story is recorded mainly in chapter 8, "A Giant Step."

The main title of this book emerged when I realized the resilient character that Asians in North America have imprinted on its history. They are a people who often turn adversity into opportunity and suffering into a lesson for self-cultivation. Thus, like a soaring crane—supple, graceful, beautiful—they, too, either rise again or surge even higher in a determined, strong, and courageous way. The word *stories* in the subtitle is interchangeable with the word *history* or *herstory* in this volume.

This book is organized in chronological order. The period covered primarily spans from the 1800s to the year 2000 CE, though chapter 1 includes some history from antiquity. In some ways, this book also bridges both shores of the Pacific Ocean and beyond. Setting a context for subsequent discussions, it begins with an introduction to Asia's geography, cultures, spiritual heritages, Asian immigration to the United States and Canada, the subsequent formation of the Asian community in North America, and the fall of Saigon. The book concludes with the historian's backward glance into the past and forward gaze into the future. In between it records the history of Lutheran ministries with Asians beginning in 1936 and provides some snapshots of Asian leaders who have made significant contributions to the church and to society.

This book covers the history of Lutheran denominations that have had and continue to have ministries with Asians in North America only. However, in the course of doing research for this book, I contacted all Lutheran denominations in North America for information. However, my own involvement in the ELCA and its predecessor bodies gives me greater familiarity with the history of these churches as compared to the more recent history of the Lutheran Church—Missouri Synod.

Titles and positions associated with the individuals are given in the first occurrence of the person's name, except in the acknowledgements and in a few cases, where they might not be warranted. Most of the Asians living in America and Canada, whether they were born in North America or overseas, have a given name in English and one in the language of their origin. In this book, for the sake of facilitating easier reading, only the person's English given name is used.

All romanized Asian personal and place names and titles are incorporated in this book as they appear in their existing written forms. This means for personal and place names in the Chinese language both the Wade-Giles and the *pinyin* systems plus some local variations are used. In the case that no previous written form exists, they are romanized in the standard form(s) accepted by the academic community.

This book can be read as an interpretive history interlaced with human stories. But *let the reader beware!* This is an incomplete history, and the stories are not always fully told for three reasons. First, not every congregation's history is recorded. My primary focus is on the initial ministries in each Asian ethnic community within each Lutheran denomination; namely, the United Evangelical Lutheran Church, the United Lutheran Church in America, the Augustana Lutheran Church, the American Lutheran Church, the Lutheran Church in America, the Association of Evangelical Lutheran Churches, The Lutheran Church—Missouri Synod, and the Evangelical Lutheran Church in America. Second, incompleteness is due to the lack of available records and some interview subjects' desire for confidentiality in certain matters, even though they were very open during the interviews and in making records available to me. The subjects' imposition was predicated on fear, justified or otherwise, of reprisal from church officials, and in one case, the subject's reluctance was due to personal reasons. Third, on occasions I was compelled to exercise judgment by withholding certain sensitive data from the reader at this time.

This book can also be read as a tribute to Asian Lutherans in North America who have made significant contributions to the Lutheran churches and society. But here again, there are missing worthies whose biographies are not recorded in this book. These individuals' humility apparently might have prevented them from responding to my request for an interview and materials.

On yet another level, this book can be read as my modest attempt to capture the history of Asians' active participation in the Lutheran churches and how these denominations, which preach love and justice, may not have been fair to them. In this respect, these Lutheran denominations and society mirror each other in promoting an unhealthy racial attitude towards Asians in North America, in spite of Asians' undeniable contributions to both. In pointing out the racism of the church, it is not my intention to create ill feelings and to seek redress for the past injustice, but to use it as background information to promote humaneness and rightness so that we *all* may live in the garden of harmony and peace and be ferried to "the other shore" in the future.

My attempt to write this history amounts to nothing more than "casting a brick to attract jade." It is my hope that someone else will eventually undertake to produce a history of Asian Lutheran congregations and congregational life in North America, to examine closely in what way Asian cultures and Western Lutheran theology may have enhanced or limited the growth of Asian congregations, and to explore the role that these congregations play in the life of Asians in North America.

1

THE OTHER SHORE

The precise location of "the other shore," besides its religious reference, is a matter of perspective. For Asians in North America, it could mean Asia—the land of our ancestors. For our ancestors, emigrants in the nineteenth and early twentieth centuries, the other shore may refer as well to North America. In this chapter the phrase is used as a symbol, referring not only to the land of Asia and its cultures but also to Asia's interaction with the outside world, to Asian immigration to the shores of North America, and to the formation of the Asian community therein.

My aim is to set a context for the unfolding stories of Asian Lutherans in North America. The description that follows is brief. The overview of geography and population reflects the postcolonial, post-World War II period only. The discussion on Asian cultures is mainly focused on where the indigenous religions predominate.

LAND OF OUR ANCESTORS

Asia is the largest and most populous continent in the world (see Figure 1), and the home of some of the world's largest urban centers. The term *Asia* is used sometimes to refer to the massive area including Asia Minor in the former Soviet Union, the Middle East, South Asia, East Asia, and Southeast Asia. In this volume it is used to refer to South Asia (or the Indian subcontinent, as it is sometimes called), Southeast Asia, and East Asia. Most of this area was either under colonial control or, like China proper, under the thrall of colonial power and influence from about the mid-nineteenth century, if not before, until after World War II. Japan, which precipitated that war in this part of the world in 1931 with the invasion of Manchuria and set out to colonize Asia for itself, fought Western colonialism and Asian forces within the context of the continent. One of the inadvertent results of the Japanese action was the liberation of these nations from both Western and Japanese colonial powers after the war.

South Asia

Despite the varying size of the states and a wide range of climatic difference, South Asia is a well-defined geopolitical region. It is hemmed in by the world's highest mountain ranges—the Himalayas—on the north; the state of Myanmar and the Bay of Bengal on the east; the Indian Ocean on the south; Afghanistan on the northwest; and the Arabian Sea on the west. This region is composed of eight states—Nepal, Bhutan, Bangladesh, Sri Lanka, Maldives, Pakistan, Afghanistan, and India—with India being the dominant nation, culturally, economically, and politically. This region, with a high population density (see Figure 2), is also one of the poorest areas in the world today.

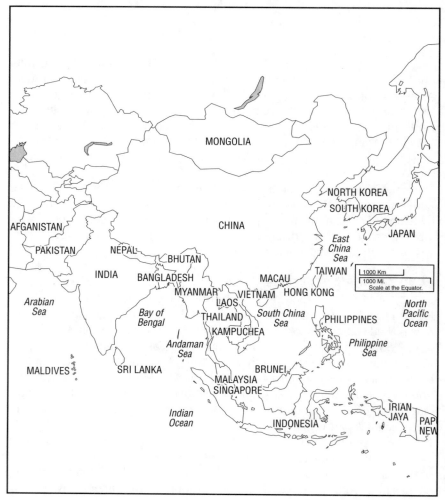

Figure 1; the States of Asia

As early as the second century of the common era, commercial intercourse occurred between part of this region, mainly India and Afghanistan, and the eastern Roman Empire. However, contact with the Mediterranean nations did not begin until the sixteenth century, with the arrival of the Portuguese and the Dutch. By about the mid-nineteenth century most of this area had come under British control or strong influence until the early years after World War II.

Religious practice in this region is predominantly Hindu and Islam. Christianity's first appearance in South Asia occurred in the fourth century, when Syriac Christian traders brought their faith with them to southern India. The Syriac trading communities existed peacefully within the context of a Hindu society as an autonomous group. Roman Catholicism's arrival in South Asia can be traced back to 1319, "marked by the visit of Franciscan missionaries." [1] Continuous Roman Catholic presence, however, did not begin until 1505 with the arrival of a Portuguese mission. Protestant Christianity entered this region in 1706 under Lutheran auspices. Today one out of every four Lutherans in Asia lives in this region (see Figure 3).

Afghanistan	25,838,797
Bangladesh	129,194,224
Bhutan	2,005,222
India	1,014,003,817
Maldives	301,475
Nepal*	25,284,463
Pakistan	141,553,775
Sri Lanka	19,238,575
TOTAL	**1,357,410,346**

* The figures for each country, except Nepal, are as of July 2000. The figure for Nepal is dated 2001.
(from CIA World Factbook, 2001.)

Figure 2; South Asia Population

Bangladesh	11,303
Hong Kong, China	41,785
India	1,621,065
Indonesia	3,794,393
Japan	32,512
Korea, Republic of South	3,125
Malaysia	84,764
Myanmar	1,525

Nepal
  Northern Evangelical
  Lutheran Church (see India)	

Philippines	27,000
Singapore	3,000
Sri Lanka	1,200
Taiwan	15,010
Thailand	2,114
TOTAL	**5,638,796**

Source: Lutheran World Information, Lutheran World Federation (2000)

Figure 3; Lutheran Population in Asia

Southeast Asia

Southeast Asia, composed of ten states— Thailand, Vietnam, Laos, Cambodia, Myanmar, Philippines, Indonesia, Malaysia, Singapore, and Sultanate of Brunei—is not a well-defined geopolitical region. Part of its land mass borders on China; the rest is blocked on its north, east, and south by water of the Pacific Ocean, and the Bay of Bengal and the Indian Ocean on its west.

Every nation other than Laos in this region is accessible by sea. The water that washes the shores of India and China is the same water that brought Hinduism, Buddhism, Confucianism, Daoism, and Islam to Southeast Asia. And because of its accessibility by the sea route, others soon came by way of this water as conquerors or as so-called defenders of freedom.

The Western encroachment on this region occurred with the arrival of the Portuguese, the Spanish, and the Dutch in the sixteenth century. The Philippines came under Spanish rule by the mid-sixteenth century, until 1898 when the United States defeated the Spanish and acquired this island state. Indonesia became a Dutch colony at roughly the same time as the Philippines became a Spanish colony. Singapore came under British control in 1819, followed by Malaysia. Indochina gradually came under French control in the nineteenth century. Thailand, however, was the only state that was not colonized in this region, but both French and British influences were felt within its borders. U.S. involvement in Indochina began before the end of World War II and culminated with the Vietnam War. April 30, 1975, marked the withdrawal of the United States from Vietnam.

Southeast Asia is a pluralistic region in terms of ethnicity, religions, and cultures. The Chinese, who command considerable economic power in this region, comprise the single largest ethnic group, ranging from three percent in Indonesia to 76 percent in Singapore. There are 25 languages with more than 250 dialects spoken in this region.

Religious practice in this region is predominantly Islam, Buddhist, shamanistic, and Roman Catholic. The first Lutheran mission was founded in 1861 in Indonesia, which has about three million Lutherans today, making Indonesia the most populous Lutheran nation in Asia.

East Asia

East Asia, composed of five nations—China, Mongolia, North Korea, South Korea, and Japan—is a well-defined geopolitical region. Siberia hems in the region on the north, with the rest of the region bordered by the Pacific Ocean on the east, the South China Sea and Southeast Asia on the south, and South Asia on the west.

East Asia has a wide climatic range, which can be divided into three zones. The north, with its short summer, is extremely cold and dry in the winter, making it unsuitable for many agricultural products. The central part is moderate in temperature, with little rainfall in the winter. The south has a rather short winter and for the most part is pleasant in temperature. It is lush and green, making it an ideal climate for producing a high yield of various agricultural products. With the exception of the extreme north and west, East Asia in the summer is hot and humid and has an abundance of rain.

China traditionally dominated this region culturally, politically, and economically. However, since the 1970s, Japan has become a major economic power here and in the world. Before the development of a modern transportation system, Korea served as a cultural, political, and commercial bridge between the continent and Japan. Though relatively poor today, Mongolia in the thirteenth century was a great power, subjugating China and Korea, and extending its military might "into the West, as far as Mesopotamia, Georgia, and Armenia in southwestern Asia, and into Hungary and Poland in Europe."[2]

This region's commercial intercourse with the West through the overland route, which begins in central China and extends to the former Roman Empire, occurred in the second century of the common era. It was through the same route that Nestorian Christianity, an Eastern branch of Christianity, entered into China in 635. In the fifteenth and sixteenth centuries mainly China and Japan felt the European expansion into this region, with the arrival of the Portuguese, the Dutch, and Roman Catholic missionaries.

The Portuguese in the mid-sixteenth century were the first Europeans to occupy Chinese territory, followed by the Dutch and the British. The major cultural clash between the East and the West during this period is best exemplified by the so-called Rite Controversy, which began in the seventeenth century and lasted for about 150 years, between the Roman Catholic church and the Chinese imperial court. The focus of the controversy was on the Chinese ancestral rite, to which Rome objected. Protestant Christianity entered East Asia in 1807, with the arrival of Robert Morrison in China. Religious practice in this region is predominantly Confucian, Daoist, and Buddhist, though shamanism and popular religion also flourish.

The civilizations of India and China are the two oldest continuous living traditions in the world today. These two civilizations exert tremendous influence on the continent and beyond. On the metaphysical level, they share a common moral universe: namely, the human, through her or his own efforts, can achieve transcendence. For Hinduism this means transcendence from suffering, anxiety, and fear into an existence beyond the cycle of birth and death. For Confucianism, this means to become fully human or to reach the ideal of sagehood. For Daoism, it is the attainment of the state of being a "true person," and for Buddhism (Zen in particular) the return to the "original mind."

On the level of popular religion, spirits and humans interact constantly. Spirits are perceived to have extra-human power. Practitioners often seek after the spirits' efficacy. And yet human beings are not powerless and helpless in the spiritual world. They often can and sometimes do employ other means, such as the service of a shaman, to control the spirits. A balance of power exists between the spirits and humanity.

On the whole, one of the salient characteristics of Asian religions is their attitude of tolerance and acceptance of other faiths. Thus, for Asians the ultimate religious truth is not to be sought through the dogmas of a given tradition but through one's experience of and with the divine in a mundane world of ordinary existence.

CROSSING THE PACIFIC

By the mid-nineteenth century, most Asian nations were either under colonial control or in the thrall of colonial powers, with Christian missionaries never too far ahead or behind. Yet colonial control was never easily won. Asia was indeed engulfed in resistance against colonialism and in coping with its impact.

These double efforts exhausted national treasuries and human resources. Nature, too, seemed to have wanted to take advantage of a weakened Asia. Floods and famines hit many parts of the continent. While Asian nations were in turmoil and their people endured suffering, white Americans under the doctrine of Manifest Destiny moved rapidly westward, pushing aside or exterminating on the way the indigenous people of North America whose land and resources they wanted. The discovery of gold at John Sutter's sawmill in Coloma, California, in 1848 attracted even greater migration to the West Coast. It created an urgency for constructing a railway and gave an impetus to economic development, the need for labor, and a dream for many of getting rich instantly. The dream was realized by a few while the opportunity for adventure remained boundless for the majority.

Asians, however, at that moment had not realized the significance of this discovery. In time gold became a symbol of sweat, tears, blood, and opportunity for Asians who emigrated and for those who continue to immigrate to this land. It likewise became what social scientists subsequently called the pull factor for Asian emigration, while the adverse conditions in Asia in the nineteenth century formed the push factor. Furthermore, the discovery of gold would record yet another shameful and violent chapter in the U.S. history of race relations.

The Chinese

Among Asian immigrants to the United States, the Chinese were the first to come as laborers, beginning in 1848. [3] At first they were welcomed as cheap laborers and looked at as a curiosity. As their numbers increased, politicians and labor movements began agitating against them, while the Christian community initiated ministry with them through teaching English as a second language and Bible studies. The Presbyterian denomination was the first to minister with the Chinese, followed by the Methodist and Congregational churches, and so forth. By the end of the nineteenth century, two Lutheran Sunday schools opened their doors to them. [4]

The life of these early Chinese immigrants was full of hardship, fears, loneliness, and suffering. They faced one obstacle after another, culminating with the Exclusion Act of 1882. This act, passed by Congress, excluded Chinese laborers from entering the United States. While the anti-Chinese movement was gaining momentum, the church, both Protestant and Roman Catholic, was divided on the issue. Some clergy took an anti-Chinese stance while others defended their presence.

After the transcontinental railroad was completed in the United States, some Chinese (soon other Asians as well) migrated to Canada where they helped build the Canadian transcontinental railroad. Their experiences in Canada reflected by and large their experiences in the United States.

With the Exclusion Act of 1882 prohibiting Chinese laborers from entering the country, a shortage ensued. The act was not lifted until 1943 when China and the United States were united in their war efforts against Japan. A quota then replaced the act, allowing 105 Chinese worldwide to enter into the United States each year.

The Japanese

The next group of Asians to come to the West—Hawaii and the continental United States—was the Japanese. [5] Official Japanese immigration began in 1868. By the end of 1880, 149 Japanese lived in the United States. In 1898 the United States annexed Hawaii. The annexation "enable[d] the 60,000 Japanese already in Hawaii to proceed to the United States without passports if they so desired." [6] The following year, 2,844 Japanese arrived in the mainland United States from Hawaii; 12,635 more came in 1900.

As the population increased, the Japanese faced the same fate as the Chinese before them. But their government, being strong at home, often lodged protests against the mistreatment of its people. This resulted in a series of "gentlemen's agreements" between Japanese and U.S. governments. But this strong government in Japan soon became a double-edged sword for the Japanese in North America.

In 1905 Japan defeated the Russians at sea. This Japanese victory somehow "stimulated anti-Japanese feeling in the United States." [7] The influential *San Francisco Chronicle*, politicians, and labor organizations agitated against them, prompting the United States to negotiate yet another gentleman's agreement with Japan in 1908 that limited Japanese immigration.

One of the consequences of this agreement was the phenomenon of "picture brides." These were marriages arranged through the exchange of pictures. If Japanese males returned to Japan to marry, they could not reenter the United States as laborers. With the arrival of picture brides, the U.S. Japanese community began to grow. Religion also had started to take root in the community almost 30 years earlier. Congregational, Methodist, and Presbyterian denominations started mission work among the Japanese in 1880. [8] The year 1899 marked the founding of the Buddhist Churches of America.

Japan attacked Pearl Harbor on December 7, 1941. On February 19, 1942, President Franklin D. Roosevelt signed Executive Order 9066, authorizing the internment of more than 110,000 people of Japanese ancestry. [9] The reasons given for the internment were "stern military necessity,…fear,…and war time hysteria." [10] But the ultimate reason was *racism*, as numerous American historians, in addition to Roger Daniels, have asserted. The Japanese-Canadians, though they were not interned, were moved to remote areas inland. As a result of the U.S. government's action, the Japanese-American community continues to be divided and polarized today over addressing the internment issue through redress.

The Koreans

Korea, "the land of morning calm," was in the thrall of colonial power toward the end of the nineteenth century. Japan and Russia were the strongest among nations contending for control. With the defeat of the Russians at sea in 1905, Japan finally consolidated its power and annexed Korea in 1910. From then on, until 1945, Korea did not exist as a nation. Life under Japanese rule was harsh.

Recognizing the hardship the Koreans faced at home, Rev. George Heber Jones, an American missionary, encouraged them to immigrate to the United States. Thus the first laborers arrived in Hawaii in 1900. [11] There was a sizable number of Christians among the early Korean immigrants, as evidenced by the first church service held on the island of Oahu in 1903. As their numbers increased, the immigrants experienced public resentment as early as 1906.

When the Koreans finally arrived in mainland America, they found the land already hostile to Asians. However, public resentment toward and agitation against them were less severe than what the Chinese and the Japanese had endured. The reasons were: (1) the Korean community was relatively small; (2) after annexation the Japanese government was able to limit Korean emigration; (3) with "anti-Oriental" laws well established by the time Koreans became noticeable to the public, the outcry against them became less frequent. Thus, the Korean community in the United States began to grow and flourish after the Korean War in 1952, due in part to the arrival of war brides and the change in U.S. immigration policy.

The Filipinos

The United States "acquired" the Philippine Islands as part of its territory in December 1898 after defeating Spain, but Filipinos were denied U.S. citizenship. However, as U.S. nationals they were allowed to serve in the U.S. Navy as well as to come to the United States. The first group to arrive consisted of about 100 young men who came to study under the *pensionado* program in 1903. [12] Three years later a group of 15 laborers arrived in Hawaii. The year 1906 marked the official beginning of Filipino presence in mainland America as immigrants. [13] The early immigrants settled mainly in Hawaii and along the West Coast, with a good number in the Seattle, Washington, area.

Like the Japanese and the Koreans, the Filipinos, too, arrived in a hostile land full of "anti-Oriental" sentiment. Hostilities against them involved politicians, labor movements, and white citizens. Hostilities grew as their numbers increased and as they crossed the racial line in marriage. In 1930, for example, the Filipinos were classified as members of the Mongolian race. The aim was to prevent Filipino men from marrying white women and to invalidate "more than 100 [interracial] marriages performed [in California] since 1921." [14]

During the years of the Great Depression in the United States, violence against Filipinos and other Asians became worse and worse. Even white persons who employed them came under violent attacks.

Meanwhile the matter of an independent Philippines was also under consideration in Congress, because the Philippines was not a profitable colony. An agreement was worked out. Thus, in March 1934 the Tydings-McDuffie Bill was signed by the president of the United States, giving the Philippines its independence within a period of ten years and prohibiting Filipino immigration all together. Following the signing of this bill more violence against Filipinos occurred.

In 1935 the first Filipino Repatriation Act was signed into law, permitting the U.S. government to provide transportation to Filipinos who wanted to go home but were unable to pay the passage. This act was extended in 1937, and the second act went into effect on July 27, 1939. Those who took advantage of this act were few in number.

Within two weeks of Japan's attack on Pearl Harbor on December 7, 1941, Filipinos were permitted to serve in the U.S. Army. In 1943 they were permitted to own land in California. Three years prior to the California action, they had won the case to own land in the state of Washington, however. And in 1946 Filipino ex-servicemen were permitted to become citizens. Up to this point the community remained small.

The Indians

Among Asian immigrants to the United States, early Asian Indians occupied a unique place in U.S. history. As they immigrated to the United States by way of British Columbia at the turn of the twentieth century, the Indians also entered a land already full of "anti-Oriental" sentiment. They immediately experienced both legal restrictions and a citizenry hostile to them. But they endured and became the first Asian group to create a biethnic and multireligious community with Mexicans. [15]

During the first five decades of the twentieth century, the Indian population in the United States was small. Most of them lived in the Imperial Valley of Southern California. These pioneers were chiefly peasants from the British province of Punjab in the northwestern corner of India. Eighty-five percent of these men professed the Sikh faith. The rest were either Muslims or Hindus.

Unlike Chinese sojourners, they decided to have families and settle in this country. The Cable Act of 1922, however, was the stumbling block. It prohibited them from selecting their mates from all races, except persons of Mexican ancestry.

These enterprising Punjabis who first came to the Imperial Valley as laborers soon became landowners (a right they later lost), and women of Mexican ancestry were among the field hands working for them. Romance between owners and field hands soon developed, thus forming an enduring biethnic and multireligious community, without religious conflicts, along the border in the Imperial Valley. Sikhism, like other Asian religions, fosters an attitude of acceptance of other faiths. These Punjabis actually encouraged their wives to keep their Roman Catholic faith. They too were the first group of Asians in North America to marry outside of their ethnicity.

Indians came to Canada beginning in 1904, not as immigrants but as subjects of England, making them, at least in theory, on par with the white Canadians. But their claim to being nationals was of no consequence, for they arrived in the province of British Columbia only to encounter a full-scale "anti-Oriental" sentiment.

ROOTING IN THE OTHER SHORE

After the dust of World War II had settled, most of the nations in Asia were either struggling to become independent or to attempt national reconstruction and nation building. In the case of China, the civil war, which temporarily subsided during World War II, resumed with vigor and culminated with the founding of the People's Republic of China on October 1, 1949. In

India, Gandhi's triumph at last freed his people from Britain. Vietnam continued to struggle against the French, with the lurking shadow of the United States never too far away. Korea, divided at the 38th parallel at the end of World War II, soon became the battleground between North Korea and the People's Republic of China on one side, and South Korea and the United Nations on the other.

On the other shore of the Pacific Ocean in North America, changes were being made by governments and Asians themselves, contributing to the growth and formation of what later could be called the Asian-American and Asian-Canadian communities.

Asian-American and Asian-Canadian Communities

The U.S. Exclusion Act against the Chinese was repealed and replaced by a quota system in 1943, followed by the Displaced Persons Act of 1948 and 1950. The latter provided some relief to nonimmigrant Chinese already in the United States by adjusting their status. By this time some Asians had already moved out of the traditional service sector into the professional arena.

Community organizations such as the Japanese American Citizens League were active in seeking to overthrow some of the unjust laws of the governments. In 1952, the U.S. government likewise passed the McCarran-Walter Immigration Act. The passage of this act marked an end of Asian immigrants' ineligibility for citizenship. But the number of Asians immigrating to North America was still small, due to the restrictive quota system imposed on them. For those who were already here, it was time for community building. The Koreans, for example, expanded their churches and established community organizations to serve their own people. Some Filipino farmers took root in the soil by becoming landowners in the Imperial Valley.

In Canada, the Asian population, though small, likewise began to take root. The Japanese, for example, were no longer concentrated in British Columbia but had moved inland to other provinces.

The 1962 Immigration Act for the first time prohibited "race, colour, or nation origin from being used as differentiating factors in approving prospective migrants." [16] This act had direct correspondence to an increase of immigrants coming from some Asian countries. This was particularly true for the period from 1967 to 1976.

Canada, under the sway of the Pierre Trudeau government, was a nation on the move. But by the mid-1970s, Canada no longer had any need for immigrants. Thus the 1976 Immigration Act was introduced. It linked the number of immigrants allowed to enter the country with domestic "manpower." This act remained in effect until the 1980s, when the Immigration Act was liberalized, making it possible for more Asians to enter Canada. Today's immigrants differ from the pioneers. They fall within the age group of 20 to 50 years old, living in metropolitan centers, such as Toronto, Vancouver, Edmonton, and Calgary. They are highly educated and are pursuing managerial or professional occupations.

In the meantime, the old-timers, too, ventured out into other professions traditionally reserved for white men, including some upper level positions in the government, both provincial and national.

There were no doubt Christians among the post-World War II immigrants. Of those who belonged to the Lutheran church, there was a good number. John Magalee, who came to the United States for higher education from Guyana, was followed by the Chu brothers, Daniel and David, who came from China for the same reason. Paul Chang, called to serve as assistant pastor at True Light Lutheran Church in New York City, was from Hong Kong. Eiichi Matsushita from Japan came to Gettysburg College and seminary to study. Clinton Chu and Roshandeen Rammarine came from South America. Philip Yang, a Chinese, came to True Light Lutheran Church as its assistant pastor, and later pastor, after he had spent some years in Japan as a student and ordained minister. By way of Taiwan, Wilson Wu came to do advanced studies at Ashbury Theological Seminary in Wilmore, Kentucky. In 1958 I arrived in Utah without a particular purpose. But a year later I was at Midland Lutheran College as a preseminary student.

By the end of the 1950s, the Asian community in North America had become multigenerational. Native-born Asian Lutherans such as Shigeru Samuel Ujiie, Paul Nakamura, Henry Wong, and Toshio Okamoto were already in ministry, with Joseph Wong, Ysuyuki Fukuda, and James Moy following soon after.

In the 1960s and the early 1970s while Canada was enjoying a period of peace and prosperity, U.S. society was shaken by the civil rights movement; civil rights legislation; and the assassinations of President John F. Kennedy, his brother, Robert, and Martin Luther King Jr. The war in Vietnam escalated as did the ever-heightening protests against it. Amid chaos and hope, Congress in 1965 passed an immigration reform bill, which provided an annual quota of 20,000 immigrants from each country.

The Asian-American community, which had long suffered separation from family members and loved ones, began to experience rapid growth. But the East and South Asians who came to the United States from the mid-1960s on were responding not only to the change in U.S. immigration policy or to reunite families. They were also responding to the global political economy and the instability of some nations in Asia. Unlike the early immigrants, a great majority of the newcomers had professional skills, intellectual capacity, financial power, and business savvy, resulting in a much greater diversity in the Asian community and in contributions to many aspects of society as a whole.

Politicians, Generals, Soldiers, and Boat People

The Democratic Republic of Vietnam was founded on September 2, 1945, in a fragmented land dominated by different interest groups within and without. The decision made at the Potsdam Conference to divide Vietnam into two zones at the 16th parallel, assigning China to control the North and Britain the South, was in theory a technical measure meant only to facilitate the disarming of the Japanese troops. It was not meant to be of consequence to the development of the country. But with the net of international interests closing in on Vietnam, the reality turned out to be different.

Internally, the Democratic Republic of Vietnam encountered resistance from different strong and powerful factions, including French strongholds, and faced difficulties in economic development, land redistribution, and education.

Externally China, under the leadership of the Nationalist Party, wanted to get rid of its uncooperative generals in the southwestern provinces by encouraging them to foray into North Vietnam. Britain, which had no particular interest in Vietnam, soon went beyond the mission entrusted her at the Potsdam Conference by reopening Vietnam to France and by allowing the French soldiers remaining there to rearm. With the British action, eight years of Franco-Vietnamese war and U.S. involvement there ensued.

The rearmed French Expeditionary Corps immediately launched a massive attack on the Democratic Republic of Vietnam, compelling its forces to abandon urban centers and to withdraw into more remote mountain and rural regions. The government of the Democratic Republic of Vietnam, meanwhile, took steps to improve the livelihood of the people and initiated the necessary procedures to stabilize the country politically. The government was able to achieve successes in these areas. Thus, during the period from 1948 to 1952, the government was able to resist the French attacks.

During the course of an eight-year war between France and Vietnam, the United States changed its basic policy of pursuing economic objectives and opposing colonialism in Vietnam. The United States began to consistently present "the war waged by the Expeditionary Corps as one 'of world interest,' as being in defense of 'the free world' against Communism." [17] Beginning in 1952, the United States supplied massive military hardware to the French Expeditionary Corps. A few months before the French defeat at Dien Bien Phu in 1954, Vice President Richard Nixon visited Vietnam purportedly to see how Operation Atlante was progressing. This visit signaled the deepening of U.S. involvement in Vietnam.

With the French defeat, a compromise was reached at the Geneva Conference. The agreement "provided for a cease-fire in the whole Viet Nam." [18] The country was divided again into two zones at the seventeenth parallel for the purpose of allowing the two forces to regroup themselves, but the unity of Vietnam was never called into question. An election was to be held throughout Vietnam but it never materialized. The Ngo Dinh Diem government in Saigon, backed by the United States, and the U.S. government deemed that the presence of the Communist leaders in the Hanoi government was incompatible with such an election. The U.S. government continued to support the Ngo Dinh Diem dictatorship.

In 1962, the U.S. government, in violation of international law, established a military base in South Vietnam. In the following year, President John F. Kennedy consented to the assassination of Ngo Dinh Diem, who by then had become a thorn in the flesh of the U.S. civilian and military officials. Ngo Dinh Diem, a Roman Catholic, was murdered in front of the altar in a church in Saigon. Three weeks later, Kennedy himself died by an assassin's bullet. With the death of Kennedy, Lyndon B. Johnson inherited the U.S. presidency. The Johnson administration ordered a massive build-up of U.S. military strength in Vietnam. At one point more than half a million U.S. military personnel were present in that country.

The Democratic Republic of Vietnam, backed by the Soviet Union and the People's Republic of China, fought U.S. and South Vietnamese forces. Meanwhile the U.S. public became more and more antiwar. The Nixon administration realized the futility of the conflict and tried to negotiate a settlement. Finally on April 30, 1975, Saigon fell.

With the collapse of the Saigon government, thousands of pro-U.S. politicians, military personnel, and those civilians who worked for the U.S. military in Indochina fled their countries, with the majority coming to North America and the United States in particular. Ordinary citizens, who had no help from the U.S. government, escaped their countries by small and large boats adrift in the open sea. They hoped to be picked up by passing ships or to land in another country. Suddenly the world witnessed another refugee problem. With the arrival of the Southeast Asians, Asian ministry in North America took on a different dimension, as chapter 11 describes.

2

SEEKING THE WAY

IN 1896 THE CALIFORNIA-NEVADA DISTRICT OF THE EVANGELICAL LUTHERAN Synod of Missouri, Ohio, and Other States, entertained an idea of a ministry with the Chinese in San Francisco, California. (In 1947 this church body changed its official name to The Lutheran Church—Missouri Synod.) This idea did not become a reality until 67 years later. In the meantime, American Lutherans from 1870 to 1910 were caught up with immigrants from Europe and immigrants from "the other shore" did not receive their attention. Within this period too the U.S. population increased by 93 million, with close to half being immigrants from Europe.

Among the newcomers, "the Roman Catholic Church received the largest number...but the Lutheran church was a close second." [1] Along with the increase in membership, the church had to deal with the attendant problems, such as overcrowded "foreign quarters in the cities, the discouraging condition of 'downtown' churches, the abandoned country churches, the multiplicity of languages, and the sudden migrations from older to newer states." [2]

During this period American Lutherans found "a deepening of church consciousness and an increase in loyalty of historic Lutheranism in doctrine and worship and practice, and at the same time a more tolerant attitude towards all Christians everywhere." [3]

For the first few decades of the twentieth century, American Lutherans were also occupied with internal and pan-Lutheran organizations, mergers, and the problems of refugee resettlement after World War I. However, the attitude of tolerance fostered earlier served the Lutheran church well in the development of the first Chinese Lutheran church in North America.

This chapter describes the first four ministries of The LCMS, covering the period from 1936 to 1963.

CHINESE MINISTRY

In 1880, two years before the Exclusion Act, the Chinese population in the United States numbered 105,465. The 1930 census reported a total of 74,954 people, a decrease of 30,511. The Exclusion Act shut out immigration; it did not permit those who went back to China to visit their families to return; and the act did not allow females to come to the United States. The population decrease was also due to death and to some immigrants returning to China to ride out the Great Depression that the United States was experiencing. And by 1930, mainline denominations had long ceased their interest in mission and ministry among the Chinese. Yet it was precisely at this juncture that an opportunity to minister with the Chinese in New York City presented itself to the Atlantic District of The LCMS. The year was 1936.[4]

True Light Lutheran Church, New York City

In 1935 a group of Chinese Christians rented "a third floor loft at 173 Canal Street, New York City, to conduct Sunday school sessions as an independent group."[5] The group called its Sunday school *Lingguang*. The Chinese character *ling* means "the spirit of a being; spirit; spiritual; divine; supernatural; efficacious." The character *guang* means "light; favor; brightness; honor." As a verb it means "to illumine." Later, when the group became a Lutheran congregation, the name *Lingguang* was adopted as part of the official name of the church. Among this group of Chinese was a white woman by the name of Mary E. Banta (1875-1971). Where did these Chinese Christians come from and why was there a white woman among them? The record reveals that these Chinese Christians were former members of Church of All Nations (CAN), a Methodist Episcopal congregation, located at Manhattan's Second Avenue and Houston Street. A social worker, Banta was a long-term employee of the same congregation, in charge of the Chinese department. The same record further discloses that by 1935 Banta had reached retirement age and, according to the policy of the church, was asked to retire.

The record in part explains why Banta was with this group, but it does not explain why the Chinese group decided to become independent. Did Banta's retirement have anything to do with the group's breaking away from CAN? Did Banta ask the group to break away so that she could continue to work with these Chinese Christians to whom she had made a commitment in her youth? Was there a fallout between the Chinese and the congregation? Was there any conflict between the pastor and the Chinese? Could the group and Banta have had some theological disagreement with the Methodist position? Unfortunately the record gives no clear answer to any of these questions. However, an examination of Banta's life and her work up to the year 1935 may provide some clues to this mystery.

Mary E. Banta, who appeared to be the only child of Rev. John and

Rachel Dusenberry Banta, was born in Upper Sandusky, Ohio, in 1875. Her father was a Methodist clergyman, who may have served a parish in Canada. But the sources that mention his service in Canada contradict themselves regarding dates. One of the sources confirms that he indeed was in Canada, but gives no date or any other evidence. [6] This same source, however, also indicates that "in 1880, her family came to New York to live." [7] That means the move occurred when Mary Banta was five years old. The second source states that Rev. Banta moved to Canada while his daughter was a young child and did not return to the United States until Banta was ten years old. [8] The third source contradicts the first two by stating that "the family moved to Brooklyn, New York, in Mary's infancy" and says nothing about her father's parish ministry in Canada. [9] While the exact dates of her father's service in Canada and of the family's moving to New York are questionable, the move to New York City itself, however, is confirmed by all sources.

As a young child, Mary Banta was an eager learner and a person of deep faith. With regard to how much education she had and how and where she was educated, the English and Chinese sources differ. According to the Chinese source she had to give up her education after she graduated from elementary school, in order to stay home during the day to take care of her sick mother. [10] However, she continued to attend an evening middle school for two years before giving up public schooling all together. The English sources mention nothing about her mother's illness or young Banta having had to give up schooling. In fact, these sources indicate that after graduation from high school, she "enrolled in the Missionary Training School." [11] Wing Jean, however, in his Chinese introduction to *The Biography of Our Mary E. Banta*, tells quite a different story. Jean states that while Banta was attending evening middle school, she heard a speech one night by a missionary who told the students how pathetic the non-Christians were and what a wretched life they lived. She was deeply moved but could not figure out what she could do to help. One day as she sat in her parents' living room reading the Bible, the word of God came to her: "My presence shall go with thee and will give you rest." [12] From that point on, young Banta dedicated herself to become a missionary evangelist. With her parents' consent she entered the branch of Brooklyn Union Missionary Training School, which was located in Hackettstown, New Jersey. After two years of training, she returned to Brooklyn to complete her training at the main campus.

As part of her practical experience during her preparation to be a missionary, she was assigned to New York City's Chinatown to work with the Chinese. She conducted English classes for a group of Chinese men at a Baptist church in Brooklyn. "These men came to her with an understanding that they did not want to accept her God." [13] Young Banta was not discouraged. Patiently she taught them English, "being careful to tell them that only

through the love and kindness of God were they now able to learn this foreign tongue." [14] Influenced by her strong faith in and love for God, the Chinese
began to inquire about her God and her religion. From this encounter, young
Banta "decided to dedicate her time and training in teaching the Chinese
people to love and understand their Saviour." [15]

However, shortly after graduation in 1901, she was "sent to Africa as
a missionary to Liberia, by The Woman's Foreign Missionary Society." [16] But
her stay in Liberia was destined to be short. Soon after her arrival, she contracted black water fever, which nearly blinded her. She returned to the
United States before the end of her first year in Liberia and spent the next
few years in recuperation.

While she was in Africa, Protestant mission and ministry to the
Chinese in New York City had quietly begun. Among those who initiated
work with the Chinese was a Dr. Theodore S. Henderson, who later became
a bishop of the Methodist Episcopal Church. Henderson started a mission
"among the foreign people known as the 'East Parish,'" [17] which later became
known as Church of All Nations. In 1905 Henderson invited Mary Banta, now
fully recovered from her illness, to take over the Chinese department. Her
influence there was far-reaching. The work of that department "includes
church-school classes from tiny tots to adult groups, mothers' meetings,
social work, and the Girls' Club, 'Daughters of China,' which has the inspiring
motto 'Living for Service.' Each organization functions under Miss Banta's
direction, and her great aim in these thirty years of missionary work has
been to instill not only an understanding of the simple gospel, but an appreciation of the responsibilities of those bearing the name of Christian." [18] The
Chinese in her care respected her as their teacher, and "their unfailing friend
in whom they place[d] implicit confidence." [19]

The relationship between Mary Banta and the Chinese was built
on mutual respect, trust, and love. Her retirement might very well have
impacted their continued presence at CAN. Wing Jean tells us that shortly
after Banta's retirement, the group of Chinese left CAN and became an
independent group. This was due to an incident of which both Jean and
other written records, in typical Chinese fashion, refuse to disclose. But in
her interview Beulah Wong, who was close to Banta, indicated that the incident Jean referred to had something to do with housing and disbandment.
After her retirement, Banta was asked to vacate the apartment that had
been rented for her by CAN. Further, with her retirement, the Chinese group
was disbanded by the church. In the meantime, Moy Gumm found a place
for Banta in Brooklyn, and together with George Gum and a group of men
formerly belonging to CAN, they rented a place at 173 Canal Street for worship. At this point Banta was invited to lead the group and to help organize
a Sunday school.

An admirer of the radio preacher Dr. Walther A. Maier of "The Lutheran Hour," Banta, at this time, requested Lutheran instruction. Dr. A. W. Meyer provided it to her and "on March 29, 1936, Miss Banta was confirmed and received into membership of the Lutheran Church." [20]

The Sunday school under Banta's direction continued to flourish to the point where a bigger space was needed. At this time in the life of this group of Chinese and of Banta, a certain "Miss Marion Klaus, a registered nurse employed by the New York City Department of Health and a member of Redeemer Lutheran Church, Newark, New Jersey," [21] entered the picture. Upon learning of the group's need for a pastor, Klaus "contacted Dr. Louis Henze, Executive Secretary of the Atlantic District, and requested the services of a pastor for the group. Dr. A. W. Meyer of Yonkers, New York, served them the following Sunday." [22]

A series of conferences were subsequently held between Atlantic District officials and the Chinese group including Banta. On March 29, 1936, the Chinese group came forth with a resolution in the name of True Light Sunday School, formally requesting assistance from the district. The resolution reads, in part:

> Whereas, we Chinese Christians and attendants of the True Light Sunday School submit this petition and plea for your Christian and spiritual guidance,... [The resolution proceeds to describe the location of the Sunday school and to state that while there are social and recreational activities available to the Chinese, there are no 'Christian teachings of their own.'] Whereas, in Christian faith we are nothing but infants and many of us are young, tender converts. We, consequently, are in urgent need of your continuous and continual assistance and spiritual nursing. We pray that you will not, for his sake, deprive us of this badly needed spiritual care. Therefore, BE IT RESOLVED, that we, the undersigned, turn over our entire work over to the Lutheran Church [Missouri Synod] for that organization to foster and guide us in this great work for Christ. [23]

Moy Gumm and Mrs. N. Thom signed the resolution.

This resolution put the district board in a quandary. The United States was deep into the Depression. Without exception, congregations were impacted by it. After careful consideration, the district board stated that "this unique endeavor among the 50,000 [24] Chinese in Greater New York presents unusual problems and puts an additional burden on our mission treasury." [25] Discussions and debates followed.

In the end, the district board concluded that this opportunity could not be neglected and that the idea of "the spreading of the pure Gospel to the Chinese is one that ought to inspire adequate financial support." [26] The district board, in the final analysis, acted by faith alone. The convention agreed with the board's decision and a resolution was passed in favor of supporting the Chinese group. The Atlantic District officially undertook the work on April 1, 1936. Banta was employed to assist the pastor.

This examination of the life and work of Mary E. Banta suggests that it was a combination of retirement, disbandment, and the determination of the Chinese group, coupled with the efforts of Marion Klaus, that brought about the birth of True Light Lutheran Church.

Initially Dr. A. W. Meyer was in charge of this mission. After serving for a few weeks (one source says two weeks) Meyer resigned. On February 9, 1936, Rev. Louis T. Buchheimer of Grace Lutheran Church, Bronx, New York, took charge of the mission as a volunteer until he officially became the pastor of the congregation in 1948. Buchheimer resigned this pastorate in July 1959 when he received "a call from the Armed Services Commission ...to go to the Far East as a member of the staff of Lutheran Service Commission." [27] But some former members maintained that he was dismissed. Regardless, his departure coincided with Paul Chang's, which is described below.

Buchheimer is remembered as a "PR man" who did "a good job in selling [LCMS] congregations about us," according to James Moy. He was not around the church much and, when he was present, he was not always approachable. He did not seem to appreciate the sort of affection that some Chinese boys tried to accord him. A former member recalled, "I was about 17 years old. A whole group of us [was] coming down the stairwell from the gym after a good basketball workout, and we were feeling good. I walked past Pastor Buchheimer and gave him a gentle love pat on his tummy and said, 'Hi pastor!' and he said, 'Don't ever touch me!' with a frown on his face. That was it. Kids do not forget things like that." Love for him had to be kept at a distance, so it seemed. On the other hand, he was also remembered by Stanley Wu, father of ELCA Council member Lily Wu, (see chapter 7), as one who understood "the business man."

The staff of the congregation was English-speaking. It was necessary to translate the Scriptures and sermon each Sunday into Chinese. Both the congregation and the staff felt the need for a Chinese-speaking pastor to work with those whose primary language was Chinese. Thus, in 1953, the congregation called Rev. Paul Chang from Hong Kong. This was an unusual move, considering that Chang had never been to the United States before.

Chang's great-grandfather was the first Lutheran in his native land—Guangdong Province, China. Paul Chang was born on June 18, 1926. His father was a physician. About his mother, nothing is known other than the fact that she gave birth to 17 children. Chang was first educated at a seminary in China [28] before receiving his B.A. degree from Hwa Kiu University in Macau in

1952. While he was serving True Light Lutheran Church, he did graduate studies at the Biblical Seminary (BS) in New York City from 1953 to 1956.

Chang proved to be energetic and resourceful. He conducted services in Chinese and built up the Chinese-speaking congregation. Then in 1959 Chang reportedly resigned to do further graduate studies at Concordia Seminary (CS), St. Louis, Missouri. His official clerical biography reveals that he entered the Teachers College in River Forest, Illinois, in 1959. Chang subsequently withdrew from the clergy roster and became a businessman, but his heart never left the church nor was his faith ever diminished, as chapter 9 describes.

If "love at a distance" was the right motto for Buchheimer during his tenure as a pastor to the Chinese, Mary Banta's would have been "love knows no boundaries." She was a self-giving woman who knew no distinction when it came to loving others, because her God gave her that love first. The following tale is illustrative of this love. A reporter once asked her what was her utmost concern for the Chinese besides teaching them English and sharing the good news with them. "Walking the children across the streets," [29] came the answer—simple, determined, dedicated. Her determination and dedication, at times, seemed to some people to be a little heavy-handed. Bruce Edward Hall writes: "Miss Mary Banta . . . seemed to have attached herself firmly to any Protestant evangelical organization over the past forty-five years that will allow her to keep fussing over Chinatown's children. When Cousin Sookie was in the second grade she even came, unannounced, to his classroom at P.S. 23 and dragged him down to the hospital to have his tonsils removed. She had decided on her own that they needed to be taken out." [30] On February 6, 1948, when True Light Lutheran Church celebrated Banta's forty-eighth year of service to the Chinese, myriad voices of Chinese and whites alike sang her praises. On that day, 160 children in Chinatown, some of whom Banta may very well have walked across the streets, remembered her. They presented her with a flower hat and a congratulatory message. But this was no ordinary flower hat. It was made out of paper currency and silver coins, brightly decorated in a floral shape. And the congratulatory message began, "We are your children, living in Chinatown....We will never forget the love, humanity, and nurture you have given us...." [31] She not only walked them across the streets, "she [also] often arranged amusements for the children and took them to clinics for physical check-ups," wrote Ruth Kwong, [32] one of several young Chinese girls who had lived with and received care from Banta. Kwong was also one of those who called her "Grandma." "Miss Banta is not only a 'grandma,'" Kwong continued, "but is a 'great grandma' today, I call her 'Grandma,' as actually she loves me more than a grandma should." [33]

Banta sometimes also protected the children based on faith more than on knowledge. Ernest K. Moy, [34] in his mature age, revealed that when he was a child, he broke a window of a shop while playing baseball on the street in Chinatown. For his crime he was hauled to court and Banta was with him, naturally. After directing a series of questions to Moy and after the boy had shown him a softball as evidence, the judge, "bent toward the boy's champion" and resumed, "'Well, Miss Banta, is he a good boy in your Sunday school?…' 'He is a very good boy, Your Honor, although sometimes I catch him eating candy during his recitation of the Sabbath lesson. I know he is sorry, and I am sure that he will be very careful not to cause any damage when he plays on the street which is the only place the children in Chinatown now have to play after school hours.' 'I believe you are right, Miss Banta,' the judge agreed and the case was dismissed." [35] Of course, it was a hard baseball that did the damage, but in her wisdom Banta had chosen not to find this out when she questioned the boy earlier.

"I regard Miss Banta as one of the finest and most consecrated Christians that I have ever known," [36] complimented Rev. Ernest J. Kunsch, a former pastor of True Light. She spent half a century giving "her time and untiring energy to the religious life of the Chinese people," observed Moy Gumm, [37] one of the two original signatories of the resolution. Her name was a household word in Chinatown. When Martha Hoffman, a Sunday school teacher at True Light from 1955 to 1959, first called on the Sunday school girls, she had no success in getting into their homes until she "learned to say the magic words, 'I'm from Miss Banta's Church.'" [38] Hoffman was right on both counts. Indeed it was Banta who built the church and her name was a magic word. After serving the Chinatown community for 67 years, Banta died in 1971. Many from that community participated at her funeral service. Others presumably remained behind tending the shops.

After the departure of Buchheimer and Chang in 1959, the congregation in the same year called Kunsch to be its pastor. Kunsch was no stranger to the congregation; he had previously served as its assistant pastor from 1949 to 1950. Within a few months after Kunsch's arrival, Martha Hoffman resigned. However, the congregation was subsequently gifted with Mrs. Wonnor Yee (nee Chan), who proved to be a boon for the parish. Not only was she fluent in both Chinese and English, she became widely known for her warmth, her dedication to the church, and her care for people.

Yee was born on October 5, 1936, in Taishan District, Guangdong Province. Her father immigrated to the United States as a young man and like most immigrants he later returned to China to find a bride. Shortly after the birth of his daughter, he returned to America. During World War II he joined the U.S. Army. After the war he went back to China and in 1948 returned to the United States with his family.

Yee grew up in a small village where life was hard, particularly during the war years. To this day Yee remembers the frightening experiences she had.

But faith and prayers seemed to have sustained her. "I learned to pray from my mother as soon as I knew how to talk. We took everything to the Lord in prayer,"Yee recalled years later.[39] Even so, she had an opportunity to attend a school organized by the Church of Brotherly Love, a Baptist group.

Yee was also an adventurous child who, at age nine, convinced her mother to let her attend school in Guangzhou, the provincial capital and a city about 100 miles from her home. "Without knowing what the big city was like, not knowing the difference in dialect, having never seen an automobile, a bus, tall buildings...I ventured joyfully, bravely to attend the elementary school division of the Union School for Teachers." [40] Yee recounted her adventure without blinking an eye.

Her first year in the United States was spent in Philadelphia where she and her mother lived with her uncle, a younger brother of her mother's, while her father worked in New York City. A year later, after the birth of her brother, her family moved to New York City. Her association with True Light Lutheran Church began the first Sunday after the family moved to New York—her father, not yet a baptized Christian, dropped her off at True Light for Sunday school on his way to work. When Sunday school was over, her father was not there to pick her up. But that did not intimidate the 12-year-old Yee, who, not knowing which way to turn, started walking home but got lost a block away. From that day on, Yee became a regular Sunday school attendee.

The next person from her family to become associated with True Light was her mother. Yee remembers well how that happened. "One Sunday afternoon in the fall of 1949,"Yee recalled recently, "my mother took my brother David for a walk on Mott Street on a stroller and she saw a parade. She followed the people and came to True Light. From then on...she attended the adult English class. True Light became our family church home."

Yee became an active member of the church and had a career at the New York University Medical Center after she graduated from college. In the meantime, True Light was in need of a Chinese-speaking person on the staff. Yee responded and served as a parish worker for two years until she was married in 1963. After her children had grown up, Yee returned to the parish to serve as a parish worker once again. Today Yee has a broad range of responsibilities at True Light, such as Bible teaching, visitation, and outreach, to name a few. Besides serving in the local parish, Yee in 1998 became a member of the Chinese Ministry Conference (CMC) for one year. The local parish, however, is Yee's first love, where she finds fulfillment and satisfaction.

In April 1966, Kunsch "left True Light to accept a call from Trinity Lutheran Church in Hawthorne, New York." [41] A year later, Rev. Philip Yang was installed as the pastor and served there until he retired in 1994.

Yang has a rich background that his official clerical record does not reveal. He was born and grew up in China, where he also received his education in law. After the founding of the People's Republic of China on October 1, 1949, Yang left China for Hong Kong, where he enrolled as a student at the Lutheran seminary. Upon graduation in 1954, Yang "immediately went to Japan for graduate study at the School of Theology in Doshisha University, Kyoto, Japan ... [and] received his master of theology degree on March 21, 1956." [42] During his student years in Japan he also taught at the Kyoto College for Foreign Languages and "served as pastor of a Chinese church in Kobe and Kyoto from 1954 to 1957." [43] Yang's pastoral ministry in Japan must have been in a lay rather than an ordained capacity. Both his official clerical biography and the 50th anniversary booklet of True Light Lutheran Church give January 10, 1965, as the date of his ordination.

In 1958 Yang received a full fellowship from Union Seminary in New York City. Two years later he was awarded the master of sacred theology degree, "followed by a semester in the New York School of Social Work at Columbia University." [44]

Yang's ministry at True Light spanned nearly 30 years. Upon his retirement he was made pastor emeritus.

True Light Lutheran Church has been an important institution in New York City's Chinatown, serving as a haven to people away from home and providing a place where the young and old can gather. By 1952, it became the largest Protestant congregation in the country with a membership of 1,185. [45] Its various programs, the programs for children in particular, no doubt, attracted and continue to attract people to become members. But as to its early days, what the older generation remembers the most were the people themselves, with their love and care for one another. "Beulah Wong and her husband were among the saints of True Light" [46] who provided others with love and much-needed attention. There were a lot of dedicated lay leaders—Donald Szetoo, Janet Szetoo, Willie Wong, Beulah Wong, and Bickie Hor, to name a few—in this congregation who added to its vitality. This congregation too has given Lutheran congregations their share of leaders— Henry Wong, Dwight Ong, Clement Lee, James Moy, Lily Wu, Fern Lee Hagedorn, Andrew Yee, and others—who in time have contributed richly to the life of the church and to their own community.

Prince of Peace Lutheran Church, Vancouver, British Columbia
From 1936 to 1955, The LCMS did not initiate any further ministry with the Chinese or any Asian group. In the meantime, the world had undergone profound changes. World War II had ended, but not without the world having experienced the most terrifying weapon of war—the atomic bomb. Most Asian nations that had been under colonial power and control became free after the war and began the slow process of nation building and devel-

opment. The People's Republic of China was founded in 1949. The following year the United States entered into the Korean conflict under the aegis of the United Nations. On the home front, fear of communism spread as politicians fanned its flames and numerous lives were ruined as a result. President Dwight Eisenhower issued an order to desegregate schools in the South. Canada was a relative calm place compared with the United States.

Ordinary people, too, were affected by the changing world, in some cases necessitating their moving from one place to another. Richard Wong, James Y. C. Lawson and his daughter, and two young Wong sisters were such individuals among numerous others. Richard Wong, a Cantonese-speaking Chinese most likely from Hong Kong, became a resident of Canada before 1950. In early 1950, Richard Wong was baptized and confirmed in Kitsilano Lutheran Church in Vancouver, British Columbia, by Rev. Carl O. Beiderwieden. [47] "In May that year, James Y. C. Lawson and his daughter Olivia, who had been members of True Light Lutheran Church, New York City, moved to Vancouver and joined Bethlehem [Lutheran Church]. Around the same time, members of Concordia congregation [Vancouver] took in two foster children, Coral and Lilly Wong, who were eventually confirmed." [48] These five individuals, who had come from different parts of the world, would become the nucleus of what was subsequently known as Prince of Peace Lutheran Church.

Lutheran work among the Chinese in Vancouver did not begin until 1955, when James Lawson transferred his membership to the interdenominational Christ Church of China. Lawson immediately organized "Lutheran Scout, Brownies, and Cub groups in Chinatown which fed into the Sunday school." [49] The Sunday school was organized and began instruction on Sunday, January 15, 1956. The first worship service took place on Sunday, February 19, 1956. Rev. Fred Gabert, pastor of Bethlehem Lutheran Church, preached the mission sermon in English. Richard Wong translated it into Cantonese, a Chinese dialect. However, preaching and services were discontinued by the end of the year, when the working agreement with Christ Church of China expired. The Sunday school continued at a local school.

This mission was given a new life when seminarian Henry Wong, member of True Light Lutheran Church, New York City, was assigned as its vicar in 1958. And in 1960 the mission called its first pastor, Rev. Paul F. Wildgrube, who resumed Chinese services on November 5, 1961. Wildgrube resigned in the spring of 1967 to become the pastor of St. Ambrose Lutheran Church, Pennsville, New Jersey. "The mission continued to be served by…[Rev.] F. Loring Younce and then [Rev.] Robert E. Kogler." [50] Rev. M. Chiong, a pastor of the Lutheran Church—Hong Kong Synod (LCHKS), subsequently served the congregation. But growth was minimal. According to the study "Chinese Lutheran Work in Canada" by Ambrose Tsui Pui Ho in 1984, Prince of Peace

Lutheran Church was then a struggling congregation with about 50 members.

In the meantime, Vancouver and its suburb, Richmond, had become a haven for the Chinese from Hong Kong. The Chinese population in the Vancouver area increased greatly from 1970 to 1990. In 1990, Rev. Thompson Tung Shing Mok of the LCHKS was called to be the pastor of Prince of Peace.

Two years later The LCMS at its convention adopted "Mission Blueprint for the Nineties" (MBN), calling for aggressive mission strategies and initiatives. As a response to the blueprint, "the Board of Directors [of the British Columbia District in the same year] approved an aggressive plan of ministry and outreach to Chinese-speaking people in greater Vancouver. The plan involved supporting a DCE (Director of Christian Education), a Christian missionary, a vicar, and a Christian lay worker for Chinese outreach in the area." [51] The plan intended to work "with Mod [definition uncertain] and Prince of Peace, the hope was to aggressively share Christ with thousands of Chinese-speaking people." [52] The plan was too ambitious to be realized in total. "Eventually, a DCE, a parish worker, and a vicar were placed into Vancouver." [53] With the added staff, the focus of the ministry shifted from Vancouver to Richmond where the Chinese population was estimated to be 30 percent in 1993.

Lutheran Church of the Holy Spirit, San Francisco

Like Vancouver, British Columbia, to its north, San Francisco has always been a major port of entry for Asians coming to North America. These two cities share geographical and climatic similarities as well as being major centers of Asian concentration. In 1963, the Chinese population in San Francisco numbered about 60,000, with "16 Chinese-speaking churches… in Chinatown." [54] This figure is questionable even if Rev. Holt had included St. Mary's Catholic Church. According to James Chuck, there were eight Chinese-speaking Protestant churches in San Francisco by 1950. In the 1950s three more were organized and in the 1960s seven more. But these seven were located outside of Chinatown. There were in reality only eight Protestant churches and one Roman Catholic Church in Chinatown in the early 1960s. The three that were organized in the 1950s were located on the periphery of Chinatown. [55] The Christian population of San Francisco was estimated at about 10 to 15 percent.

Also in 1963 the California-Nevada District decided to actualize the dream it had for the last 67 years, when the district's Lutheran Women Missionary League (LWML) at its convention allocated "$4,200 to begin work in Chinatown, San Francisco." [56] And on May 28 of the same year, the mission board of the district called Rev. Wilbert Holt as a missionary-at-large to the Chinese in San Francisco.

Holt was born on November 11, 1918, in Oak Park, Illinois. He received his theological education at Concordia Seminary (CS), Springfield, Illinois, and did graduate studies at Concordia Seminary (CS), St. Louis, Missouri, and the Lutheran School of Theology, a United Lutheran Church in America seminary, at Maywood, Illinois. After that, in November 1945, he set sail for China as a missionary. Due to the political change in mainland China in 1949, Holt moved to Hong Kong where he continued to work among Chinese refugees from the mainland until he was called to San Francisco.

Holt faithfully served Lutheran Church of the Holy Spirit from 1963 until his retirement in 1994. The congregation was located in the heart of Chinatown for the first six years before moving to its present location at 1725 Washington St., about one mile away from Chinatown. The congregation has an extension in the Sunset District of San Francisco.

As the congregation developed, it required more staff. In 1967 Amy Hau joined the staff as a parish worker. Hau is a talented person with an interesting background. She was born into a Christian family in Hong Kong where she grew up. After completing Form Six at St. Paul College, Hong Kong, she took a position as a secretary to the director of the Lutheran World Federation's (LWF) Hong Kong office. After five years on the job, she was selected to go to Europe as a LWF's Hong Kong representative to raise funds for poor people in Hong Kong.

She proved to be an excellent fund-raiser and the trip was a great success, which made a deep impression on her boss. Later she was asked to go to the United States to speak to congregations on behalf of LWF. She was full of energy and enthusiasm. Within a relatively short period of time, she had spoken to more than 200 congregations. On one of the occasions, she met Holt, who was very impressed by her personality, her ability to do simultaneous translation, and her commitment to the Christian faith. Holt subsequently asked her to work with him at Lutheran Church of the Holy Spirit. Hau was not yet a Lutheran. Nevertheless, she accepted the invitation and became a Lutheran after her marriage to Mr. Mui, a member of the congregation.

Her service as a parish worker had a humble beginning. One of her responsibilities was to work with the youth. There were only four students in the congregation at that time. She spent long hours working with them and others. She often brought these four young people to the small neighborhood parks to meet other youth. The young people gradually became friends and, at this point, Hau-Mui would invite the entire group to church for social activities and snacks. Her commitment to the faith and her hard work paid off. For from this humble beginning, Hau-Mui in time built 10 active groups of considerable size in the church today.

When she was asked about the secret of her success, Hau-Mui maintained that there is no secret at all. Throughout her 32 years as a parish worker, she has but three goals for her ministry: First, to enable others to have a firm relationship with Jesus; second, to equip the youth through Bible studies; third, to help the youth to enter the ministry. These goals are undergirded by love, which is the theme of her ministry. As to her third goal, the congregation thus far has given The LCMS nine pastors.

Today Hau-Mui is not only involved in ministry at the Washington Street location, but she is also serving Sunset District Chinese School, which is part of the ministry of Lutheran Church of the Holy Spirit.[57] Sunday services began at the Sunset extension on Easter Sunday 1999.

In 1969, Deaconess Carol Lee Halter joined the staff. Halter "developed a park ministry, child evangelism program, vacation Bible school programs, and the Laguna Honda convalescent hospital ministry. She also began and developed the first English Youth Fellowship, now called Faith Fellowship."[58] In 1981, Halter left the staff and was commissioned as a missionary to Hong Kong.

When Holt retired in 1994, the congregation, two years later, called Rev. David Chan, a 1996 graduate of CS, St. Louis, to be its pastor. Chan was born in Hong Kong in 1960 and came to the United States in 1969. He came to this ministry having spent nine years working for the Bank of America before enrolling in the seminary. He was also one of the nine sons of the congregation who dedicated themselves to ministry.

JAPANESE MINISTRY

By the end of 1942, the United States had experienced heavy losses in its two-pronged war against Germany in Europe and Japan in the Pacific Theater. The U.S. Army was in need of men. Thus on January 28, 1943, Henry L. Stimson, Secretary of War "announced a new policy of 'inherent rights of every faithful citizen regardless of ancestry to bear arms in the national defense' which was a plan to form an all-Japanese-American combat team with volunteers from the United States and Hawaii to be designated the 442nd Regimental Combat Team."[59] Another provision was made to allow those eligible Japanese to leave the internment camps, providing that they would move inland. Taking advantage of this opportunity, some young Japanese moved to the twin cities of Minneapolis and St. Paul, Minnesota, while others volunteered for the Army. Some of the young soldiers were sent to Camp McCoy in Wisconsin for training.

In the meantime, a Lutheran couple by the name of Daniel and Ann Schoof of Faribault, Minnesota, befriended a number of these Japanese men. Through a certain "Tommy," the Schoofs "came in contact with some Japanese-American young men who were in training at Camp McCoy, Wisconsin."[60] While the Schoofs were befriending the Japanese-Americans, who had accepted their Lutheran faith and worshiped with them in their church, Toshio Okamoto, their future pastor, was an elementary student in a parochial school in Chicago.

First Japanese Lutheran Church, Los Angeles [61]

The roots of this congregation, initially named First Japanese Lutheran Church but subsequently changed to St. Thomas Lutheran Church, are traceable to Minnesota, a state known for its countless lakes, and to Wisconsin, a state noted for the potency of its wild ginseng. As fate would have it, Daniel Schoof died in 1949 or 1950. The young Japanese families, which the Schoofs had befriended, by now had returned to Los Angeles. Upon hearing the death of Dan, as they knew him, they implored his widow, Ann, to move to Los Angeles. Mrs. Schoof heeded their entreaty and moved to Los Angeles.

By the time she arrived in Los Angeles in the early 1950s, several of the Japanese families living in the San Pedro area had joined a Lutheran church. There were also a few families living in Los Angeles. Mrs. Schoof guided them all to Hope Memorial Lutheran Church in Los Angeles, a small multiracial congregation consisting of white, African-American, and Japanese-American members.

Upon hearing that Toshio Okamoto was in training for the ministry at CS, St. Louis, and would soon be available for internship, Mrs. Schoof requested the district's Mission Board to assign him to Los Angeles. Okamoto arrived in Los Angeles in the fall of 1954 to serve his vicarage at Hope Memorial Lutheran Church. After graduation in 1956, Okamoto was called as a missionary-at-large by the Southern California District to work among Japanese-Americans. Soon after Okamoto arrived in Los Angeles, Mrs. Schoof recontacted her Japanese friends and encouraged him to begin a Saturday night Bible class and a social hour in her home. Okamoto was persuaded. Later a Saturday night school was established, using vacation Bible school as a model plus 30 minutes of conversational Japanese. The school was housed at Hope Memorial Lutheran Church, some members of which also volunteered to help.

Within a few months, about 75 children were enrolled in Saturday night school and about 30 families with whom firm contact had been established. This small but significant nucleus decided to hold its first worship service on March 17, 1957.

In the 1960s, America witnessed the burgeoning of suburbs, which would soon change the city life of a large number of Americans, including this group of Japanese-Americans who worshiped together. By 1960, half of this group had moved to the suburbs, though the families that had chosen Gardena and El Monte as their places of residence continued to come to Los Angeles to worship. Okamoto began to wonder how long they would continue to make such a trip Sunday after Sunday. When one of his members told him that there was a Lutheran church just blocks from where he lived, Okamoto again wondered why he could not worship there.

He also began wondering whether they were building a "Japanese church or the Church with Japanese." He gradually came to the conclusion that the mission of the now St. Thomas Lutheran Church "was to introduce Japanese to the faith, introduce them to congregational organization, train them for active Christian and congregational life, and 'seed' them to existing Lutheran congregations." He likened the "mission to a 'hallway,' —we'd get them in, get them acquainted, and send them on." But neither the congregation nor the Southern California District shared his vision. Having failed to convince the congregation and the district, Okamoto thought the next best thing to do was to get "the Los Angeles group settled in with Trinity Lutheran Church in Los Angeles, so we could concentrate our efforts with the Gardena group." The shared vision of the congregation and the district, however, was to remain one Japanese church.

In retrospect, Okamoto felt that the clash of visions had much to do with their upbringing. He recalled that "the Japanese-Americans we served were a people of two cultures, with one culture decidedly prominently 'different.' They were born in America but also born into and raised in West coast Japanese communities. They spoke the language; ate the food; were immersed in Japanese culture. They suffered much discrimination, culminating in relocation during the early years of [World War II]. They were a wary bunch."

Okamoto's parishioners indeed were quite different from him. His parents were *Issei* (first generation) who had come to the United States after World War II. They settled in Pittsburgh, Pennsylvania, and worked as housepersons for individuals who were employed by the local steel company. They had no West Coast connections, though his mother had come through Seattle. His father, who had come through New York, never set foot on the West Coast. Later the family moved to Chicago where Okamoto was born on December 3, 1931. In Chicago the family lived on the Northwest side, with no other Asian within five miles. At home they "spoke English ... ate sauerkraut and spaghetti, goulash and borscht." And on holidays, the family "had ham for Easter, turkey for Thanksgiving, standing rib for Christmas, pickled herring and pickled pigs' feet for New Year's Eve." He and his siblings attended school with whites. Wherever they went, whatever group they joined, they were the only Japanese. Growing up, he did not know the difference and did not care. A year after he was born, his "mother was in the first adult confirmation class of the new neighborhood [LCMS] mission." Subsequently, the children "were also confirmed and became members of the Lutheran church."

In 1964 Okamoto left St. Thomas Lutheran Church to accept a call to Our Master Lutheran Church, Inkster, Michigan, where he served for ten years before becoming pastor of Our Redeemer Lutheran Church, Muskegon, Michigan, from 1974 to 1990. While serving Our Redeemer Lutheran Church, he was elected Counselor of Circuit 28 of the Michigan District, serving from 1985 to 1989. At the end of his term, he was elected second vice president of the district, a position he occupied from 1989 to 1992. In 1990, he became the pastor of Hope Lutheran Church, DeWitt, Michigan, until his retirement at the end of 1999. In 1991 he was named cochair of the district's "Growing in Vision and Mission," a program of stewardship emphasis. And since 1992 he has been the first vice president of the district.

In 1960 Okamoto married Sachiko Kohara, a Hiroshima survivor. Together they have three children, one of whom, Dr. Joel Philip Okamoto is on the faculty of CS, St. Louis, in the field of systematic theology.

In 1965, [62] St. Thomas Lutheran Church moved to Gardena, a suburb just outside Los Angeles. After Okamoto left, the congregation was served by a succession of white pastors. But the church closed its doors in 1998 and the building was sold to a Korean Baptist church.

From 1936 to 1963, The LCMS initiated four ministries with Asians in North America, with varying degrees of success. Meanwhile, within The LCMS the wind of conflict was gathering force, culminating in the church splitting in the 1970s. This cloud over The LCMS definitely affected as well as contributed to the development of the ministries, as described in chapter 5.

3

MISSIONARIES AT HOME

MISSIONARIES FROM THE BRITISH EMPIRE DOMINATED THE TRANSNATIONAL religious movement in the nineteenth century. American missionary activities at that time were primarily "aimed at evangelizing the American West." [1] It was not until the closing of the frontier that American churches began to turn their attention to foreign missions. Finally "the torch was passed to the Americans during the World Missionary Conference at Edinburgh in 1910." [2] In East Asia, China became the primary focus of these missionary efforts, though Japan also saw an increase of missionaries. For example, in 1906 there were 1,037 missionaries in China, but 10 years later the figure was 2,862. During the same period, Japan witnessed an increase from 594 missionaries in 1906 to 858 in 1916. Lutheran churches in America were also caught up in this transnational religious movement and some of these Lutheran missionaries, in retirement or in forced withdrawal, likewise made an impact on mission and ministry with Asians in North America.

This chapter describes how a United Evangelical Lutheran Church (UELC) missionary to Japan and an Augustana Lutheran Church missionary to China influenced Asian ministries in the United States.

JAPANESE MINISTRY OF THE UNITED EVANGELICAL LUTHERAN CHURCH

Before the United States' entry into World War II against Japan, the UELC had two missionary couples in that country, Dr. and Mrs. J. M. T. Winther and Rev. and Mrs. Ditlev Gotthard Monrad Bach, in addition to Miss Maya Winther. In early 1941 Miss Winther had already come back to the U.S. on furlough and it was doubtful that she would return upon completing her leave. By June of the same year, Dr. and Mrs. Winther had likewise returned to the United States and the Bachs were expected to come back soon thereafter.

The Forty-fifth Annual Convention Report of 1941 of the UELC raised a number of questions regarding what could be done with these missionaries and how they would be supported a year after their return (in other words, after July 1, 1942), as well as the possibility of taking "up a mission among the Japanese people on the Pacific Coast. There are many of them in such cities as San Francisco and Los Angeles ... in [and] around Fresno." [3] The report went on to say that since they would continue to "receive their salaries for one year...this situation will afford an opportunity to make a survey of the possibilities of mission work among the Japanese people ... [and it confidently concluded that] undoubtedly Rev. Bach would be happy to make such a survey." [4]

In October of the same year, the Bachs were present at the Thirty-seventh Annual Convention of the Pacific District. The district president's report gave no hint that Bach had been assigned to another ministry or did he mention that Bach was surveying the Pacific Coast for a possible ministry site. However, the following year's report mentioned that in the "distribution of the balance on hand [from last year,]" $25 were allocated to "Rev. and Mrs. D. G. M. Bach for their work among the Japanese in Concentration Camps." [5] But the report did not indicate exactly where the Bachs were doing their ministry. In Bach's own "Biographical Record," it was recorded that he served as a missionary among the Japanese-Americans in Fresno, California, from 1941 to 1942 and 1947 to 1956.

According to the available information, there was no concentration camp in or near Fresno, but the city did serve as an assembly center. Could the person making the district report confuse an assembly center for concentration camps? Possibly. But Lester E. Suzuki in his book, *Ministry in the Assembly and Relocation Centers of World War II*, a comprehensive and authoritative volume on the subject, never mentions Bach's ministry anywhere. It is likely that after Bach returned from Japan he and his wife settled in Fresno and did some unofficial ministry at the Fresno assembly center. His ministry was no doubt interrupted after the people from the assembly center were relocated to different concentration camps. The Bachs themselves moved to Colorado where he served as a teacher of Japanese at the Colorado University from 1942 to 1946.

Fresno Area Nisei Ministry

At the end of World War II, the Bachs returned to Fresno, but for a fairly long period of time Bach was too ill to carry on any ministry. The Board of Foreign Missions (BFM) at its annual meeting held February 18, 1947, in Minneapolis deliberated on both Bach's health and his ministry. (By this time, Bach had recovered sufficiently well from his long illness.) BFM concurred that he was well enough "to work again even if not with his former capacity." [6] Even so BFM did not think he was well enough to return to Japan. Bach himself also recognized his own physical limitation, expressing interest in ministry closer to home: as a missionary to the Japanese in California "with the idea of connecting converts with already established congregations."[7]

BFM stated that it had received "assurance that the pastors and congregations in the Fresno area will give him their moral backing."[8] BFM also reported that the Board of Foreign Missions of the United Lutheran Church in America (ULCA) "offers to pay him $1,000 a year provided the United Evangelical Lutheran Church will supplement it."[9] After some discussion and debate the following resolution was passed:

> Whereas, the condition of the Rev. D. G. M. Bach's health does not permit his return to Japan,... [the resolution proceeded to describe Bach's willingness to work in Fresno and the Fresno area pastors' backing, the UELC's conviction in evangelizing the Japanese, and the ULCA's offer of a disability allowance of $1,000. The resolution continues,] BE IT THEREFORE RESOLVED, that the Rev. D. G. M. Bach be engaged to serve as missionary in the Fresno area and that the United Evangelical Lutheran Church supplement by $1,000 the equivalent amount offered by the U.L.C. [ULCA] [10]

Bach began his ministry with the *Nisei* (second generation) after the BFM meeting. But this ministry seemed to be doomed to failure from the beginning. In the following year, for example, the author of the report to the Forty-fourth Annual Convention of the Pacific District sounded an alarm by pointing out that "the work among the Japanese ... is practically impossible."[11] The author further maintained that it was "inhuman" to expect the missionary to "build without tool, or without funds." [12] Nevertheless, the Bachs continued to conduct classes in their home twice a week.

The same report also pointed out that Bach was able to break down "the mountain of prejudice," as evidenced by the Del Rey congregation, which in the end might have contributed to the closing of the Nisei ministry, as detailed below. The author of the report likewise challenged the San Joaquin Valley congregations to adopt and support this mission.

In the meantime, the matter of supervision came up among district officials. It seems that the working relationship between the district and Bach was breaking down and the local officials did not know how to handle him. Thus, they decided to send a delegation to attend the Board of Home Missions (BHM) meeting on February 14-16, 1950. The delegation and BHM discussed Bach's activities along with the matter of supervision. At the end of the discussion, the following motion was passed: "That we respectfully request the Church Council to transfer the supervision of the work among the Japanese on the West Coast to the Board of Home Missions." [13]

The matter of funding soon also entered into the discussion. The executive secretary of the BFM in 1951 or 1952 called attention to this matter. BFM offered a resolution calling the transfer of financial responsibility to the BHM. [14] The BHM accepted this responsibility to the tune of $3,000 a year.[15]

While the matters of supervision and finance were discussed and transferred from one unit of the church to another, the district in 1952 "purchased the Rosedale School in the locality between Easton and Del Rey," [16] with the intention of making it into a residence for the Bachs and a worship-social center for the ministry. At the same time, the district sounded an alarm. It seems that an evaluation was about to take place and the district warned that that must not be done by the district board alone, but that every concerned individual should be involved, and that Bach himself would welcome an open discussion on the convention floor. What brought all this about was the district board's own uncertainty of the mission after a site visit.

Besides offering classes twice a week in his home and trying to win the valley congregations' welcome to the Nisei, what else did Bach's ministry consist of? It seems that by 1952 he had visited a large number of Nisei along with publishing a piece called the "Nisei Lutheran," necessitated by the fact that the Nisei community was so tied down by work "that it is all but impossible to gather them for regular meetings." [17] In addition, Bach also had an interdenominational radio program aimed at the Issei, a regular visitation program for shut-ins, various social activities at his home, and classes in English and in citizenship. Further, Bach was also cooperating with Pella Lutheran Church in Del Rey in ministering to the Nisei.

The Nisei membership at Pella as of 1952 was reported as follows: "baptized 9, confirmed 1. No Nisei were taken in during 1952. Two Nisei were dropped. The average attendance of Nisei members at morning worship services: 4. During the year 6 Nisei infants and 4 Nisei adults were baptized. Confirmed: 1 Nisei child, 1 Nisei adult. About 10-12 Nisei children are enrolled in the Sunday school. 2-3 attend Bible class. There were no Nisei children enrolled for confirmation in 1952. 4-5 Nisei children attended the vacation Bible school." [18] From this confusing report one can deduce that the maximum Nisei membership at Pella stood at 20.

At the same time in Bach's report to BHM, in which he listed his various activities, he also admitted that the past year had been one of crisis for him and his wife and questioned the UELC's sincerity in this mission. Bach did not explicitly state the nature of the crisis. But from the tone of report, it seemed that he was having a disagreement with someone. For example, at one point he wrote, "then 'the word of the Lord came to us' and said: you have been calling other people stupid, and they are; but have you thought of the fact that you yourself are being stupid: you have not yet understood that God uses the stupidity of human beings to work out his plan." [19]

BHM at the same time received the following request from Pastor A.

P. Andersen of Pella Lutheran Church. Because of its significance, it shall be quoted in full: "In order to avoid and forestall any difficulty and conflict, which I see could be probable, as well as possible, in the future, I make this special request of the Board of Home Missions—that two matters be definitely understood and adhered to in the work among the Nisei, namely: (1) That there be no transfer of Nisei members from the Del Rey congregation to the Rosedale unit. (2) That all instruction in Christianity and ministerial acts be done by the local pastor of the Del Rey Church. This is to include all Nisei in the Del Rey area." [20] The conflict between Bach and Andersen now becomes very apparent. And Bach's sarcasm does not stop here, as we shall soon see.

By the end of 1953, the renovation of the Rosedale property was just about completed and ready for use. In the same year, the Nisei themselves had an idea as to what could be done with land surrounding the building. They hoped to build small cottages for their aged and donated an initial sum of $600 for this purpose.

In the meantime, BHM disavowed the work in the Fresno area as "a regular home mission work" and put it into a category of "special work in American Missions." [21] In retrospect, this political move put the mission in position for termination. Bach's own personality may very well have contributed to the uncertainty of the mission, the disavowal of ownership, and the termination. In the process of terminating this ministry, the church received some help from the most unlikely quarter—Supreme Court of the United States, which declared segregation illegal in 1955.

The Report on Home Missions to the Fifty-ninth Annual Convention quickly pointed out that "because of the ruling by the Supreme Court paving the way for nonsegregation toward minority groups such as Negroes, Jews, Indians, Mexicans, and Orientals the Church is facing the problem of rearranging its work wherever it ministers to these groups." [22]

Without knowing the details of the UELC's ministry to the "Negroes," the "Jews," the "Indians" and the "Mexicans," the historian must accept this statement at face value. But when it comes to the "Orientals," namely the Japanese in this case, it was clearly stated from the beginning that Bach's ministry was to integrate the Nisei into existing white congregations. In fact a year before the Supreme Court action, BHM passed the following motion, "The work among the Nisei shall not be done with the view of establishing a separate Nisei congregation but it shall attempt to integrate the Nisei Christians into the congregations of the community." [23] (This motion was passed probably in response to Bach's request to organize a Nisei congregation.) Therefore one must question the intent of this statement regarding the "Orientals," particularly in view of the fact that a year later, BHM at its annual meeting cited "the policies established by the National Lutheran Council government nonsegregation"[24] as an excuse to transfer Bach's work into a different category.

In 1955 Bach was not old enough to retire and be eligible for pension and Social Security. BHM, at its annual meeting held in March that year, proposed to offer him a two-year term at a salary of $3,500 per annum. That meant Bach would retire at the close of 1956 or shortly thereafter. It was not certain that this decision was communicated to Bach. In the meantime, the Rosedale property was transferred from the Pacific District to the UELC. The Bachs were supposed to stay on at Rosedale.

When Bach learned of the decision, he was not at all pleased. In an October 3, 1956, letter to Rev. K. M. Matthiesen, executive secretary of BHM, Bach said, "also it appeared in print somewhere that the decision to retire Bach as of end of 1956 was UNANIMOUS as far as the Board was concerned. This was an unfortunate misstatement, when we know there was a minority dissent."

From this point on, if not before, the relationship between Bach and Matthiesen only got worse, with verbal assaults and name-calling. In another letter to Matthiesen, dated January 30, 1957, Bach called him a "liar" and proceeded to lecture him on his stupidity. On his part, Matthiesen withheld Bach's rent allowance and possibly accused him for teaching heresy.

Bach was not intimidated. He admitted, "I am a heretic because I interpret the Lutheran faith as best I can to the Nisei." Then he went on to accuse Matthiesen for being so theologically ignorant and financially so greedy. Bach continued, "you who do not know the first rudiments of theology, and that the only glasses you are wearing consist of a dollar sign." Based on financial reasons, Matthiesen some years back had objected to Bach's desire to organize a Nisei congregation and told Bach to "cut out the complaints." To which Bach now let Matthiesen know of his bitterness: "Karl," he continued, "I could forgive you for all this if you were not so inexcusably stupid. I suppose some day I shall even be forgiving you for that. Your very stupidity is the guarantee."

Bach further accused Matthiesen of running the church like a general would run an army. The concluding sentence of this letter makes it quite apparent that Matthiesen was trying to force Bach to do things his way, but Bach refused: "you are forcing me to turn my back to you and say, 'Kiss my fanny.'"

While Bach and Matthiesen were exchanging personal verbal insults and other forms of unbrotherly rivalry, the Pacific District board sealed the fate of the ministry with a resolution, which, in part, reads: "BE IT RESOLVED: (1) That this work be continued by the local churches. (2) That we do not place a pastor at the Rosedale Lutheran Center. (3) That as of May 1, 1959, we discontinue the work at the Rosedale Center. As to the property, the district board will study what best usage can be made of same and present to next year's convention." [25]

Politics, local and national, personality conflicts, ignorance of the needs of the Nisei, and the "missionary mind" finally were responsible for the closing of this mission to the Nisei.

CHINESE MINISTRY OF THE AUGUSTANA LUTHERAN CHURCH

The Augustana Lutheran Church, which was known as the Augustana Synod until 1918, originated from Sweden. In 1870 Augustana joined the General Council, another church body, but it retained considerable powers in matters such as ordination of ministers, missions, at home and overseas, and so forth. For missions in East Asia, it began sending missionaries to central Henan Province, China, in 1905.

During the first half of the twentieth century, China was a war-torn nation, with the Communist Party finally achieving victory in 1949. The change of political wind compelled the Augustana Lutheran Church to evacuate its missionaries from China proper by the end of that year. Most of the evacuated missionaries returned to the United States. But some moved to other parts of Asia. Among them were Dr. Victor E. and Mrs. Evodia Swenson, [26] who had served in China proper from 1913 to 1949. In 1952 they decided to go to Taiwan, where they served until retirement in 1957. After retirement they moved to Pasadena, California.

Pasadena is the home of a number of institutions of higher learning, including the California Institute of Technology, initially known as Throop College of Technology. These institutions attracted a large number of Chinese students. By 1960, the Chinese population in Pasadena became quite noticeable. Seeing so many Chinese in their midst, Mrs. Swenson, felt that her dream of someday establishing a Chinese congregation might have a chance to come true. After some consulting with her husband, they together turned to a young man by the name of Wilson Wu for help.

On January 1, 1960, Wu arrived from Wilmore, Kentucky, where he had been doing graduate studies at Ashbury Theological Seminary, to begin the ministry in Pasadena. Wu was charged to work with the students, with the intention of eventually organizing a congregation. But Wu's work was not connected with or supported by the California Lutheran Conference of the Augustana Lutheran Church, or any other church body. It was a ministry under the private sponsorship of the Swensons. They provided Wu a place to live in their home. To support himself and his family, which was still in Taiwan, Wu sold plastic products produced by a factory owned by the LWF in Hong Kong. Part of his earnings would be returned to the LWF to help refugees who were in Hong Kong. In a sense, Wu was one of the very first, if not the first, Asian Lutheran "worker priests" in North America.

The relationship between the Swensons and Wu dates back to the time when they were all in China. Wu, whose parents were converted to Christianity by the Swensons, is a second generation Augustana Lutheran by birth. His father was a merchant in real estate and the coal business, while his mother assumed the traditional role of Chinese women.

Wu, standing at six-feet-two-inches tall, with a square face and broad shoulders—tall and big for the Chinese of his generation, was born on October 18, 1928, in Zhengzhou, Henan, China. During the first two decades of his life, Wu experienced one civil war after another, not to mention the devastation brought about by World War II. This culminated in the Communist party's takeover of China in 1949. But faith sustained the Wu family through thick and thin.

While destruction and chaos were everywhere in China, Wu's parents were determined to give their young son an education. Thus, from his primary to high school years, they sent him to a mission school organized by Augustana missionaries. Wu's schooling, however, was often interrupted either by the raging wars or by the advancing Communist army. The family from time to time had to move to the countryside to escape from the conflicts.

In 1948, as the Chinese civil war was coming to a decisive end, LWF decided to evacuate all missionaries and some natives from Zhengzhou. Wu climbed onto the last LWF chartered plane leaving China for Hong Kong. Shortly after arriving in Hong Kong, Wu began his theological training at the Hubei-Shekou Lutheran Theological Seminary, which by then had been relocated to Hong Kong, and which was also the predecessor of the now Lutheran Theological Seminary of Hong Kong.

After graduation in 1952, Wu was assigned to serve in a church in Hong Kong for six months before moving to Taiwan to develop a church in Fengshan. In 1957, he received a full scholarship to study at Ashbury Theological Seminary, where he spent the next three years.

Though hard at work in this ministry but without authorization and support from the California Lutheran Conference and being a "worker priest" working with a transient population, Wu was not successful in fulfilling Mrs. Swenson's dream. The dream, however, did not die but was carried on by Wu into the Lutheran Church in America.

Neither Bach nor Wu succeeded in establishing a congregation. But their labor had contributed to heightening the consciousness of Lutheran denominations about Asian presence in North America.

4

ANOTHER BEGINNING

THIS CHAPTER DESCRIBES THE JAPANESE MINISTRIES OF THE UNITED LUTHERAN Church in America (ULCA) and a Chinese ministry of the Lutheran Church in America (LCA). Before going into detailed description of the ministries, a brief general background of each church is presented to provide a context for the reader.

JAPANESE MINISTRY IN THE UNITED LUTHERAN CHURCH IN AMERICA

The ULCA came into being in 1918 as a result of the merger of the General Synod, the General Council, and the United Synod of the South. It soon became the largest Lutheran body in the United States and its influence was to be reckoned with in the ecclesiastical world. Two of its predecessor bodies—the General Council and the General Synod—cooperated in mission work in Japan. Even so, the ULCA itself was not ready to initiate ministry with persons of Japanese ancestry in North America. Consideration to working with the Japanese was given only after the church came under pressure from two sources—the Synod of California and the newly organized Japan Evangelical Lutheran Church (JELC) in Japan.

Request from the California Synod

Sometime during the biennium of 1934 to 1936, the Board of the American Missions (BAM) of the ULCA received a request from the Synod of California asking BAM to "consider the sad condition of the thousands of Japanese on the Pacific Coast." [1] While acknowledging that this was a "neglected field of evangelization" and promising to give it "serious consideration," BAM did nothing more than make a preliminary study of the situation on the Pacific Coast. BAM gave "unfavorable financial condition" as the reason for not honoring the synodical request in the 1938 report to the Eleventh Biennial Convention.

The Home Mission Committee (HMC) of the Synod of California was not pleased by BAM's lack of action. In its report to the 1937 Annual Convention, this committee expressed frustration over a "serious problem" in "oriental" work in the cities of Los Angeles and San Francisco. It further stated that BAM had assured the committee of cooperation in this endeavor, and yet nothing had happened.[2]

Thus, four years later HMC once again submitted a request to BAM asking it to inaugurate work among the Japanese in the city of Los Angeles. This request was not honored either, because missionary S. O. Thorlaksson could not leave Japan for the time being, as described below. HMC's desire to initiate work among the Japanese was not realized until 1953.

Appeal from Japan

Even though HMC did not realize its desire immediately, it did get some help from an unlikely quarter. During the biennium of 1936 to 1938, BAM received an appeal from the newly evangelized JELC in Japan, requesting the board to begin mission work among the Japanese in America. The appeal was formally adopted at JELC's annual convention and forwarded to BAM via BFM.

It appeared that this appeal had quite an impact on BAM's thinking, for it "ordered an immediate investigation of the possibilities in this field."[3] The impact of this appeal was further seen in the following statement on the BAM report: "This situation [on the Pacific Coast]... should rebuke us and stir us to action."[4] This swift change of minds and hearts of the BAM staff seemed to be due to a sudden realization that, in this case, it was the "recently evangelized" church that was calling the "mother church to the spiritual needs of its nationals in our own country!"[5]

Board of American Missions Plan

Having committed itself to the field, BAM set out to secure a person who was knowledgeable of the Japanese in America to do further investigation of the situation. In cooperation and consultation with BFM, BAM secured "the services of Missionary Thorlaksson."[6] He made a favorable full report to BAM, recommending that the work among the Japanese be confined to those persons who were born in America, because there was no ministry being carried out among them by other denominations.[7] The Women's Missionary Society of the ULCA was highly interested in this mission and appropriated enough funds to begin this ministry. With the backing of this group, BAM decided to rely on the church in Japan to find a qualified missionary to staff the mission. The church in Japan identified missionary Thorlaksson who had done the investigation of the field earlier.

By this time the relationship between the United States and Japan had become strained, making it impossible for Thorlaksson to come back immediately. And by the time Thorlaksson finally returned, the entire Japanese population had been placed in 10 concentration camps in different parts of the United States. The effort to minister with the American-born Japanese was aborted, but not entirely given up. "As far as possible," stated a BAM report in 1942, "our workers are keeping in touch with these groups and will continue to do so until such time as conditions will permit the beginning of an organized work among them." [8] The organized work as stated earlier, would not take place until 1953. The same report also mentioned that a pastor Knutden, who was a BAM mission developer in Gardena, California, "was permitted to visit and preach at one these [concentration] camps," [9] attracting large crowds at both Japanese and English services.

Hostel Ministry

True to its word, BAM continued to look for opportunities to provide ministry with the Japanese. That opportunity came in 1943 when the U.S. government decided to draft eligible internees to join the military and to allow others to leave camp, providing that they would move inland. The latter would need transitional places to stay "until jobs and permanent homes [were] provided." [10] BAM looked at the opportunity to provide hostel services to the Japanese as the most promising ministry that would give permanent results, surpassing "the many efforts of the Christian churches in America to minister to the spiritual and moral welfare of Americans of Japanese parentage suffering under war restrictions." [11]

After consulting with the Interdenominational Committee of the Federal Council and having secured financial support from the Women's Missionary Society, BAM opened a hostel in Minneapolis toward the end of 1943. [12] An experienced missionary to Japan now on enforced war furlough was hired to head the hostel. [13] The efforts were quite successful. The report for the first five months of operation gave a detailed breakdown on the total number of persons using the facility, number of meals served, the cost per meal, the average number of days each person stayed, as well as her or his religious affiliation. And to everyone's delight, the 1944 report continued that "excluding the original outlay for the property and the missionary's salary, the hostel is practically self-supporting." [14] The service was discontinued after the war.

Local Effort

While HMC made repeated requests to BAM to inaugurate work among the Japanese on the Pacific Coast, St. Paul's Lutheran Church in Los Angeles decided to take the matter into its own hands. The pastor of the congregation [15] in 1936 or 1937 made a survey of the Japanese population residing in that city and estimated the total to be about 25,000. With this information in hand, the congregation initiated a Sunday school for Japanese children. It was reported in 1937 that there were 12 children of Japanese parentage in its Sunday school.

HMC was pessimistic about the potential success of this ministry. Indeed, in its 1937 report the committee unequivocally stated "if this work is to be continued with any assurance of success there must be a trained leader and financial assistance by the church at large." [16]

The outcome of this ministry seemed to bear out the committee's pessimism. Several factors appeared to be involved: (1) there was no financial support from the church-at-large, though BAM pledged cooperation; (2) there was a pastoral change in 1940 and the congregation was headed by an interim pastor for some time; (3) there was indication that the 1936 earthquake might have damaged the building; (4) there was a decline in membership. [17]

It is evident from the above accounts that the prewar efforts to minister with the Japanese were not successful. The hostel ministry, though successful in meeting the needs of the moment, was short lived. The work among the Japanese would not resume until 1953.

Los Angeles-Based Ministry

The majority of Japanese internees returned to the West Coast shortly after World War II. When a BAM missionary arrived in Los Angeles in 1953, the Japanese population in that city was estimated at 35,000, with "about twenty organized Japanese churches scattered over the city, most of them with two pastors, one for the Issei and one for the Nisei." [18] There were Buddhist temples located in that city as well.

What then was the purpose of the BAM mission in this city? Why should it take so long before this mission materialized, in view of the fact that conversations regarding ministries to the Japanese on the West Coast had been on going for about 16 years? Would BAM on its own have commissioned this mission? The following pages provide some answers to these questions and a description of the mission.

The decision to begin a ministry with the Japanese in Los Angeles after World War II can be traced to the recommendation regarding mission "among Orientals in the U.S.A." of BFM. At its February 3-5, 1947, meeting BFM passed the following recommendation, which, for the sake of providing the reader with proper context and background, is quoted in full below:

> ... voted (a) that whereas the work of the Board of Foreign
> Missions among the Japanese people in Japan is related to
> the spiritual conditions of the Japanese people of the
> United States, the Board of Foreign Missions respectfully
> calls the attention of the Executive Board of the United

Lutheran Church to the great need and opportunity for Lutheran work among the Japanese in the United States. (b) that since this is not in the province of the Board of Foreign Missions, we suggest that the Executive Board delegate this work to some agency of the U.L.C.A. or refer it to the National Lutheran Council. The Committee on Boards and Committees RECOMMENDS that the secretary be requested to report to the Board of Foreign Missions and to the Board of American Missions, that missionary work among Orientals in this country is at present the prerogative of the Board of American Missions. [19]

This recommendation was transmitted to BAM, which in its 1950 report to the convention mentioned nothing about it or the work among the Japanese on the West Coast. It seems what BAM did was once again spend time and energy investigating the field, as evidenced in its 1952 report, which stated that BAM "recognizes the need for Lutheran work among Asiatics on the Pacific Coast and during the biennium has made an extensive investigation of such need and is still seeking ways and means to do the mission work that should be done in this field." [20]

Meanwhile during the 1952 convention, Thorlaksson, "moved that 'this convention encourage the Board of American Missions to occupy the field of Oriental Missions in the United States and Canada.'" [21] Before World War II he had investigated the field for BAM and was recommended by the JELC to undertake the work. Debates and discussions ensued, followed by a substitute motion introduced by Rev. J. J. Scherer Jr., which stated "that we encourage the Board of American Missions and the Board of Social Missions (BSM) to put on a more intensive program of evangelism amongst the Orientals of the United States and Canada." [22] The convention adopted the substitute motion.

BSM seemed to have taken this motion seriously. The Committee on Boards and Committees presented to the Executive Board at its January 1953 meeting the following report and recommendations: "At a meeting of the Board of Social Missions on November 13, 1952: 'It was moved that the Board of Social Missions send an inquiry to the Executive Board of the U.L.C.A. as to the most desirable procedure of the carrying out the recommendation of the 1952 Convention of the U.L.C.A.' [the said recommendation was stated]." [23] The Committee on Boards and Committees, having presented this report, proceeded to make its own recommendation, which reads in part: "the Executive Board indicated that the most desirable procedure will be (1) for the Board of American Missions to state its views and present intentions regarding this subject in a memorandum addressed to the Executive Board and (2) for the Executive Board to share this memorandum with the Board of Social Missions. After these steps have been taken, it can be determined later whether a conference between the two boards will be needed or not."[24]

At the Executive Board's April meeting, the Committee on Boards and Committees again presented the following report and recommendations, which seem to be important enough to warrant quoting it in full:

> Under date of February 25, 1953, the Board of American Missions transmitted to Secretary Reinartz the following memorandum regarding evangelism among Orientals in reply to the request of the Executive Board at the January 1953 meeting 'for the Board of American Missions to state its views and present intentions regarding this subject': Complying with item (1) of the Executive Board's recommendation concerning evangelism among Orientals, the Board of American Missions has long felt a responsibility toward the Orientals on the Pacific coast. In fact at one time it was sponsoring work among them until evacuation during the World War ended it. A quest for proper personnel to supervise the work has finally resulted in our employment of the Rev. L. S. G. Miller, D.D. to head it up. Our view for his task is primarily to ascertain the need for and response to Lutheran work among Orientals. Practically his primary purpose is to get the pastors of existing churches interested in and to work among these people and correspondingly to help interest the Orientals in membership in existing churches. Wherever there is such a concentration of them as to make it embarrassing to existing congregations to have so many of the Orientals unite with them, the Board will consider supporting the organization of separate congregations. As to the part of the Board of Social Missions should have in this task we have no knowledge at present. It is our opinion on the facts at hand that the Orientals are self-sufficient citizens and need nothing in the field of social welfare work beyond that of any group of Americans.[25]

This BAM memorandum raises three interesting points. First, what does BAM mean by the following sentence, "wherever there is such a concentration of them as to make it embarrassing to existing congregations to have so many of the Orientals unite with them, the Board will consider supporting the organization of separate congregations"? Second, what were the facts at hand that caused BAM officials to have such a strong opinion on Asians' self-sufficiency? Third, did BAM officials include "Negroes," "Mexicans," and "Indians" in their reference to "any group of Americans"? In retrospect, is this the "model minority" myth in the making? ("Model minori-ty" is a sociological theory referring to how Asians in America have "made it" and therefore don't need social services or external support from the gov-ernment.) BAM officials never gave as much as a small hint to what they meant by the second point. But the first would come back to haunt them.

The memorandum was forwarded to BSM, which at its April 23, 1953, meeting indicated "its desire for a conference with the Board of American Missions 'to discuss the need of social missions work' among Orientals." [26] BSM obviously saw the "Orientals" in a different light. The conference between the two boards was held on September 3, 1953. Among the items reviewed by the participants was BAM's "'view and present intentions' regard-ing this subject." [27]

The conference, in the end, approved "the following statement (paragraphs 1-3 inclusive) in the February 25, 1953, memo of the Board of American Missions [quoted above]." [28] The conference further recognized the BSM's readiness to render "assistance in evangelism among Orientals...and to encourage all congregations to include in their 'responsi-bility list' members of any and all minority groups." [29]

BSM at its November 12, 1953, meeting seemed to have picked up the racial overtone of BAM's statement in its memorandum, for when the matter came under discussion, BSM "voted its approval of the findings with the understanding that the reference in the statement 'Wherever there is such a concentration of them as to make it embarrassing to existing congre-gations to have so many Orientals unite with them' carries no element of race prejudice but refers to practical problems of administration and organ-ization within the congregation.'" [30]

BSM was not the only one to raise the question concerning BAM's statement. The 1954 convention itself was concerned with BSM's interpretation of it and "asked whether the phrase, 'race prejudice,' and 'practical problems of administration and organization within the congregation' were synonymous or contrasting." [31] After some discussions and debates the convention approved the following resolution: "That the Executive Board be instructed to present an interpretation or clarification of the next to the last paragraph of Item xi, 3, on page 310 (of the Minutes of the 1954 ULCA convention)." [32]

The committee consulted with both executive secretaries of BAM and BSM "to gain full and accurate information as to the intention behind the disputed words." [33] The conclusion was that the "practical problems" referred to were *linguistic* and not *racial*, and "that the original phraseology 'carried no element of race prejudice.'" [34] An incredible explanation, since the mission was supposed to integrate into existing congregations the English-speaking Nisei or those Japanese who would have no problem with English.

While the bureaucrats, committee members, and convention delegates debated over the intent of the BAM memorandum, the work among the
Japanese in Los Angeles had already begun with the arrival of Miller in May
1953. A month later, Paul T. Nakamura, a seminarian who would graduate in
early 1955, joined him. They formed a good team, but "the results [of their
work] are not calculable by statistics because the largest part of the work
[was] concerned with securing the interest and welcome of existing congregations for the Orientals in the coastal area as well as directing interested
people from Asia into such congregations." [35]

Miller and Nakamura had an unenviable task. The "coastal area"
referred to ranges from San Diego, California, to Vancouver, British Columbia,
not to mention that locally they had to "conduct a Sunday school in the parsonage of the missionary which not only evangelizes the children but wins
the good will and interest of parents toward Christianity." [36]

As summer slowly changed to autumn, the two teammates were
becoming good friends. Miller during the next two years would play a significant role in the life of Nakamura, as his friend, confidant, and mentor.

Miller carried on the ministry after Nakamura returned to seminary
to continue his preparation. In Nakamura's absence, Miller wrote to inform
him how much the children, the few they had in Sunday school, missed him
and how he himself longed to hear Nakamura's whistling, which was something the latter was so fond of doing as he approached the missionary's
home. In another letter, he told Nakamura of his survey trip on behalf of
BAM along the coast from Los Angeles to Vancouver, with a side trip to
Spokane, Washington. In other letters he kept Nakamura informed of what
was happening in the lives of the individual adults who had occasionally
attended worship services with them.

Nakamura in turn shared the joy of his relationship with a certain
young woman by the name of Kiku (Kikuno Miyagi), who eventually married Nakamura and became his "inspiration and partner in the ministry." [37] He
also confessed to a poor grade he got in one course. In his response, Miller
advised Nakamura on the matter of romance and sympathized with him
regarding the low grade. Miller and Nakamura's relationship was platonic as
well as professional and without the presence of self-interest.

Lewis Samuel Godfry Miller (usually known as L. S. G. Miller) was born
on August 23, 1881, at Salem, Virginia, the son of Rev. Lewis G. M. and Mrs. Laura
Campbell Miller. After completing his education at Roanoke College and the
Lutheran Theological Seminary at Philadelphia, Pennsylvania, in 1901 and 1907
respectively, he was ordained in 1907. After ordination he was commissioned
as a missionary by the United Synod of the South and in 1908 began his long
service overseas at Fukuoka, Japan. Two years later he assumed the position of
dean at the Kyushu Gakuin at Kumamoto until his retirement in 1952.

He returned to the United States during the war years and served parishes in Elberton, Georgia, and Laurel, Mississippi. After the war, he was the first Lutheran missionary to return to Japan where he helped to reorganize the Japan Lutheran Church and continued his post at the school. The Emperor of Japan, with the Order of the Sacred Treasure, Third Grade, decorated him in 1951. [38] This was then the highest decoration that was given to a foreigner.

When he retired in 1952, the Japanese people and officials alike honored him. "The Kumamoto Prefectural Governor published the merit of Dr. Miller's work in the field of Christian education.... [And] the Japanese mourn [his departure] today." [39] He was recalled to service in 1953 and finally retired at the close of 1956. After retirement he returned to his beloved Virginia and died on August 29, 1977, in Winchester, Virginia.

Miller's young friend came from a different and fascinating background. His ministry would eventually cover, as of this writing, as many years as that of his "old" friend. Nakamura also has the distinction in being the first native-born Asian-American Lutheran clergy to minister with the Asians—in this case the Japanese-Americans—in North America.

Paul Takeichi Nakamura was one of nine children born to Mr. and Mrs. Teikichi Nakamura, who emigrated from the Prefecture of Yamaguchi, Japan, to Hawaii. The Nakamuras were Buddhist by faith, which they demonstrated by "caring for their family shrines daily and attending the monthly service," their son Paul recalled. When Paul Takeichi, their eighth son, was born on July 13, 1926, they were living in the sugar cane district of Waialua, which is situated on the North Shore coast of Oahu.

Young Nakamura's life, at the risk of oversimplification and stereotyping, was idyllic. As a child, he would roam in the banana and sugar cane fields, walk along paths shaded by papaya trees and wedged in by lotus ponds, and explore the streams alongside the paths.

His parents, being immigrants, worked diligently to support their family. Mama Nakamura ran a small store called "Nakamura Store" in town, while Papa Nakamura was a proud owner of a small fish market, "plus peddl[ed] the fish on his truck equipped with an icebox." [40] The children slept on the floor, spreading their futons each night and folding them every morning. Crowded as they were in a small house, they got along well. Nakamura attributed this to his parents, who "never showed anger or used harsh words. They were very tolerant and caring." [41]

The elder Nakamuras' attitude of tolerance was extended beyond their household to other religions. The tenets and values of their religion were important to them, but they never verbally taught them to their children. They lived out those tenets and values in their daily life. When their young son, Paul Takeichi, was in second or third grade, his Chinese friend

took him to an Episcopal mission Sunday school, with the elder Nakamuras'
blessing. When he was in fourth grade his brother, Masuo, took him to the
Japanese Congregational Church where he was eventually baptized. Young
Nakamura was an active member of that church.

The year 1946 was decisive for young Nakamura. He went to the
island of Kauai as a member of his church's deputation team, a group of
young persons who went to other churches to witness the faith. During this
trip he felt the call and decided to dedicate himself to God as an ordained
minister of the church.

To accomplish his goal he enlisted in the U.S. Army so that he could
get his college education and seminary training paid for with the GI Bill.
After a period of training at the Army language school at the Presidio in
Monterey, California, in October 1947, he was sent to Japan. In January 1948,
he was assigned to the Counter Intelligence Corps in Tokyo. In May he was
sent to Okinawa, where he completed his term of service that summer.

In the fall of 1948, the Congregationalist Nakamura was studying at
Gustavus Adolphus College, a Lutheran institution in St. Peter, Minnesota.
Three years later he became a first year student at Andover Newton
Theological Seminary in Newton Centre, near Boston. After the first semester
there, he transferred to Augustana Lutheran Seminary, Rock Island, Illinois.
After one semester at Augustana he returned to Andover Newton, but the
ecumenical Nakamura transferred back again to the seminary in Rock
Island in the winter of 1953. This time he not only stayed at Augustana for
good, but also decided to join a local Lutheran congregation. He became a
Lutheran in the same year. It was while he was at Augustana Lutheran
Seminary that BAM assigned him to do summer work with L. S. G. Miller in
Los Angeles in 1953.

Even though BAM's objective for Miller's work seemed to be clear,
Miller in his wisdom discussed the method of approach with his young associate. Their discussions centered on the following questions: "Should we
attempt to organize a new segregated Japanese congregation ... or should
we take the method of integration as the Board wants, and more so, as the
Christian way of approaching the whole work?" [42]

Nakamura spent part of that summer doing field research and com-
piled a report in which he stated "the program of integration is undoubtedly
the best." [43] In the same report Nakamura provided a glimpse into the fruit of
their labor that summer: "Approximately thirteen to fifteen children were sent
to vacation Bible school at St. Mark's Lutheran Church. Then on Sundays, a
Sunday school in the neighborhood is conducted in Dr. Miller's home." [44]
Nakamura went on to state "the work is very slow.... The greatest handicap is
the lack of an adequate meeting place." [45] Nakamura further sensed the enor-
mity of the task facing Miller. Thus, he concluded his report with a recom-

mendation: "that if possible, an aide—probably a parish worker or an intern preferably a Nisei, be sent to assist Dr. Miller throughout the year." [46]

No aid was sent to assist Miller, but in the summer of 1954, Nakamura was back in Los Angeles assisting Miller and whistling even more blissfully. For it was in this summer that he met Kiku, who was attending Holiness Church. Kiku was born in Hawaii and spent the war time years in two concentration camps in Arkansas—Jerome and Rohwer. They were married in 1955, after Nakamura's graduation from Augustana Lutheran Seminary in the same year.

In the summer 1954, too, there were telltale signs that Dr. Howard Anspach, pastor of St. Mark's Lutheran Church, Los Angeles, was having health problems, which were confirmed later by Miller in his letters to Nakamura. After graduation, Nakamura again returned to Los Angeles to work with Miller until the latter finally retired at the close of 1956. Miller's retirement coincided with that of Anspach's.

Ordained in 1955, Nakamura worked with Miller and in 1957 was called to be the pastor of St. Mark's Lutheran Church, which by this time had become a congregation of people from the African-American, Japanese-American, and Anglo-American communities. Nakamura's ministry at St. Mark's eventually became the foundation of the Japanese ministry in Torrance, California. But the historian is getting slightly ahead of the story. Instead, this history next turns to a ministry in the San Francisco Bay area, some 400 miles north of Los Angeles.

San Francisco Bay Area Ministry

On September 27, 1954, Miller wrote a letter to Nakamura, telling him, among other things, about the possibility of a call for him after graduation and that Miller and his wife had taken Kiku, the future Mrs. Nakamura, "to hear Bishop Lilje." Toward the end of this long letter, Miller stated that there was "a Lutheran Nisei Theological student at Hamma, Mr. Ujiie." He believed "the Board [BAM] could interest him in work among the Nisei rather than for him to go to Japan." He also intimated to Nakamura that he had written "the Board several letters about him." Further he told Nakamura that Ujiie "seems quite a fine fellow and the [professors] at Hamma seem to think a lot of him." Finally, he told Nakamura something about Ujiie's personal life. Miller continued: "He is married and has three children. Had quite a war experience and after the war was connected with the army courts in Yokohama as interpreter and investigator."

When the Miller letter arrived in Nakamura's mailbox, Ujiie was busily wrapping up his final year at Hamma Divinity School, Columbus, Ohio, and hoping to go to Japan as a missionary. But in the 1955 Field Record of the ULCA there was an entry that reads: "San Francisco, Oriental. Approved for

Entrance, 9/14/55. Entered, 6/1/55." [47] The Field Record, however, gives no hint as to who was assigned to this ministry. Was the person assigned to this ministry the one whom Miller had hoped for and had spent so much time and energy trying to interest BAM to take notice of? Of course it was he.

His full name is Shigeru Samuel Ujiie, the son of a railroad section foreman and a schoolteacher. The record of the Pacific Southwest Synod, which states that he was ordained in 1955 and entered the synod in 1956, confirms my assertion. The same record also gives his address at 1505 California St., Berkeley, California, a city directly across the bay east of San Francisco.

Ujiie was born in 1921 in Shoshoni, Wyoming. His parents were originally from northern Japan, which distinguished them from the majority of other immigrants who came from southern Japan. The first stop in their journey was Hawaii. When his father finally came to San Francisco some years later, he was unable to integrate into the Japanese community, consisting of southerners. During the day he worked and at night he studied English. When his English was proficient enough, he moved to Wyoming to work for the railway, rising to the position of section foreman within a short period. But his charges spoke Spanish only. Thus, he had to learn Spanish as well, giving rise to a unique phenomenon. When his son, Sam—as his colleagues and friends call Shigeru Samuel Ujiie—was old enough to speak, his first language was Spanish.

Ujiie had a usual sort of childhood, attending school first in a one-room schoolhouse. His mother, however, wanted him to enter into the medical profession. Thus, when he was ready for college, he was sent to the University of Nebraska, Lincoln, where he spent one year. He then transferred to Midland College, a Lutheran institution in Fremont, Nebraska, to pursue his studies in the field of humanities. He became a member of Salem Lutheran Church. While he was at Midland College, he declared himself to be a pre-seminary student and worked at Pathfinder Hotel and Hahn's Bakery to support himself. It was also at Midland where Ujiie met and developed a life-long friendship with Levon Spath, who had a distinguish a career as a missionary to Argentina. When World War II broke out, the college registered Ujiie at Western Theological Seminary, which was also located in town, in order to get a deferment. He was drafted anyway because he himself did not choose to be deferred.

The Army assigned him first to the Philippines and then Japan, where he ended up in the intelligence unit of the occupation forces. While in Japan he met a young woman, who would later become his wife. When he informed his superiors of his intention to marry her, they transferred him to the War Crimes Defense of the Judge Advocate Section of the 8th Army. After they were married, his wife refused to live in the dependent housing in Yokohama, and instead they had a place on the outskirts of Yokohama called Nakayama.

After his discharge from the army, Ujiie took a civil service examination in order to stay in Japan. He worked in the Defense Section until March 1946. Their home became the center where young Japanese would come for English lessons. Ujiie taught them, using the Bible. "It turned out more like an evangelism session than anything else," Ujiie recalled years later. At the same time, he felt that he had neglected his calling. So he resigned his position and entered Wittenberg College in Springfield, Ohio, instead of going back to Midland, because "Wittenberg and Hamma [which was next door to Wittenberg] had provided a lot of missionaries to Japan." [48] Being a missionary to Japan was Ujiie's goal.

In his senior year at the seminary he was interviewed by the staff of BFM for a possible position as a missionary to Japan. During the course of the interview, Ujiie pointed out the shortcomings of the missionaries at that time, "such as being condescending to the Japanese, [by] trying to make Americans [out of them]…[and] missing the boat of indigenous church." [49] Besides that he also "criticized some of the missionaries, because they lived loftily. [He] felt that missionaries should be part of the people." [50]

His criticism was not accepted "warmly." Ujiie strongly felt that this pointed out the fact that if he would give up his American citizenship, he might have been accepted to go to Japan. But "his pride in the United States could not allow him to give up his citizenship." [51] As a compromise, he accepted the call to serve the Nisei in the San Francisco Bay area.

His task, like that of Miller's and Nakamura's, was to integrate the Nisei into existing congregations and to work with congregations enabling them to become receptive to the second-generation Japanese living in their midst. He was under the guidance of Rev. Milus Bunker of Grace Lutheran Church in Richmond, a neighboring town.

To fulfill his charge, Ujiie attended Lutheran churches in the area. He discovered that these churches generally were very much interested in foreign missions and the missions to Japan in particular. His wife, being Japanese, "was a scapegoat" and objectified as a token. These churches from time to time would call on her, not with the idea of integration, but they were interested in her knowledge in flower arrangement and tea ceremony as well in her readiness for "display." Besides serving in the Bay area, Ujiie was also asked by Miller to go to the Fresno area, about two hundred miles southeast of Berkeley, to work with the migrant workers and with D. G. M. Bach in the Fresno, Dinuba, and Hanford areas.

Ujiie, likewise, worked with the staff of the Lutheran Student Center, located next to the campus of the University of California, in bringing foreign students from Japan and the Nisei students to the center. To Ujiie's distress and discomfort, Lattie Kohe, the assistant director of the center, was always ready to welcome the exchange students but he believed she ignored the Nisei.

In the meantime, there was a large concentration of Japanese in Richmond Annex, just a few miles north of the Ujiie residence, where St. James Lutheran Church is located. The St. James leadership invited him to work with the congregation. Ujiie spent two years there, before the pastor resigned to accept a call to Hollywood Lutheran Church in Los Angeles. The council president asked if he would accept a call to serve the congregation. Before Ujiie could give an answer, the president of the synod intervened, preventing the congregation from calling him.

The Proceedings of the Sixty-Ninth Annual Convention of the Evangelical Lutheran Synod of the Pacific Southwest, May 9-12, 1960, recorded under the heading "Special Missions" the following item in two terse statements: "The special work among the Japanese in the Bay area and Northern Conference was terminated by the Board of American Missions. Pastor S. S. Ujiie now serves as an assistant at St. James, Richmond."

The work of Ujiie, like that of Miller and Nakamura, in the Bay area could not be calculated by statistics. In the main, the churches were not interested in the Nisei. Ujiie attributed the lack of interest to the social reality of the time—whenever there was a large concentration of minority members in a given place, the dominant society would become discriminatory and prejudicial.

In later 1961, Ujiie served as an assistant pastor at St. Mark's Lutheran Church where Rev. Paul T. Nakamura was pastor. In November 1962, Ujiie became the pastor of Faith Lutheran Church, Long Beach, California until retirement in 1992, but to this day he continues to serve the church as pastor without salary. When he began his ministry, his salary was $350 per month. When retired, he drew a monthly pension of $600 per month, necessitating an additional part-time job as a Protestant chaplain at St. Mary Medical Center in Long Beach.

This historian concludes that the ULCA's ministry to the Japanese on the West Coast cannot statistically claim to be successful nor could it be said that BAM initially was all that interested in the ministry. However, in retrospect, what can be stated is that these early efforts paved the way for the subsequent development of Japanese ministry in North America.

CHINESE MINISTRY OF THE LUTHERAN CHURCH IN AMERICA

In 1962 the United Lutheran Church in America and the Augustana Lutheran Church merged to become the Lutheran Church in America. At the time of the merger, the Chinese population in the United States had grown from 150,005 in 1950 to 237,292 in 1960. And by this time, more and more Chinese were moving out of the traditional Chinatowns into the suburbs. The suburb Monterey Park, about seven miles east of Los Angeles, saw a rapid increase in the number of Chinese residents. But there was neither a Chinese

Protestant nor Roman Catholic church in Monterey Park.

This section briefly describes the birth of the first LCA Chinese Lutheran church in North America.

Faith Lutheran Church, Monterey Park, California

The previous chapter describes how a couple of former missionaries to China tried, with the help of Wilson Wu, to establish a Chinese congregation in Pasadena, California, and why such a dream was not realized after three years of hard work. Sometime during those three years, the rest of Wu's family immigrated to the United States to join him. They settled in Monterey Park and attended St. Paul's Lutheran Church.

In 1962 Wu approached Rev. Howell Foster, pastor of Good Shepherd Lutheran Church, Buena Park, California, about the possibility of becoming a member of the ULCA and beginning a ministry in Monterey Park. He was advised to wait until after the merger between the ULCA and Augustana. Wu waited. After the merger it was agreed among synod officials that for Wu to qualify for admission into the church as a candidate for ordination, he needed to spend one year at a U.S. Lutheran seminary. This was to fulfill the requirement of the church, even though he had had graduated from a Lutheran seminary in Hong Kong and had done graduate studies at Ashbury Theological Seminary. But Wu agreed and spent the academic year 1964-1965 at Pacific Lutheran Theological Seminary (PLTS), where I was a second year student.

I noticed that Wu would fly back to Southern California every other weekend and inquired about Wu's frequent return. I learned that before Wu enrolled at PLTS, he had already organized a school for Chinese children, located at St. Paul's Lutheran Church, which necessitated his bimonthly journey to Monterey Park.

After Wu completed his Lutheran year at PLTS, he received a call to serve St. Paul's Lutheran as its associate pastor. Rev. Philip Ellman was the pastor. Wu was ordained on June 13, 1965.

As associate pastor, Wu was responsible for outreach into the Chinese community. And by this time there were more than 30 families that had become active in the school. William E. Wong—Bill—was one of the first students. Wu tried to integrate the Chinese into the congregation. Some responded positively, while others were intimidated by the English service and refused to come.

Wu realized that to reach the Chinese he had to provide services in that language. The Chinese responded positively to Wu's initiative. The group Wu gathered had to leave St. Paul's Lutheran Church to find another place for worship, because the latter had decided to expand its facility by adding a sanctuary. The group worshiped in a local school for about six months before moving to the chapel at the headquarters of the Southern California District of The LCMS. Meanwhile, the Chinese school remained at St. Paul's Lutheran Church. The group was formally organized as Faith Lutheran Church on Reformation Sunday 1968.

Officials of the Pacific Southwest Synod of the LCA felt quite uncomfortable, according to Wu, in having one of its own congregations worship at an LCMS facility and urged St. Paul's Lutheran Church to provide worship facilities for the newly-organized Faith Lutheran Church. The Chinese congregation moved back to St. Paul's in 1968.

The two congregations coexisted for nearly a decade. Then in 1977 Faith Lutheran Church was given a month to vacate the premises. The congregation had no place to go. The Division for Mission in North America (DMNA), LCA, tried to intervene. Howell Foster, assistant director (Western Region), Department of Church Extension, DMNA, and I met separately and jointly with the two groups. But it was too late for intervention. When the local Methodist congregation learned of the plight of Faith Lutheran Church, the Methodists made their congregation's basement available to the group for worship and to carry on Faith's educational program.

Meanwhile, negotiation was taking place between the congregation and DMNA for a loan so that the congregation could purchase a building for its ministry. The negotiation was successful. The congregation purchased the Living Water of the Tabernacle Church building at 115 West Newmark Ave., Monterey Park. On April 23, 1978, Faith Lutheran Church and its school moved to this location.

This was the first Asian Lutheran congregation in the LCA to have its own building for ministry. For this reason, it became an important site for future LCA and American Lutheran Church (ALC) Asian Lutheran gatherings.

With the establishment of the Lutheran Church of the Holy Spirit and Faith Lutheran Church, the district's and Mrs. Swenson's dreams to organize a Chinese congregation were in some ways realized. Without their visions and dreams, who knows what would have happened to the Lutheran Chinese ministry of The LCMS in San Francisco and to Wilson Wu?

Mary E. Banta, D. G. M. Bach, Louis T. Buchheimer, Wilbert Holt, Amy Hau-Mui, James Y. C. Lawson, L. S. G. Miller, Paul T. Nakamura, Toshio Okamoto, Shigeru Samuel Ujiie, Henry Wong, Richard Wong, Wilson Wu, and Wonnor Yee were pioneers. The path on which they trod was rugged and rough. The valley they crossed was deep. But they walked on, paving the way a little at a time for those who would follow in their footsteps. Today the valley has not been transformed into a plain, nor has the rough road made straight and level. However, because of these individuals' persistence and unceasing efforts, the ruggedness of the path has been somewhat diminished and the valley is now less abyssal.

Bach, Banta, Buchheimer, and Miller are no longer with us, but we still can sense their legacy and presence. Lawson and Richard Wong may still be with us, although this can't be stated with certainty. Holt, Okamoto, Ujiie, and Henry Wong are now retired but not inactive. Ujiie, for example, continues to serve as a volunteer chaplain at St. Mary Medical Center in Long Beach. Hau-Mui, Nakamura, Wu, and I are still in active ministry. In the stillness of the night, this historian, who has gotten to know them much better through this writing project, can surely hear their collective voices urging me forward.

Before another group of Asians takes the next step, the churches themselves would experience internal traumatic changes and external challenges. Both changes and challenges could thrust the institutions forward or force them to retreat. In one case, two would march forward into the uncharted waters of a rough sea, while in another, one would retreat from it, with a branch thrust forward, as the next chapter unveils.

5

MOVING AHEAD

U.S. SOCIETY IN THE 1960S AND 1970S FACED AN UNCERTAIN FUTURE. THE WAR in Vietnam went from bad to worse. President John F. Kennedy, his brother Robert, and Martin Luther King Jr. were assassinated. Race riots erupted across the nation. President Lyndon Johnson opened the gate to immigrants from all over world on an equal basis for the first time in U.S. history. Student protests against the unpopular war in Vietnam escalated and Johnson decided against running for a second term. Inflation was out of control. Richard Nixon was elected president but was forced to resign during his second term due to the Watergate scandal.

Canada enjoyed a period of economic growth and opened its door to immigrants. But the door was shut once again when the government decided that there was no need for their labor any longer.

During this period, too, Lutheran churches in North America witnessed changes and challenges from within and without. One of the most obvious changes was membership. From 1970 to 1977, the LCA, the American Lutheran Church (ALC), and The LCMS lost a total of 344,811 members, which prompted these Lutheran churches to come to terms with factors of social change, their positions on social issues, and matters of mission and ministry.

This chapter describes the events that took place within the Lutheran ecclesiastic world and shows how the churches responded to the various changes and challenges in ministry with Asians in North America from 1965 to 1977.

THE LUTHERAN CHURCH—MISSOURI SYNOD

In 1962 The LCMS held its biennial convention in Cleveland, Ohio. The convention elected Rev. Oliver R. Harms as president. "Observers described the Cleveland convention as a turning point in the life of the

Missouri Synod, signaling a move away from rigidity in theology and isolation in church life toward more openness in both theology and mission,"[1] as well as in interchurch and interagency relations. Indeed, under Harms's leadership The LCMS not only helped to create the Lutheran Council in the United States of America (LCUSA) but also remained an active member until 1987 when the organization was dissolved due to the formation of the Evangelical Lutheran Church in America (ELCA). It was also under Harms's administration that a proposal to establish fellowship with the ALC was introduced.

Harms's leadership drew both acclaim as well as criticism. His critics were opposed to the proposed fellowship with the ALC and they plotted to remove him from office. That opportunity came in 1969 when the biennial convention was held in Denver. Harms's critics were well organized there, even with campaign managers on the convention floor.

A few months before the Denver convention, Dr. John H. Tietjen, Harms's choice, was elected president of CS, St. Louis, Missouri. Dr. Jacob A. O. Preus was then president of Concordia Theological Seminary (CTS), Springfield, Illinois, and the critics' choice as the candidate to replace Harms. The Preus campaign took issue with the proposal to enter into fellowship with the ALC.

Preus was elected president of the synod, but the convention also passed the resolution to enter into fellowship with the ALC, a slap in the face of the Preus camp. Observers maintained that Preus was now without an issue with which he could unify the synod. But soon biblical research and criticism became a major issue in The LCMS, and the faculty at CS became the scapegoat of the Preus camp. The issue pitted the faculty and Tietjen on one side and the Preus camp on the other.[2]

This dispute led to the mass exit of the faculty and administrators of CS. They organized a seminary in exile—"Seminex"—which led to a split of The LCMS and the formation of the Association of Evangelical Lutheran Churches (AELC) in 1976. The AELC, in 1978, issued a call to the ALC and the LCA for Lutheran unity. The result was the merger of these churches in 1987 and the birth of the ELCA in 1988.

What's in the NAME in St. Louis

The period from 1969 to 1976 was a tumultuous, divisive, and traumatic time in the institutional life of The LCMS, causing the synod to retreat to the days before the election of Harms. The retreat to some was a necessary return to orthodoxy. To others it was a return to irrationality, old politics, corruption of power, and unnecessary control. In the midst of this contentious dispute, a group of district mission executives reaffirmed their commitment to mission and to one another at a conference held March 24-26, 1975, in St. Louis. They constituted themselves into an organization called North

American Mission Enablers (NAME).

This NAME conference had two goals: (1) To renew their fellowship with one another as individuals entrusted with servant roles in facilitating God's mission in North America; (2) to stimulate dialogue about their situations, ideals, and ongoing work to the end that they would be better equipped to plan for quality of ministry in a diverse society. [3] The group promised to care for one another, "to share views, skills, knowledge, resources ... and to prepare one another for tomorrow." [4] The conference also articulated three objectives reflecting a diversity theme.

At the conclusion of the conference, the participants agreed on a *Declaration* pronouncing themselves to be NAME, and stating the purpose of this fellowship, including "supporting the pursuit of God's mission at the local level." [5] The participants further declared through the *Declaration* that "together we shall pursue these simple goals 'for the common good' ... CARING ... SHARING ... PREPARING." [6] Each of these three goals is further spelled out in the document, which ends with the ambitious statement, "and [we] will seek to develop a concept of interdependence of mission on the national and world scene." [7]

For this reason, LCMS districts continued to develop local missions and ministries, even during the darkest days of the dispute initiated by the Preus camp. The commitment of district mission executives, too, had implications for Asian ministries in North America.

LCMS MISSION EXPANDED

National politics and theological disputes notwithstanding, LCMS districts moved ahead with ministry developments on the local level, including four new Asian ministries from 1971 to 1977. Two were Chinese—one in San Francisco and the other in San Jose, California. [8] The other two—a Korean ministry in Los Angeles and a Filipino ministry in Hawaii—are described in greater detail below.

Korean Ministry in Los Angeles

Trinity-Central Lutheran Church in Los Angeles was the first Korean Lutheran church of The LCMS. The idea of having a Korean church in Los Angeles was conceived by Dr. Shang Ik Moon [9] when he moved to southern California in the early 1970s. The purpose of Moon's coming to the area was not to organize a congregation but a church-related college. [10] However, when he realized the number of Koreans living in this region, he became excited and eager to have a Korean Lutheran church planted in Los Angeles. He submitted the Korean mission idea to the Southern California District for consideration. Both the district president and the mission executive were very interested in Moon's idea. They consulted with the mission board of The

LCMS, which approved the proposal.

When the matter of staffing the ministry came up for discussion, Moon turned to Dr. Young Hwan Hong, who was then studying at Christ Seminary (formerly Seminex) in St. Louis for an S.T.M. degree. Hong was no stranger to Moon, for his mother was a member of Hong's congregation in Seoul, Korea. On June 1, 1979, the Southern California District and The LCMS called Hong to be a missionary-at-large for Korean ministries in the district.

Hong was born in Korea and had a Presbyterian background. When he was a graduate student at Han Kuk Theological Seminary, a Presbyterian school in Seoul, he took a course on Lutheran theology from Dr. Won Young Ji. Both Ji and Hong made a favorable impression on each other. Hong graduated from the seminary in 1963 and immediately enlisted in the army, in which he served for the next three years. After Hong's discharge from the army, Ji, who was then teaching at Yonsei University, called Hong to explain his vision of the new seminary[11] in Seoul. Ji further offered Hong a full four-year scholarship to attend Lutheran Theological Academy (LTA) and the Graduate School of Theology at Yonsei University concurrently. Hong accepted Ji's invitation and became a Lutheran in 1966. He received the Th.M. degree from the university in 1969, one year before he obtained his diploma in theology from LTA.

Two days after his graduation from LS on January 10, 1970, Hong was assigned to plant a new Lutheran church in Seoul. Hong methodically surveyed the neighborhood to which he was assigned to do ministry, visited the community leaders, and introduced himself and the Lutheran faith to his neighbors. To enable his neighbors to become better acquainted with the Lutheran faith, he advertised in newspapers and distributed tracts from door to door. Next, Hong brought his neighbors' children to his home for Sunday school. And before long he extended his ministry to the junior and senior high school as well as to college students. Then he held worship in his home, which was soon filled to capacity. At that point, Hong proposed to the Korean Lutheran Church (KLC) and The LCMS that a new church building be constructed for this growing congregation. Both churches agreed. The congregation built a multipurpose building.

Hong was successful. He was ordained as a Lutheran pastor on January 12, 1971. On February 5, 1971, he married Youngja Lee and twenty days later he dedicated a new church building, the very first in the KLC.

Be that as it may, Hong had his heart set on further theological education in the United States. Thus in 1973, he resigned from his pastorate in Korea and came to CS, St. Louis, for advanced studies. In 1976 he moved to Christ Seminary to continue his education.

Hong's work as a missionary-at-large required long hours in his ministry. He not only met the challenges, but in the 1980s he also continued to pursue his theological education at the California Graduate School of Theology, from which he received his Ph.D. degree in 1988. Hong's ministry extends beyond the local parish and the teaching of Korean candidates for the colloquy, as chapter 15 describes.

Filipino Ministry in Hawaii

"The dream of a special Lutheran ministry among Filipino ethnic groups in Hawaii goes back to the late 1960s. At that time much preparation was done by Pastor Dennis Kastens and the Lutheran Mission Council of Hawaii. Lack of staff made it impossible to begin any specific work until November, 1977." [12] The result of Kastens's field study was shared in 1969 with the president of the Lutheran Church in the Philippines (LCP), who "felt then that the work in Hawaii ... was imperative." [13] But there was neither money nor staff for this ministry.

By 1977, the Filipino population in Hawaii numbered about 130,000 to 140,000, with 80 percent being Ilocano (which refers to the people from Ilocos, a place north of Manila), living on the five main islands. With the promise of partnership between the district and the national mission board, it was decided that the time had come to enter this ministry. For the solution to the staff problem, the Hawaii Circuit of the California-Nevada-Hawaii District (CNHD) looked to the Lutheran Church in the Philippines. But that church, being young, was itself having problems staffing the ministries. "The alternative seemed to point to the reactivation of a retired but still capable worker." [14] A letter was sent to Dr. Alvaro A. Carino, a retiree, inquiring whether or not he would be interested in serving this mission for up to two years. Carino consented.

Carino was born on September 19, 1908, in San Juan, Luzon, Philippines. In 1928 he came to the United States for his secondary education at St. Paul [High School] in Concordia, Missouri. From there he went to Valparaiso University and CS, St. Louis, and did graduate studies at Northwestern University. He was ordained on September 27, 1942, at St. Martini Lutheran Church in Chicago, where he also served as an assistant pastor for two years. Subsequently, he became an "institutional missionary" in the Chicago area in 1944 and served as student pastor at the Chicago Medical Center at the same time. In 1946 he became an instructor at the Luther Institute in Chicago. Later that year, he was commissioned as the first missionary of The LCMS to the Philippine Islands. He served in a variety of capacities, including positions such as conference secretary, vice chairman, district chairman, and president of the LCP.

His task in Hawaii was to introduce Lutheranism to the Filipinos by means of radio broadcasting, visitation, newspaper articles, community involvement, gathering a worshiping community, and directing Filipinos into existing congregations. Carino's first 18 months in the field were busy, as he tried to do what was expected of him. But some of the expectations, based on untested assumptions, were unrealistic. For example, the "18 Month Evaluation" stated "we anticipated that it would be fairly easy to gather a worshiping community. We have found that there is much preevangelism to be done prior to even enunciating that expectation." [15] Another area of miscalculation was funding for this mission, which was predicated on rapidly being able to gather a community that would be working toward partial support." [16] The financial crisis was already in evidence before the 18-month evaluation. In a letter dated March 3, 1979, from Rev. Robert F. Meyer, pastor of Trinity Lutheran Church, to Rev. Roger Leenerts of the Board for Missions and Rev. Theodore (Ted) Iverson of CNHD, Meyer called attention to the financial problem.

In the 18-Month Evaluation, a series of 10 proposals was articulated, such as installing Rev. Leonardo Bugtong (pronounced "boogtong") to continue this mission after Carino had completed his term of two years and a request to the "supporting bodies for a five year commitment to … this ministry." [17]

Who was Bugtong and how did he become involved with this ministry? In a letter dated June 6, 1978, from Rev. Arnold G. Steinbeck, a counselor in Circuit 11—Hawaii, to the executive committee of the board of directors of CNHD, the matter of future staffing for this mission was mentioned. Steinbeck further stated, "we find a dire lack of staffing possibilities available." [18] The committee once again explored the possibility with the LCP, which "finds itself in a situation of 'field white [sic] unto harvest' with 'few laborers' qualified to work in that field, or in this new field.'" [19]

In the same letter, Steinbeck mentioned the availability of Bugtong [20] and stated, "we have been in contact with Rev. Roger Leenerts of Synod's Board for Missions… [who] concurs with the possibility of calling Rev. Bugtong… [and that] Bugtong himself [is] currently studying at CTS, Fort Wayne, Indiana." [21] Then acting on behalf of Circuit 11, Steinbeck requested that the executive committee "issue a Divine Call to the Rev. Leonard Bugtong," [22] for two years, extendable, beginning on August 15, 1978, and concluding on August 14, 1980, with the missionary arriving on September 1, 1978, or sooner.

Bugtong and his family arrived in Hawaii in August 1978 [23] to assume this ministry prior to the departure of Carino and his wife. Bugtong was born on December 30, 1933, in Atok, Benguet, Philippines. After receiving his A.A. degree in 1956, he enrolled in the Lutheran Seminary in Manila in the fall. He graduated from the seminary in 1961 and was ordained and installed on June 4 as pastor of Holy Cross Lutheran Church (1961-1966) in Candon, Ilocas Sur. He then served as pastor of St. Stephen Lutheran Church (1966-

1969) and as a district missionary to the Atok-Tublay area among the Benguet tribe (1969-1971).

While in the Philippines he also served as district president of the North Luzon District for two terms from 1967 to 1971 and concurrently as a member of the board of directors of the Lutheran Philippines Church for two terms. He likewise served as a member of the Lutheran Seminary board of control for two terms from 1964 to 1968.

Bugtong was busy. But he was determined to continue to pursue his education. Thus in 1970, he obtained his B.A. degree from Baguio Colleges Foundation. A year later he immigrated to Canada with his family. There he served as pastor of St. Peter's Lutheran Church in New Hamburg and St. Paul's Lutheran Church in Tavistock, Ontario (1973-1978). He likewise served on the Ontario District mission board for several years, and from 1974 to 1978 he was the pastoral advisor of the LWML of the Ontario District. For his contributions to the church in Canada, he was listed in the second edition of *Who's Who in Religion*. And in 1980 he received his S.T.M. degree from CTS.

Bugtong continued the work started by Carino, broadcasting five minutes a day (except Sunday), visiting the community, having small group Bible studies, and so forth. The radio broadcasting program generated interest: some of his listeners called in wanting to know more about the gospel and the Lutheran church. In the meantime, Iverson, in a letter dated March 28, 1979, to Robert Meyer raised some doubt about the "media ministry." He stated, "I think that it is fair to say that the St. Louis people are really anxious that this be some kind of a media ministry. I am not convinced that that is the way to go." [24]

The ministry was slowly moving ahead. Bugtong in a letter dated February 14, 1980, to "Dear Friends in Christ," informed donors and friends about the mission. He gave some figures that he had gathered through personal contacts, such as having "202 individuals' [names] in the files." Out of this figure, two regularly attended services at Good Shepherd Lutheran Church and his cottage meetings. Most of the people whom he contacted were Roman Catholics, but some also liked what they heard on the radio. "It helps them as well as their children, according to one woman.... She [also] sends [the message] to her relatives in the Philippines." [25] Bugtong went on to relate similar tales. Although his ministry consisted of few in number, the message reached far and wide.

While Bugtong served in ministry, the Circuit 11 committee members were clearly mindful of financial uncertainties. In a letter dated April 20, 1979, to Iverson, Meyer raised the concern. Subsequent letters written by others to different officials of the district and the synod continued to raise the same concern.

Bugtong in the meantime forged ahead, albeit not without difficulties. On September 19, 1980, his letter to "Partners in Mission," reported that while his radio work had been on the air since his arrival, the time for broadcasting on KISA (a Filipino station) had been changed three times and he received more feedback from this station than the other. With the help of Good Shepherd Lutheran Church where he had served as an interim pastor, he held regular cottage meetings. Though attendees were few in number, Bugtong was encouraged enough to think that he could soon offer an "information class for them." And then there were services held for "a small group [of] both adults and children at Cane Street, Wahiawa." Bugtong went on to describe movingly how a Mrs. Cecil Corpuz, who had heard him on the radio, had walked for miles to come to the Sunday service at Our Savior Lutheran Church in Aiea, and how another one had called and spoke with him for more than one hour on the telephone. The letter concluded with a list of five proposals to the Philippine Mission Committee.

From a statistical perspective, Bugtong's ministry did not seem to have increased membership in the Lutheran churches in Hawaii. The committee that oversaw his ministry, in the meantime, wanted to expand his radio work to the island of Hawaii, where 15 percent of the 80,000 inhabitants were Filipino. And by this time, the very same committee that had instructed Bugtong that the purpose of his "work in Hawaii was not to build a church but to integrate Filipinos to the existing Lutheran churches wherever they are located" [26] seemed to have changed its mind. The committee wanted an organized congregation to support the ministry.

In another letter, dated November 16, 1981, Bugtong reported that four individuals had called with various requests: to ask him for prayers, to listen to confessions, to bless a newly built house, to request scripts of his radio messages to be used in the person's own church. By now the ministry was in its fourth year and apparently reaching some individuals, but far from the number that would be needed for organizing a congregation that could contribute financially to the ministry in some way.

But support for ministry occasionally came from outside sources. On April 19, 1982, Mrs. Heather Ott, projects chairman of the Ontario District's Lutheran Women's Missionary League, wrote to Rev. Orval M. Oswald, then president of the CNHD, seeking his approval regarding the women wanting to support "Rev. Leonard Bugtong's Radio Ministry to the Phillippines [sic] in Hawaii." Oswald gladly approved the request.

"At this point in time," recalled Bugtong, "there were several cottage meetings being conducted in Wahiawa, Aiea, and Kalihi. Attendance varied from 15 to 25 in each meeting." [27] But there was no worshiping community on Sunday. There were, however, conversations regarding what was the best possible situation for Bugtong and the ministry. Meyer obviously thought that Bugtong could spend part of his time at his parish—an idea to which Iverson responded favorably. He thought that Bugtong should be listed as "Associate Pastor of the congregation." [28] Iverson went on to discuss financial support for Bugtong and advised Meyer to share an outline of the proposal with his committee.

By August 15, 1982, the ministry was approaching the end of its fifth year. On this very same day, Bugtong sent an upbeat letter to "Brothers, Sisters and Friends." He reported that there were now 16 adults and eight children at Trinity Lutheran Church and five adults at Whitemore Village, where he taught (presumably a Bible study class). The Sunday school "at Liliha Alley has been moved to the church at Kuakini Street." [29] Here too Bugtong was upbeat in reporting the total attendance of 16 children. The Thursday cottage meeting at 1504 Haloa Drive, likewise, seemed to be doing well. Bugtong maintained, "this is a caring support group which enjoy[s] the fellowship of Word and *pupus* (light snacks) after the study." [30] By now he was using another radio station, KNDI, which "remains to be a strong arm in Evangelism...[and] has brought [him] closer to the Filipino community." [31] He was known to the community as "Father Bugtong," who in the minds of the people was an old man. But when they would finally meet him, "they were a bit surprised to see a younger man." [32]

From the prospect of qualitative ministry, Bugtong was no doubt quite effective. In a February 3, 1983, letter to Leenerts, Meyer confirmed this historian's conclusion. Meyer stated that "Pastor Leo Bugtong has ably carried on this work. Several Filipino families are now attending Trinity in Wahiawa through the work of this Lutheran Philippine Mission of Hawaii." [33]

Just as things seemed to be going well, Louis Y. Nau, Asia secretary of the Board for Mission Services, expressed surprise "that the Lutheran Church in the Philippines has really ignored this vital extension of the Lord's work among their kinsmen [sic]." [34] How long the LCP had ignored this mission Nau did not state, but in the same letter he promised to "work on that aspect of this ministry." [35] In his "Field Visitation," Nau also reported that Bugtong essentially had no written material in Ilocano (a dialect as well as a region of the Philippines) to work with, adding difficulties to his ministry. [36] Financial support was another issue.

Nevertheless, Bugtong carried this ministry forward for the next dozen years. The work among the Filipinos in Hawaii was never easy. For one thing, they belong either to the Roman Catholic Church or to the Philippine Independent Church. For another, they are immigrants who, by and large, are eager to establish themselves in the new environment in order to avoid welfare at the expense of their spiritual life.

In 1996 The LCMS appointed a new mission executive whose philosophy of mission, according to Bugtong, seemed to be at odds with this local initiative. This coupled with the decline in mission giving contributed to the closure of this ministry in 1996. Bugtong took early retirement in December the same year. A year later his car sticker read, "Goodbye tension, hello pension."

Be that as it may, Bugtong voluntarily continues to lead the group's Bible class in Ilocano each Sunday. Following the study, the group attends worship at Trinity Lutheran Church.

THE AMERICAN LUTHERAN CHURCH

By the early 1970s, the ALC realized it needed to take a position on race in the United States. On October 14, 1974, the General Convention, the highest ALC policy-making body, adopted the statement "Racism in the Church," which urged congregation members to engage in "careful study, prayerful self-examination, and constructive action to eradicate all traces of racism within The American Lutheran Church." [37] The statement further directed divisions, offices, and agencies of the church to practice fair employment policies in relation to "minorities."

In a sense, the statement on racism could be seen as the ALC getting itself ready for ministries among persons of color, though not so much for their sake. The statement clearly stated, "In its own self-interest The American Lutheran Church must wake up to and correct its white racism. Black, brown, red, or yellow persons may not need The American Lutheran Church. The American Lutheran Church, however, needs nonwhite persons within its membership and its leadership." [38]

This statement had little immediate impact on Asian ministry. Up to the adoption of this statement by the Church Council, the ALC had no organized Asian ministry nor was there a strategy to develop any future ministry with Asians. On the local level, however, a small number of individuals seemed to have a different idea. This local initiative occurred in Hawaii.

Chinese Lutheran Church of Honolulu

Since the liberalization of immigration by the Johnson administration, a large number of Chinese had come to the United States by the early 1970s. In Hawaii, in the autumn of 1972, about 5,000 Mandarin-speaking Chinese lived on the island of Oahu. At about the same time, Rev. Donald W. Baron arrived in Oahu to serve as a faculty member without call at Lutheran Bible Institute. When he realized the size of the Mandarin-speaking population on the island, he called on Rev. Norman Hammer, pastor of Prince of Peace Lutheran Church, Honolulu, to suggest that together they initiate a Mandarin-speaking fellowship within that congregation. Hammer agreed. Eventually the fellowship evolved into the present Chinese Lutheran Church of Honolulu.

Before the evolution of the congregation is described, it may be instructive to show how another former missionary, in this case due to prejudice and discrimination at home and abroad, became involved with the development of this Chinese ministry in Hawaii. Rev. Donald William Baron was that missionary.

Baron was born on May 6, 1931, in Queens Village, Long Island, New York. At age four, he was baptized into Grace Episcopal Church, Jamaica, Queens, New York, but attended a Christian Science Sunday school until age 12. On March 25, 1945, he was confirmed at the Evangelical Lutheran Church of the Redeemer, Queens Village. He attended Gettysburg College, Gettysburg, Pennsylvania, from 1950 to 1951 and graduated from Gordon College, Beverly Farms, Massachusetts, in 1953. He received his B.D. degree from Luther Theological Seminary, St. Paul, Minnesota, in 1959, after having spent a two-year internship in Hong Kong.

After completing his theological training, he spent the next two years at Yale University, studying the Chinese language. In 1961 he entered Taiwan National University in Taipei, Taiwan, and in 1966 received an M.A. degree in Asian studies from the University of Hawaii.

He served as a missionary to Taiwan from February 1966 to November 1969 and as a pastor of Prince of Peace Lutheran Church, Margate, Florida, from November 1969 to September 1972. His ministries in both Taiwan and Margate, recalled one of his colleagues, were difficult. His wife was Chinese, and they experienced prejudice and discrimination in both places, necessitating in part their move to Hawaii.

Since he could not serve on the pastoral staff at Prince of Peace Lutheran Church, he recommended Ruth Yuan, a parish worker for 25 years at Truth Lutheran Church in Hong Kong, to assist Hammer. In early 1974, Hammer extended an invitation to Yuan who was in a quandary, not being sure if this was the right move for her. For the next four months, Yuan prayed. Then one day, the words of God recorded in Genesis 22:14 came to her:" 'The LORD will provide.'" On September 17, 1974, Yuan arrived in Hawaii to begin the ministry with the Mandarin-speaking Chinese.

On November 3, 1974, the Mandarin fellowship had its first worship service in the library of Prince of Peace Lutheran Church's retirement home, with more than 60 persons in attendance. Fourteen months later in January 1976, Rev. David W. J. Chao of the Taiwan Lutheran Church (TLC) accepted an invitation to serve the group as assistant pastor. But the group could not afford to pay Chao, who had a wife and four children. To support himself and his family, Chao and his wife operated a small Chinese restaurant for the next 16 months, until May 1977 when the group received program support from the Division for Service and Mission in America (DSMA) of the ALC.

Chao, a multitalented individual, has an interesting background. He was born on April 5, 1930, in Hankou, China. Yet when he speaks, one can't tell he is a Southerner. His Mandarin is flawless. His family was originally from Linsan County, Fujian Province. His grandfather, for reasons unknown to Chao, moved to central China and settled in Hankou. That was where Chao spent his first years. During World War II the Chao family moved from place to place, never being able to settle in a given locale for very long.

Chao attended school wherever and whenever the family could find a school for him to attend. His first year of junior high school was spent at the school for orphans established by the Bethel Mission of China. This was the first time he set "foot into the saving and gracious gate of God." [39] And before he "knew the meaning of baptism, [he] was baptized on Easter Sunday in 1944." [40]

After the war, the family moved back to Hankou. Chao entered the Light of Righteousness Middle School in Xinyang, Henan, for his senior high school years. Lutheran missionaries had organized the school. The advancing Communist army interrupted his education. In 1949 he left mainland China for Taiwan by himself. He found work in a theatrical company. Because he is an enthusiast of literature, art, music, drama, and poetry, this line of work suited him well. But he had reservations about the lifestyle of the artists and performers—"too romantic." [41] Subsequently, he resigned to work at various odd jobs while preparing himself for the high school diploma examination, with the hope of going on to higher education.

His own plan did not seem to coincide with what God or what his former teacher wanted him to do. In 1952 his former middle school teacher, Miss Cora Martinson, an American missionary, sent him a letter from Hong Kong saying that a Bible institute was being established in Kaohsiung, a city in southern Taiwan and encouraged him to dedicate himself to God by attending that school. Chao received his diploma from the institute in 1954 and in 1958 his B.Th. degree from the Lutheran Theological Seminary of Hong Kong. He was ordained on September 20, 1959, in Taiwan where he was the pastor of Panchiao Lutheran Church. He resigned in 1963 and enrolled at Hamma School of Theology in Springfield, Ohio. Two years later he was awarded the M.Div. degree.

Returning to Taiwan in 1965, he began a career as producer, acting director, general director, and executive director of various Christian and non-Christian radio and television programs, as well as films. From 1973 to 1975, he was a lecturer in the Department of Communication of Hong Kong Baptist College. And from March 1976 to September 1980, he was the pastor of the now Chinese Lutheran Church of Honolulu. In 1980 he returned to Hong Kong to take a position as lecturer in the Department of Journalism and Communication of the Chinese University of Hong Kong. Chao's publications include books, songs, and TV drama scripts. He also served as a member of various committees and boards of professional organizations.

Chao returned to the United States in 1985 to assume the position of administrative director of *Kairos* Communication Service, USA. [42] In 1995 he became the general secretary of *Kairos* Communication International, USA. In the same year Concordia College in Bronxville, New York, in recognition of Chao's work, honored him with an honorary LL.D.

During Chao's tenure as pastor, the Mandarin fellowship moved to the Lutheran Church of Honolulu campus and became an organized congregation. After Chao's departure in 1980, the pastorate was vacated 10 months before Rev. Simon Lee was called to be its pastor. In the meantime, Ruth Yuan retired in March 1981.

Lee was born in Hong Kong in 1947 and received his theological training first at the Alliance Bible Seminary. In 1976, he received his theological degree from Lutheran Theological Seminary of Hong Kong. Later he did graduate study at Luther Theological Seminary, St. Paul, Minnesota, where he earned an M.A. degree in pastoral counseling. [43] Under Lee's leadership, the congregation continues to flourish. From its inception through 1998, for example, the congregation had baptized a total of 626 people—460 adults and 166 children. And in the past few years, more than a dozen individuals from this congregation have dedicated themselves to ordained ministry. [44] For their theological training, a number of them attended or are attending Lutheran seminaries.

Social Ministry in Los Angeles Chinatown

When Jacob A. O. Preus was investigating the faculty of CS, one of the Chinese pastors of the synod quietly transferred into the ALC. This pastor, who prefers not to be named, was subsequently assigned to engage in social ministry in Los Angeles's Chinatown. As a result of this ministry, a small congregation was born. This congregation later became part of Faith Lutheran Church in Monterey Park. But this pastor's work in Los Angeles's Chinese community cannot be measured statistically, because his assignment was to serve with his presence and assistance to social service agencies and local organizations. His presence was appreciated and well spoken of by the people in Chinatown.

THE LUTHERAN CHURCH IN AMERICA

Among the three major Lutheran bodies making preparation for "minority" ministry, the LCA appeared to be the most systematic, beginning with the statement "Race Relations" adopted by the Second Biennial Convention in Pittsburgh, Pennsylvania, July 2-9, 1964. The opening statement in this document acknowledges what the "racial revolution" had done to the church but also describes the church as facing a time of "opportunity and hope." The document stated that "at the heart of the life of the church is prayer" [45] and offered a series of prayerful petitions. The LCA recommitted itself "in obedience to the Lord of the church and in repentant acknowledgment… [and issued] a renewed call to action."[46]

The Second Biennial Convention also created the Coordinating Committee on Race Relations (CCRR) "charged with the responsibility 'to explore ways of implementing the actions of the church in race relations' and to develop recommendations for constructive programs and projects to be carried out by the various program units of the church."[47] As if to demonstrate the church's seriousness in the matter of race relations, this committee was chaired by the president of the church and its membership "was comprised of the chief executive, or his appointee, of each board, commission and auxiliary plus one additional person appointed by each unit."[48] The various units "in most instances [appointed] representatives of minority groups"[49] to the committee.

CCRR sponsored a consultation on the Black Manifesto in 1969 and a conference on black economic development in the following year. Two years later, in 1972, the Consulting Committee on Minority Group Interests (CCMGI) was created by the biennial convention held in Dallas, Texas, "in response to a resolution submitted by Carver Portlock of the Southeastern Pennsylvania Synod."[50] And by action of the Executive Council of the church, CCMGI replaced CCRR.

In a memorandum dated February 6, 1973, to the members of CCMGI, Rev. Robert J. Marshall, then president of the LCA, stated that the very same convention also "adopted a bylaw which requires the Division for Mission in North America to provide staff services for a Committee on Minority Group Interests that brings together minority group persons with representatives of churchwide agencies."[51] Rev. Massie Kennard was appointed to staff the committee. The memorandum went on to relate, "the committee has been chosen in order to represent the various areas in the territory served by our church. It has also been appointed to represent various minority groups including Blacks, Puerto Ricans, Chicanos, Cubans, American-Indians, Canadian Indians and Orientals."[52] As for the "Orientals," Wilson Wu was appointed to represent them. Bill Wong replaced Wu in 1978.

One of the committee's major accomplishments was the recommendation, adopted and commissioned by the 1974 convention, of an inventory of the LCA "to determine the status of minorities in the institution."[53] The LCA completed the inventory in 1976 with the publication of a document entitled, "An Inventory of the Lutheran Church in America: Race Relations." The inventory revealed a slow increase of "Orientals" in the church from 1964 to 1974, but there was no "Oriental" holding any synodical position and only one holding an executive position on the churchwide director level. Ministries on the local level always seemed to move ahead of the institution. There was no exception in the LCA.

New Life Chinese Lutheran Church, Vancouver, British Columbia

Census data published in 1971 reported that there were 58,260 Asians in the Vancouver area, with the greater concentration in Vancouver City proper. But the Canadian census does not indicate to which ethnic groups these Asians belong, making it difficult to provide a precise figure for each Asian ethnic group. The general wisdom at that time was that most of the Asians were Chinese. At that time too the Chinese in Vancouver comprised the largest single group of Chinese in Canada, followed by the Chinese population of the greater Toronto area. Thus it may just be quite natural that the first Chinese Lutheran congregation of The LCMS was in Vancouver, followed nearly two decades later by a second, which was part of the LCA.

New Life Chinese Lutheran Church officially began in July 1974. The seed, however, was planted a year earlier at Augustana Lutheran Church when a student from the Lutheran Theological Seminary in Saskatoon spent one month serving as missionary at that church. Augustana was a unique congregation then. In 1973, the congregation had not had a pledge system for three years and yet, in the third year, the members' contributions were the highest in its history! Thus the congregation planned to initiate a ministry with the Chinese in partnership with the Western Canada Synod and DMNA. The congregation, for its share, was prepared to commit "the use of its facilities and $1,000 to the basic cost of the ministry." [54]

In his report to the 1975 synod convention, the dean of the British Columbia District mentioned, "New Life, Vancouver was the name chosen for the new Chinese congregation being readied for organization under the direction of Herman Liu." [55] The dean's report went on to say that the group later rented accommodations from Windsor United Church, possibly implying that the group, within a short period of time, had outgrown the facilities at Augustana. Indeed, within some eleven months Rev. Liu had gathered a group of "some fifty potential members, a Sunday school, youth group and women's group." [56] The congregation was organized on October 26, 1975. By 1977 the congregation had a baptized membership of 97, plus 30 students in its Sunday school.

Liu was born on December 23, 1929, in Hubei, China. Later in life he recalled an incident, which he interpreted as a religious experience—"the hand of God sparing him for some special purpose in life." His father was a merchant. When Liu was five years old, his father's store caught fire early one morning. A neighbor rushed into the burning store, hoping to retrieve something of value. What this neighbor saw inside were some blankets on a bed. He brought them outside—and found Liu inside the blankets. Based on this experience, Liu decided not to seek wealth in life but to seek to give his life "to saving others." [57]

His father died a year after the fire destroyed his store. Liu's mother brought him up in the Buddhist tradition, but there is no evidence that Liu knew much about Buddhism. When interviewed by the *Western Canada Lutheran*, he informed the reporter that he saw the broken Buddhist statues in a temple and thought, "if the idols cannot protect themselves, how can they protect me?" [58] —not realizing that this was his own Christian projection and not the Buddhist understanding.

When he entered high school, he met some young Christians who "introduced him to a kind pastor." [59] At 17 he was baptized, all the while protesting "he knew too little [about Christianity]." [60] He decided to dedicate himself to God.

Three years later the People's Republic of China was established. Liu and other fellow-students fled to Hong Kong where he became destitute and homeless, and endured starvation. It was at this juncture in his life that he met Rev. Charles Reinbrecht, an American Lutheran missionary, who arranged for him to attend the Bible Institute in Hong Kong.

Whether or not Liu graduated from the Bible Institute is uncertain. His biography, dated July 30, 1973, makes no mention of the institute, but states that he received diplomas from the Lutheran Theological Seminary in 1956 and Chung Chi College in 1964, and a B.A. degree from Hwa Kiu College in 1972. All of these institutions are in Hong Kong. He further received the S.T.M. degree from the Lutheran Theological Seminary in Saskatoon in 1974. He was ordained on July 21, 1974, at Augustana Lutheran Church in Vancouver.

In between attending seminary and colleges, he served as a preacher, an assistant minister, and an evangelist in charge of the Leprosy Mission in Hong Kong. For three years prior to his coming to Canada in 1972, he was a chaplain and welfare assistant at the Fanling Hospital in the New Territories. At the suggestion of Miss Carol Martinson, he went to the Lutheran Theological Seminary at Saskatoon to prepare himself for ordination. With a grant of H.K. $10,000 from LWF, he flew to Canada.

Academically and financially, theological education in Canada was hard on Liu. He had to work at various jobs to support himself and his family in Hong Kong, not to mention overcoming language difficulties. It was then that he contacted the Western Canada Synod for a student loan. This contact led to one month of missionary work at Augustana Lutheran Church in Vancouver and the subsequent development of the LCA's first Asian ministry in Canada.

Liu is a scholarly clergyman with a religious mind and a sense of humility. He is also a lover of literature and art, as well as a master of calligraphy.

Lutheran Oriental Church, Torrance, California

St. Mark's Lutheran Church is located next to the University of Southern California campus, where Paul T. Nakamura spent 15-1/2 years as its pastor, from 1957-1973. Nakamura had an eventful pastoral ministry there, including an opportunity to work with the LCA's lay associate program, the first of its kind in that church body.

However, in the fall of 1973 he took a year off from parish ministry to enter into a Clinical Pastoral Education (CPE) training program. Consequently, Nakamura had to move out of the parsonage. On moving day his friend Yoshimitsu (Yosh) Hokama, whom he met in the summer of 1954 at the boarding house where he himself was staying, showed up with a truck to help move him and his family into Mrs. Miyagi's (Kiku's mother's) home. The friendship between Hokama and Nakamura had enormous significance in the development of Lutheran Oriental Church.

Nakamura spent the academic year 1973-74 at the California Hospital and the Santa Monica Hospital. By this time, Nakamura had met all of the few Asian pastors of the synod. And while he was being trained at the California Hospital, he and Wilson Wu decided to meet with Rev. Carl Segerhammer, president of the Pacific Southwest Synod, to discuss possible ministries in the Asian communities.

On the day of the meeting, Nakamura and Wu were accompanied by several representatives from their respective communities. Sensing the amiable atmosphere permeating the room, Nakamura years later recalled that he asked Segerhammer point-blank, "Is there room for Asian ministries in our church?" [61] Without giving the question a second thought, Segerhammer said, "Yes, there is." [62] Hokama was one of the representatives at this meeting. As they descended the stairs of the synod office at the end of the meeting, Hokama—not yet baptized into the Christian faith—turned to Nakamura and said, "Paul, if you go into this [Japanese] ministry, I'll back you all the way." [63]

After completing CPE training, Nakamura decided that Gardena was the place for the Japanese ministry. By the early 1970s, the Gardena-Torrance area was already a suburb of Los Angeles with a fairly good size Japanese population. Furthermore, this population growth was pretty much assured with companies from Japan continuing to establish North American branch offices there. By this time, too, Hokama and family had moved from Monterey Park to Torrance, where he and his wife, Dorothy, had just begun their beauty products distribution business.

This ministry began "on December 7, 1975, the Second Sunday in Advent, with about 30 persons of Japanese-American heritage gathered in the warehouse of International Beauty Distributors [owned by Yosh and Dorothy Hokama], in Gardena [a city next to Torrance], for their first worship service." [64] Though this new ministry started without official sanction, the synod sent Nakamura a check for $5,000 as a token of encouragement. The worshiping group called itself "Lutheran Oriental Circle," a name the group used for nearly two years until on Thanksgiving Day, 1977, it was changed to Lutheran Oriental Church. That same year the group was given partial financial support from DMNA, LCA. In 1979 this faith community was received into the Pacific Southwest Synod as an organized congregation.

Between 1974 and 1975, Nakamura served as an interim pastor at Emanuel Danish Lutheran Church, Los Angeles. To support his growing family and to keep the Japanese ministry moving ahead, Nakamura also worked at the International Beauty Distributors, his friends' company. In mid-1976 he returned to Emanuel Danish Lutheran Church as its interim pastor, while simultaneously carrying on the work among the Japanese in Torrance.

The Nakamuras' determination to carry out a ministry among Japanese-Americans and the Hokamas' generous support had a lot to do with the ministry's beginning and subsequent success in meeting the spiritual needs of that community. The Hokamas were an honest, a hard-working, and a congenial couple with open minds. Born in Hawaii, Yosh Hokama attended the University of California at Los Angeles (UCLA). He and Nakamura met as students and formed a friendship that lasted until Hokama's death in 1999. After graduating from UCLA with a degree in philosophy, Hokama started a number of businesses with varying degree of success. But nothing seemed to change his attitude on friendship and honesty. His outlook on life was always friendship and honesty first. Their business, International Beauty Distributors, was built on these priorities. "His friends remembered how they paid off their debts and fulfill[ed] their obligations," observed Nakamura, "and they came to support them in this new venture." [65]

Through their company and personal commitments, the Hokamas provided space, human resources, and finances for this ministry at its inception as well as throughout much of its development. Hokama was finally baptized into the faith in 1976, followed by Dorothy and their children. "Besides the Hokamas," said Nakamura, "all of our people participate in supporting the ministry and in assisting in worship every Sunday. They are a wonderful group of Christians ... you should see how hard they work during the year at the church, particularly when the annual bazaar time comes." [66]

Lutheran Oriental Church and its pastor subsequently played a significant role in the Redress Movement. At this point, however, the focus of this history turns to other Asian Lutherans not directly connected with congregational ministry, but who, nevertheless, have been contributing richly to the life of the church and the community.

6

SNAPSHOTS: GENERATION ONE

ASIAN LUTHERANS HAVE BEEN IN THIS COUNTRY FOR QUITE SOME TIME. THE book *Seasons of Light* reported that "early Hawaii Chinese Christian history records stories of Chinese evangelists trained in the Lutheran missions of China who entered into service with the Congregational or Anglican Churches"[1] in the later nineteenth century. However, Asian Lutherans did not enter into ordained ministry in the Lutheran church until the second half of the twentieth century, beginning with John Magalee and Daniel Chu. Since then many Asian Lutherans have come forth, struggling for recognition and self-determination against the mighty forces of injustice and racism in the church and in society. In the course of their collective struggle, some individuals seem to have fared better than others.

In this chapter and the next, the aim is twofold: (1) To show the reader snapshots of what it means to be Asian Lutherans in North America at a given time, by recounting the experiences of several Asian Lutheran leaders, lay and ordained; (2) to pay tribute to these women and men who have courageously, resiliently, and faithfully marched and, in most cases, continue to move forward in ministry. This presentation does not divide them according to their Lutheran denominational affiliations (ELCA or LCMS). However, for the sake of convenience, two generational groupings are used. Rather than categorized by chronological age, these groupings designate the period in which the people emerged as leaders in the church or made their presence felt in society.

This chapter covers "generation one," which includes the period from 1950 to 1977. By the end of this period, fewer than 10 Asian Lutheran congregations and ministries existed in North America. But Asian Lutheran leadership, besides those who were serving Asian Lutheran parishes, had already penetrated other aspects of ministry.

JOHN MAGALEE

Rev. John Magalee, a grandson of indentured servants in Guyana, South America, was in 1950 the first person of South Asian heritage to be ordained by a predecessor body of the ELCA. His grandparents were brought over to Guyana as indentured servants from India. His parents became members in the Lutheran Church of Guyana. In the early 1940s, Magalee came to the United States to study. He attended Gustavus Adolphus College, St. Peter, Minnesota, and Northwestern Theological Seminary, St. Paul. "He served as pastor of St. Paul Lutheran Church, New York, and then as a United States Army chaplain until his retirement in 1986." [2]

DANIEL CHU

Rev. Daniel H. S. Chu was the first Chinese clergy to serve as pastor of an all white congregation among all Protestant denominations in North America. Chu also has the distinction of being the first Chinese Lutheran ordained by an American Lutheran church as well as being the first Asian clergy to serve as a missionary under BFM of the ULCA.

Born on March 20, 1918, in Sinyang, Henan, China, Chu is a third-generation Lutheran. His grandparents were among the first to be converted to the faith by Lutheran missionaries in the early nineteenth century. His father, Rev. Chu Haoran, was among the first group of Chinese to become pastors in the Lutheran tradition. The elder Chu graduated from Lutheran Theological Seminary in Shekou, China, in 1916 and later became the first president of the Lutheran Church of China. Before Chu was born, his parents, having given birth to three daughters, prayed to God for a son. Should God answer their prayers, they would dedicate this son to God's service. Thus when Chu was born they were convinced that God had answered their prayers and dedicated him to God's service. They decided to give young Chu the best education they could provide in order to prepare him for ministry. They sent him to several boarding schools in China.

Japan invaded China after Chu's first year at Cheloo University. During his senior year, young Chu, swept up by patriotism like many others, joined the army to fight Japanese aggression. During his years in the military, Chu traveled extensively throughout the nation, visiting different war zones and seeing the suffering of his own people first hand. This experience and a shipwreck incident changed Chu's life. "He became more convinced than ever that God's love and patience was humanity's salvation." [3]

After the war, young Chu asked the Lutheran church to give him a chance to go to the United States to study for ministry. He arrived in Springfield, Ohio, in August 1948 and spent two years and one summer at Hamma Divinity School and Wittenberg University, plus one summer at Union Theological Seminary in New York City. In 1950 he was awarded a B.A.

degree from the university and a B.D. degree from Hamma in 1951. [4] After graduation he returned to China by way of Europe and the Middle East, arriving in Hong Kong on December 11, 1950. By this time the People's Republic of China had been established for more than a year.

While he was in Hong Kong, his father discreetly told him not to return to the mainland. Chu "stayed in Hong Kong under the support of the Board of Foreign Missions of the ULCA, working to expand the Lutheran ministry in the Hong Kong area." [5] While Chu was working in the colony, the ULCA "at the 1952 convention voted 'to open a field of work in Malaya'." [6] By the fall of 1953, there were already five American missionaries in Malaya.

In the same year, Chu was ordained in Hong Kong by Rev. Charles Reinbrecht on behalf of the North Carolina Synod at the request of the BFM, ULCA. Chu was assigned to Malaya as a missionary. He served in that capacity for about two years.

In August 1955 under a new congressional bill allowing two thousand "communist affected Chinese refugees to immigrate to America," [7] Chu and his family returned to Springfield, Ohio. Two months later, Chu was installed as pastor of St. Luke Lutheran Church in town. Chu subsequently spent his pastorate in Michigan and Washington State. In 1981, while he was serving as pastor of Resurrection Lutheran Church in Tacoma, Washington, he was asked to develop a Chinese ministry in Federal Way, Washington. He served the mission until 1983 when he retired. The Chinese ministry was subsequently closed.

Chu's services to the church go beyond congregational ministry. He was a member of the Board of Pensions and member of BFM for a total of 22 years. He also served as the first chair of the Asian Caucus of the LCA. Chu, likewise, was an advocate for Asian ministries in the church, particularly after the 1960s when the influx of immigrants from Asia began to increase drastically. Among his Chinese colleagues, he is affectionately known as "*Chu dage*" (big brother Chu), whose wisdom and experiences have benefited the younger generation of Asian Lutherans in North America.

EIICHI MATSUSHITA

Rev. Eiichi Matsushita (1930-1984) had a complex personality and a keen mind. Born on March 20, 1930, in Tokyo, Japan, into a *samurai*-turned-merchant family, Matsushita appeared to have retained a great deal of the warrior class's characteristics. By the time he was born, the warrior class had undergone great changes, which had begun during the Tokugawa period (1603-1868). Indeed, though the *samurai* then continued to wear their traditional two swords as their badges of rank, they no longer resembled a standing army but rather a group of civil bureaucrats. They had become men of the writing brush instead of the sword.

During this period of prolonged peace, "rural as well as urban Japan was developing far beyond the normal limits of a feudal society." [8] With a flourishing economy, the merchant class soon emerged as one of the dominant social forces in the society. Some *samurai* bureaucrats soon joined the merchant class.

Exactly when the Matsushita family joined the merchant class is not known. His father, however, was a factory owner, who expected his eldest son, Eiichi, eventually to take over the family business. But Matsushita's own intellectual orientation was toward the humanities and social sciences. Thus after receiving his A.B. degree in sociology from the Keio University in Tokyo in 1954, to his father's disappointment and chagrin, he embarked on a journey to the United States in search of further education. He entered Gettysburg College in Gettysburg, Pennsylvania, in the fall of 1954 and obtained yet another A.B. degree in sociology two years later. In the fall of 1956 he entered Lutheran Theological Seminary at Gettysburg, where he prepared himself for ministry and from which he obtained his B.D. degree in 1960, with a major in sociology. His B.D. thesis, a sociological study, was on St. Mark's Lutheran Church, Los Angeles, where Paul T. Nakamura served as pastor.

After graduation Matsushita briefly served as an assistant pastor at Bethany Lutheran Church in Bronx, New York, before moving to California, where he stayed at St. Mark's Lutheran Church with Nakamura for a few months. Nakamura remembered him as a person of deep faith and of compassion. From 1961 to 1962 he was an assistant pastor at Faith Lutheran Church, Long Beach, California, where S. Samuel Ujiie was the pastor.

His ministry at Faith was difficult, recalled Ujiie. The church was located directly across the street from the Golden Stars, a home for mothers whose sons were killed in the Pacific or in Europe during World War II. As a person from Japan, Matsushita was not the object of their affection. Matsushita from time to time was quite distressed. At such times he would confide in and consult with Mrs. Ujiie, who was also born in Japan and whose family belonged to the same social class as Matsushita's. But Matsushita eventually won the residents of Golden Stars over with his deep faith and compassion.

From 1962 to 1963, he was the director of the Philadelphia Planning Study under the auspices of BAM. By 1962 Philadelphia had already experienced urban flight and its attendant problems, leaving the downtown and surrounding churches in a state of rapid decline. The Philadelphia Planning Study was sociological in nature, focusing attention on how to prevent churches from further decline and to enable them to become self-sufficient neighborhood institutions serving the community. Within a year, Matsushita published his influential study in four volumes with detailed recommendations. The result of his study was the formation of the Center City Parish, a coalition consisting of more than 30 congregations.

The Philadelphia Planning Study was one of the most significant contributions that Matsushita had made to the LCA. This study brought him tremendous personal satisfaction. It was also a step that Matsushita needed in order to make his knowledge known and available to the church.

While he was doing the study, he did not neglect his personal life. Thus in December 1962 he married Heidrum Bohn, a woman of German parentage. Together they had two daughters—Sabine Uta, born in January 1964, and Suzanne Taka, in April 1967.

The Philadelphia study also earned him a place in church bureaucracy. Headquartered in Chicago, BAM appointed him in 1963 to the position of assistant secretary for church planning. It was in Chicago that he eventually got acquainted with Martin L. Yonts, a white person, and Massie Kennard, an African-American. The threesome formed a friendship that lasted throughout their entire lives.

Matsushita held the above-mentioned position until 1968. In that year he became secretary for strategy planning, a position he held until 1972. Meanwhile the LCA restructured itself in 1972, grouping smaller units into divisions. The work of BAM came under the umbrella of DMNA, under which was the Department for Research and Study. Matsushita felt that he was the best-qualified person to head the department. But he was passed over for the directorship, which caused him to become bitter about the institution. He had told me he considered the move unjust and racist. Instead, he was given a position of assistant director for research and planning. However, Matsushita said he felt vindicated in 1976 when he became the director of the Office for Church and Community Planning, a position he held until his death in 1984.

In his professional life, Matsushita pioneered a study of membership and population trends of the Lutheran churches in the 1960s. In 1964 he published "A Theoretical Explanation on Church and Community," followed by numerous studies of LCA congregations and an article on "Population Growth Zero Point" in 1973. During the last years of his life, "Matsushita concentrated on congregational spot studies, which included the use of membership trend graphs and age-sex pyramids, and site evaluations of new and existing congregations." [9] Matsushita "was a founding member of Census Access for Planning in the Church, a consortium of denominations and church-related agencies." [10]

Matsushita shared his knowledge and new findings not only with the central LCA staff but also with pastor-developers of new congregations. At their training sessions, he would teach them how to understand the communities in which they would serve and what to look for that would help them in their ministries. He would also describe the characteristics of different types of congregations, including the "point-of-breaks" [11] and the "balloon"[12] theories.

Matsushita was an articulate man with an aesthetic sensitivity that few people possess. He also had a wry sense of humor that seemed to have carried him forward in the dark moments of his life, particularly in the last few years when his health deteriorated rapidly. He was a collector of Japanese wood block prints, a genre that I also appreciate. Whenever we had a chance to get together at each other's home, we would view our collections.

Matsushita was a loyal subject of Japan. Even though he spent most of his life in the United States, he refused to become a citizen. His loyalty to Japan, however, was not uncritical. In fact he often voiced his criticism against his beloved homeland. But should he deem that someone else's criticism against Japan or his people was unjustified, he would not hesitate to defend either. He was often critical of the Green Peace organization that accused Japan of killing whales. Matsushita was not for killing whales, but he strongly felt that Green Peace was too one-sided. To him whaling was what kept some Japanese alive.

He was a family man. He and Heidi loved their children. Their second daughter, Suzanne, was born a mentally challenged child. But they refused to institutionalize her. Heidi gave up her career to stay home and care for Suzanne. Their love for children went beyond their own; they often had foster children staying with them. Among the children for whom they had cared was an African-American boy named Peter. The Matsushita family fell in love with him and adopted him.

Matsushita's work involved much weekend travel, causing him to miss worship at his own church more often than not. And with his failing health, even if he did not have to travel over the weekend, he would stay home and rest. But he did occasionally accompany his family to church. On those occasions, more often than not, the ushers would try to separate him from his family. He did not look like one of them. The ushers' action infuriated Matsushita, making him not want to attend worship at his home congregation on Sunday.

To some people such as Lily Wu, Matsushita's presence exuded a sense of calm and confidence. That was true. But some others had also experienced his wrath. Nowhere was that more evident than after he had gotten wind of the content of the Foster report. In 1980 in his capacity as assistant director (Western Region), Department of Church Extension, DMNA, Howell Foster made a trip to Asia to become familiar with church life in that part of the world. Upon returning to America, Foster wrote a report on his trip, as it was a customary thing to do within DMNA. In his report, Foster mentioned that the Japanese were a violent people. Matsushita was furious and demanded that the report not be circulated. He felt that Foster misportrayed his people. DMNA officials were in a quandary. Ultimately, they decided not to publish the report. In reality, Foster's portrayal of the Japanese as a violent people was most likely based on incomplete information. Matsushita's objection perhaps reflected, more than anything else, the search for elusive beauty in a world of constructed truth by the brokenhearted at the sky's edge.

With a portrait on a banner in the Heritage and Hope Village, Matsushita was among 37 individuals honored by the ELCA at its 1997 churchwide assembly in Philadelphia. "The people depicted on the 20 banners," the information on the Heritage and Hope Village map read, "represent many thousands more who have served our church in the United States and the Caribbean in the 250 years since Henry Melchior Muhlenberg declared to that first Lutheran Synod 'Ecclesia Plantanda' (the church must be planted)." It was most fitting that the church would honor him in the city where Matsushita made his first significant contribution to the institution as its pastor and churchwide staff.

MABEL LAI YING CHIN MOY

Dr. Mabel Lai Ying Chin Moy is a quiet, well-balanced person with an immense intellectual capacity (she reads Paul Tillich's theology for recreation!), numerous skills, and a wide range of interests, including but not limited to mountaineering, tennis, anthropology, archaeology, and international and Daoist studies, all of which she puts to good use in her professional endeavors, family life, and service to the church.

One of seven children of immigrant parents, Moy was born on March 3, 1934, in New York City. In 1944 the family moved to the Brooklyn section of the city. Her father owned a restaurant in Manhattan and her mother stayed home caring for the ever-growing family. Her parents were generous and gracious to relatives, friends, and new immigrants from China. There was always a place in their home for all who needed a room for a night or longer. Childhood was a happy one for Moy. The church entered into her life early. "A Christian and Missionary Alliance Church," she recalled recently "on the next block [where they lived] was operating a nursery school program. They invited our parents to send the children there." [13] A nursery school program was followed by Sunday school, from which she received loving care but not much of anything else. In fact, she and others "rebelled against the moralistic injunctions against playing cards and going to the movies, because that is exactly what [they] did after church: [they] went to the movies and [they] loved to play cards."

When the family moved to Brooklyn, a friend and classmate invited her to go to her church—an independent charismatic church. Moy accepted the invitation and became a faithful Sunday school student and a regular attendee of Sunday morning and evening services. Her parents became quite concerned, particularly when she contemplated baptism. They did not think that she should be "'buried' in [her] religion"! As far as her parents were concerned, "being taught to live a good life is one thing; extreme involvement was another." But to Moy, especially when she began to assert her independence, "the church and church members were a loving and supportive community for [her]."

After high school graduation in 1951, Moy became a student at Brooklyn College, where she studied history and from which she obtained her B.A. degree in 1955. On December 21, 1957, she married James Moy. In 1962 Columbia University, New York City, awarded her an M.A. degree in education and ten years later she received her Ph.D. degree in educational psychology from Ohio University, Athens, Ohio. In addition, she received a certificate in Japanese flower arrangement from the William Rainey Harper College in 1992, a certificate in the liberal arts from the University of Chicago in 1994, and an A.A.S. degree in architectural technology from Harper College, Palatine, Illinois, in 1996.

During various stages of her professional life, Moy served as a sixth-grade teacher, university instructor, college professor, consultant, and research associate. In her spare time she has also taught *taijiquan*, a Daoist art of spiritual exercise and is a practitioner of *ikenobo ikebana*, the art of Japanese flower arrangement.

Moy's spiritual journey, as we have seen, began with the Missionary Alliance and an independent charismatic church. When she was in college, she "connected with the InterVarsity Christian Fellowship," an evangelical group on campus. The other group on campus was the Student Christian Association, a more "mainline" organization. There were Lutheran leaders in both groups. This was her first exposure to Lutherans. Shortly after her graduation, she was introduced to James Moy, who was preparing for ministry at Valparaiso University. And by this time she was already attending BS (now New York Theological Seminary) in New York City, "contemplating the possibility of becoming a missionary." Her marriage to James changed her plan. After they were married, they joined a ULCA congregation and she was "duly baptized and confirmed in that church."

Her involvement with the Lutheran church heightened in 1980 when the LCA held its biennial convention in Seattle. Moy was the coordinator of ushers for "the Eucharistic Service at the Seattle Opera House." On the national level, Moy was a member and vice-chair of the Division for World Mission and Ecumenism (DWME) management committee. She was a delegate to the LWF assembly in Budapest, Hungary, as well as "part of an international team to evaluate the work of Lutheran World Service in India."

She and her husband were participants in Transcultural Seminars (sponsored by LCUSA; for details see chapter 10), the June 1982 Consultation on Preparation for Ministry in an Inclusive Church (sponsored by Consultation on Theological Education of the ALC, the AELC, and the LCA), and other events. In every case, Moy puts her training, knowledge, and skills to work for the good of the whole.

WI JO KANG

Rev. Professor Wi Jo Kang in 1968 became the first Asian Lutheran to be appointed to the faculty of a Lutheran seminary in North America. Born on March 10, 1930, in Jinju, Korea, Kang was a product of a compassionate Buddhist mother and a stern but loving Confucianist father. He lived in a Buddhist village about one hundred miles west of Pusan. His mother often took him to the nearby Buddhist temple when he was young. Thus, Buddhism had a strong claim on his early life. Through his father, he also learned the Confucian virtues with which he became conversant all his life. Growing up in such a multifaith family was no problem for Kang, because Asian religions and their adherents, in actual practice, are rather inclusive.

When Kang was born, Korea was no longer an independent nation but a colony of Japan.[14] Korean life under Japanese rule was hard and harsh. Korea was made into a chief rice supplier to Japan. Like other Koreans under Japanese rule, Kang was forced to learn the Japanese language, which would one day serve him well in his academic career. After World War II, he also learned English in school, which in time would become a symbolic boat ferrying him from Buddhism to Christianity.

The Korean War interrupted young Kang's life and education. Even so, he became a student at Busan Teachers College in Korea in 1948, after his basic education in his hometown Jinju. Because of his proficiency in English, Kang became an interpreter in the 7th U.S. Infantry Division from 1950 to 1953. During his tour of military duty, Kang became acquainted with some Lutheran soldiers in his unit and from whom he learned about Christianity. A soldier by the name of Robert Bendixen from Plainview, Nebraska, and his pastor Rev. Theodore Stolp were especially instrumental in Kang's becoming a Lutheran Christian.

While he was in the army, Bendixen introduced him to Stolp. Through correspondence with Stolp, Kang studied Martin Luther's Small Catechism and basic church history for three years. At the end of the period, he accepted the Christian faith and dedicated himself to ministry. In the spring of 1954, Kang arrived at St. John's College in Winfield, Kansas, to prepare himself for ordained ministry under the sponsorship of Stolp and the congregation he served, with the hope that he would "return to Korea to teach and to preach the gospel."[15] After his graduation from St. John's, Kang entered CS, St. Louis, from which he obtained his B.A. degree in 1957 and the M.Div. degree in 1960.

Two years before Kang graduated from the seminary, The LCMS entered Korea as a foreign mission field. Kang had high hopes that after he received his M.Div. degree the church would call him back to Korea to serve. But that did not happen. He continued his education at the University of Chicago, where he studied world religions and history of Christian mission and from which he obtained an M.A. degree in 1962 and a Ph.D. degree in 1967.

After he had completed his course and language requirements for his doctoral degree, Kang went to Columbia University in New York City to do research for his dissertation. While he was there he encountered financial difficulties. But his professors at the University of Chicago were able to arrange for him to be hired as an instructor by the Department of Religion at Columbia University from 1964 to 1966. In the fall of 1966, he was appointed assistant professor of religion at Valparaiso University in Valparaiso, Indiana.

Ordained in 1968, he was in the same year called to CS, St. Louis, as an assistant professor of history of religions and missions. A year later, Preus was elected president of The LCMS and Kang's life eventually took a drastic turn. In 1972 he was promoted to the rank of associate professor. In 1974 Kang joined the majority of his colleagues and students at Seminex (later Christ Seminary-Seminex), where he taught until 1978. But the enrollment at Seminex was not large enough to support the faculty. Thus, Kang became a part-time adjunct professor of Asian civilization in the Department of History at the University of Missouri at St. Louis from 1974 to 1976. Finally in 1978, he returned to Korea hoping that the Lutheran church there could use him. In the end, he was disappointed that "the Korean Lutheran Mission did not want to use [him] to teach in the seminary or to be involved in the church." [16] Kang remembered that "it was [a] terribly sad and difficult time [in my life and career]. I became a homeless person in my homeland." [17] Fortunately Yonsei University offered him a position as visiting professor in the College of Theology and the Seoul National University did likewise in the Department of Religion.

He returned to the United States in late 1979. In the spring of the following year Kang was appointed Endowed Chair Professor of World Religions and Mission at Wartburg Theological Seminary in Dubuque, Iowa. In the same year, he transferred his rostered membership from The LCMS to the ALC. In 1988 he became the Wilhelm Loehe Professor of Mission at Wartburg, a position he held until his retirement in 1998.

Kang is a prolific scholar. He authored several books, translated one—*Religion of the East* by Joseph M. Kitagawa—into Korean, and coedited two others in English. Among his books, *Christ and Caesar in Modern Korean: A History of Christianity and Politics* and *Religion and Politics in Korea under the Japanese Rule* are highly acclaimed scholarly works. In addition to the books, Kang was a regular contributor of scholarly articles to various journals, as well as a regular presenter of papers at academic conferences.

As a churchman, Kang also served on the Division for World Mission and Interchurch Cooperation (DWMIC) advisory board of the ALC and the boards of the Division for Ministry (DM) and the Division for Higher Education of the ELCA.

MARGARET TSAN

Sister Margaret Tsan is the first Asian Lutheran deaconess in North America. She was also a trailblazer in theological education in another Lutheran church. Born in Beijing and raised in Hong Kong, Sister Tsan, as she is commonly known, is the youngest in her family, which includes six brothers and five sisters. Her father was a professor. Her mother died when she was seven years old.

She received her education in Hong Kong from 1938 to 1968, except for the years 1947 to 1951 when she went back to mainland China. Brought up a Buddhist, she became a Christian in 1948. Miss Gertrude Woodrich, a German missionary, Miss Anna Lankoetter, a German deaconess, and Miss Cora Martinson, an ALC missionary, had considerable influence in her life and vocation.

In 1960 Tsan applied for admission to Lutheran Theological Seminary of Hong Kong but her application was denied. The seminary did not accept women. Undeterred, she requested an appointment with the president and recounted "the resurrection story of Jesus as he first appeared to women and told them to tell others the Good News." [18] She was admitted to the seminary from which she obtained her Th.B. and B.D. degrees. After her graduation, Tsan served for a number of years in educational institutions and service agencies.

Tsan left Hong Kong for Canada in 1968 where she enrolled at Lutheran Theological Seminary in Saskatoon, Saskatchewan. When she graduated in 1970, she became the first woman graduate from that seminary to receive a master of sacred theology degree. Three years later she was set apart as a deaconess of the LCA. Since then, Tsan has dedicated her life to God's service through educational institutions, parishes, and social service agencies.

DAVID YUAN-PIN CHOU

Professor David Chou, an educator and an active layman, was born into a traditional Chinese family on March 5, 1922, in Muping Prefecture, Shandong, China. At age 15, he became a baptized Episcopalian. After completing his high school education, he went to Tokyo, Japan, where he studied applied chemistry at the Tokyo Institute of Technology and received his B.Engr. degree in 1948. Following graduation he did graduate studies at the

University of Tokyo until the spring of 1951. He then came to Ohio State University, Columbus, Ohio, to continue his graduate work. After receiving his Ph.D. degree in 1954, he taught at Saint Augustine's College in Raleigh, North Carolina, for two years before joining the faculty of Lenoir–Rhyne College, Hickory, North Carolina. He served there as professor and chairman of the chemistry department for 32 years until his retirement in 1988. Presently he holds the title of Professor Emeritus in Chemistry.

In 1951 he attended the Students' Volunteer Movement Conference held at the University of Kansas and met his future bride, Mary Ann Sung. A Lutheran from China, she was a nursing education student at the University of Minnesota. After they were married in 1953, Chou joined the Lutheran church and remained active in the church on all levels.

At his home parish, Chou served as a member of the congregation council and social ministry committee, as well as a delegate to the synod assembly numerous times. On the synodical level, he was a member of the world mission committee, minority ministry task force, inclusive ministry committee, and synod transition team. Chou also was elected to Lutheran Theological Southern Seminary board of trustees from 1986 to 1991.

In 1989, Chou was elected to the Asian advisory committee of the Commission for Multicultural Ministries (CMM) for two years and elected to the board of the Division for Global Mission (DGM) in 1997.

KYUZO MIYAISHI

Rev. Kyuzo Miyaishi, commonly known as Frankie-San to his colleagues and to prisoners, is an exceptional man with an unusual ministry. He spent 28 years as a tentmaker in prison, ministering to inmates at the Central Correctional Institution in South Carolina until it was closed in 1994.

Miyaishi was born on September 17, 1929, in Tokyo, Japan. When he was 15 years old, he joined the Japanese navy. After his discharge, Miyaishi resumed his education, graduating from the Hosei University in Tokyo at age 32.

In 1961, he came to America to attend Columbia Bible College in Columbia, South Carolina. After spending one semester at the college, Miyaishi transferred to Lutheran Theological Southern Seminary in January 1962 and obtained a master of religious education degree in 1966. In the same year, he became an adult academic instructor in the educational department of the Central Correctional Institution, serving in this capacity until 1975. While working at the correctional facility, he also attended the University of South Carolina from 1976 to 1980.

Miyaishi was ordained by the South Carolina Synod, LCA, in May 1973, as a tentmaker minister to serve at the Central Correctional Institution, which was "the most overcrowded prison system in the nation." [19] In 1975 he joined the library staff. When the facility was closed in 1994, Miyaishi joined the Health Services of the Department of Corrections, serving as a minister to AIDS victims and the dying in the state prison system.

After having spent more than 30 years serving the prisoners, Miyaishi is convinced "that longer imprisonment is not the answer" [20] to social problems. To him, imprisonment destroys a person mentally and spiritually and such destruction was the most frightful experience that Miyaishi faced daily in his ministry.

Miyaishi, who is rather shy and private, pays little attention to his own personal welfare and the world outside the prison walls. He is man for others. Parker Evatt, a commissioner of the South Carolina Department of Correction, unequivocally stated, Miyaishi "gave his life for his prison work." [21]

CLEMENT W. K. LEE

Rev. Clement W. K. Lee is one of the first Asian Lutherans in North America to enter into media ministry. Throughout his career, Lee has made his technical knowledge available not only to the Lutherans but also to a wider ecumenical circle.

A quiet and thoughtful person with a sense of humor, Lee was born on February 7, 1938, in Brooklyn, New York. His grandparents were immigrants to the United States in the late nineteenth century. His mother was born in Chicago and later became a member of True Light Lutheran Church, New York City. She was buried in the Lutheran Cemetery in Middle Village, New York. His father was born in Sacramento, California. Lee became a Lutheran through a close friend who introduced him to True Light Lutheran Church, where he was baptized. Lee was active in the local congregation in his youth.

When he responded to the call to enter the ordained ministry, Lee chose to prepare himself at Concordia College in Portland, Oregon. The college awarded him the B.Th. degree in 1958 and he obtained the M.Div. degree from CTS, Springfield, Illinois, in 1962. In the same year, he was ordained and served from 1962 to 1965 as an associate pastor at Our Shepherd Lutheran Church, Birmingham, Michigan.

His ministry took a different turn in 1965 when he was appointed associate executive director of the Lutheran Center of Greater Detroit and concurrently as associate communication director of the Metropolitan Detroit Council of Churches. Lee served in this capacity until 1967. He subsequently accepted the position of media operations director of the American Bible Society, New York City.

In 1971 LCUSA called him to be media relations director. Lee's responsibilities at LCUSA included but were not limited to the "council's film, filmstrip, and television productions, as well as its unique program of media interview arrangements for newsworthy Lutheran spokespersons."[22] While he was serving in this capacity, Lee pursued graduate studies in media at the New School University in New York City and from which he obtained an M.A. degree in 1976.

Busy as he was, Lee also served as "an editor of the Detroit and Suburban Lutheran Newspaper and the Religious Public Relations Council counselor... [and] independently, as a media consultant for an architectural newsletter, 'Window;' Concordia College, Bronxville, New York; Wheat Ridge Foundation; Council for a Livable World Education Fund; and Physicians for Social Responsibility."[23]

In 1982 Lee became telecommunications director of the LCA, a position he held until 1987 when the LCA was dissolved to become part of the ELCA. In the same year Lee transferred his membership from The LCMS to the AELC, and joined the Episcopal Church in the USA as its electronic media director. He held the position until 1998 when he was appointed as media services director of the same church.

Since he joined the staff of the Episcopal Church in the USA, Lee has concurrently served up to the present as a telecommunications adjunct staff specialist in the Anglican Communion office in London.

Lee has received numerous awards for his work, including "the silver medallion of the International Film and Television Festival for a film commissioned by the USA National Committee of the Lutheran World Federation,...the Detroit Press Club Foundation Award for a radio documentary on the work of a prison "half-way house... [and] a Columbus Film Festival award."[24]

Lee's "ecumenical involvements have included service as chairman...and vice chairman"[25] of numerous boards, commissions, and committees. He also holds membership in a number of professional associations and societies.

Even though he has spent nearly all his professional life in media ministry, Lee has not forgotten the parish. Thus in 1990, he became a pastoral associate of Good Shepherd Lutheran Church in Scarsdale, New York, and in the same year he became a member of St. John's Episcopal Church in New York City. He continues to be active in both churches.

7

SNAPSHOTS: GENERATION TWO

THIS CHAPTER CONTINUES THE THEME OF CHAPTER 6 BUT COVERS THE PERIOD from 1978 to 2000 and introduces the second generation of Asian leaders. Within this period, some Asian congregations reached maturity, producing a cadre of highly qualified lay leaders. Together with other Asian leaders who worshiped in congregations other-than-Asian, the younger generation of ordained Asian Lutheran clergy as well as the first generation veterans would exert strong influence within and beyond the church.

FENG SHAN HO

Dr. Feng Shan Ho (1901-1997), a courtly, quiet, thoughtful, daring, and generous intellectual and diplomat, was a charter member of Chinese Lutheran Church in San Francisco, California. Ho was born on September 10, 1901, in Yiyang, Hunan Province, China, and became fatherless at the age of seven. The Norwegian Lutheran Mission in China helped him and his family, and Ho himself received his secondary education in their schools. After graduating from the College of Yale-in-China, Ho sailed for Germany to further his education. In 1932 the University of Munich awarded him the Ph.D. degree, magna cum laude, in political economics. In 1935, he joined the government and its foreign service.

In May 1938, Ho was appointed Consul General in Vienna, Austria, and witnessed the eruption of anti-Semitism in full force. Ho commiserated with Jewish people in their suffering. During the early Nazi occupation of Austria, Jewish people were given a chance to immigrate to other nations, provided that they would turn over everything they owned. The desperate Jews tried to obtain visas from the foreign consulates in the city, but most did not offer any help.

Ho, however, decided on his own to help Jewish people by issuing them visas to Shanghai, China. He continued to do so, even after he was ordered to stop issuing visas. Thus, during the years 1938 and 1939, Ho saved thousands of Jews. After the war, Ho served as ambassador to Egypt, Mexico, Bolivia, and Colombia.

In 1973 Ho retired and moved to San Francisco where he became a member of Chinese Lutheran Church and remained active until the end of his life. He was a well-respected member whose advice on congregational and other matters was often sought by others. In retirement Ho occasionally would entertain in his home Asian Lutheran leaders who came to San Francisco for meetings. He also wrote his memoirs: *Forty Years of My Diplomatic Life,* which was published in 1990.

In recognition of his service to Jewish people during World War II, Temple Emanu-El in San Francisco honored him with an exhibition in April and May 2000. He was also "one of the 75 men honored at the United Nations for issuing exit visas, transit visas, and other documents that saved thousands of Jews from murder at the hands of the Nazis." [1]

JULIET HSIA

Ms. Juliet Hsia was a graceful and articulate layperson who brought a wealth of knowledge and experience to a church trying to be fully multicultural. Born into the Malayan multicultural society before World War II, she was nurtured by the multicultural environment. She obtained her secondary education in Chinese and English at a Roman Catholic convent school, before setting sail for boarding school and college in England. Moving from a multicultural society to an Anglo culture was not easy for Hsia, but she adjusted well in a short time.

She was baptized in the Church of England. But being a vulnerable teenager away from home, she committed herself to Jesus Christ as a born-again Christian at a student Christian conference in northern England. Later she married a converted Christian in London. She was blessed with five sons and six grandchildren.

In 1962 Hsia moved to Connecticut where for 10 years she was active in the Calvary Baptist Church and in Chinese community services. In 1977 she and her family moved to Hawaii. She worked as a genetic counselor and administrator for Medical Genetic Services at Kapiolani Medical Center for Women and Children in Honolulu until she retired in 1998.

In Hawaii the Hsia family decided to bring up the children in the Lutheran tradition. They joined Calvary-by-the-Sea Lutheran Church. Through the years, Hsia had served as chairperson for the music and worship committee, mission and ministry committee, and as president of the congregation for three terms. She also helped the congregation to implement the "Caring Evangelism" and "Prayer Ministry" programs.

In addition to serving her own congregation, Hsia was also a two-term member of the synod council of the Pacifica Synod and a one-term member of the synod committee for multicultural ministries. Her church-wide activities were equally impressive. She served as a member of the steering committee of CMM and participated in brainstorming sessions and special conferences of the Commission for Women (CW). She was one of two ELCA delegates to the international LFW Women's Caucus in Mexico in 1989 and was nominated for the ELCA Church Council in 1997. In retirement Hsia continued to give her time and talents to the church locally, synodically, and nationally until she died in September 2000.

LILY R. WU

Ms. Lily R. Wu is the first Asian American woman to serve on the highest elected governing board—the Church Council of the ELCA—of any Lutheran body in North America. She was elected to the Church Council at the 1997 churchwide assembly, then to the executive committee. She became chair of the planning and evaluation committee in November 1999. Other firsts in her church life include being primary author of *Eternal River*, a first curriculum by and for Asian Lutherans in the United States and project manager and editor of *No Hate Allowed*, a first ELCA resource for congregational action against racial hate crimes. In 1989 she was the first Asian-American woman to receive a "Disciple for Justice" award from the ELCA's CMM. In 1998 she received an Honorary Chair Award from the Lutheran Human Relations Association of America at its 45th anniversary celebration and a Mary L. Chrichlow Leadership Award from CW of the Metropolitan New York Synod.

Wu is a quiet, diplomatic writer and editor. Born on July 16, 1952, into a Christian family in New York City, Wu has lived all her life there, except for a short two-month sabbatical spent in Seattle, Washington, in 1997, working with Lutheran Peace Fellowship. Her maternal grandfather was a Methodist minister in Canada who later settled in Portland, Oregon. Her mother, who "also chose Christian service as her life's work," [2] served as a teacher and interpreter in mainland China and colonial Hong Kong before World War II "and later worked with Chinese young people in Nanaimo, British Columbia." [3] Her father was a graduate of Pui Ying High School, a Christian institution in Guangzhou, China, "and ... Huron College in South Dakota in the 1930s." [4]

Her parents settled in New York City after their marriage. Her mother became an English teacher and served as a church organist and youth leader. Her father was a businessman. Mrs. Wu later also served as a deaconess at First Presbyterian Church in New York City's Chinatown. Lily Wu became a Lutheran because of an English-speaking youth program at True Light Lutheran Church which was not only the largest Chinese Protestant church in North America, but had also "really become a major influence in Chinatown since its founding in 1936." [5] It was there that she met Fern Lee Hagedorn in her early teen years.

The Wu family "lived in a third-floor walk-up tenement in Chinatown in a one bedroom railroad flat apartment." [6] Both her mother and the environment had a strong influence on Wu's faith, her appreciation for diversity, and her career. When Wu was six years old, her mother took her "to the public library [where she become so captivated that she] borrowed and read the entire fairy tale and fantasy section from the Chatham Square Chinatown branch—10 books at a time, which was the borrowing limit." [7] Wu read the books aloud to her dolls after lining them up on the fire escape while she herself sat on the window sill, from where she could see the diversity of people "walking around on the street below." [8]

After high school Wu attended Pace University, New York City, where she obtained her B.A. degree in English literature, cum laude, in 1974. She went on to Queens College, Flushing, New York, and was awarded a master of library science degree in 1976. In the same year "New York City froze the hiring of public librarians." [9]

Fern Lee suggested that she work for the LCA. Her first job entailed packing "a bulletin insert called 'Acts of Thanksgiving' into jiffy bags and [labeling] them for mailing all over the country." [10] This job gave her a sense of the size of the LCA and its operation and led to a position as a writer-researcher in the Department of Interpretation, DMNA.

In 1980 Wu joined the staff of Lutheran Immigration and Refugee Service (LIRS), New York City. LIRS is the second largest resettlement agency in the United States. She served as an assistant for sponsorship promotion (1980-1987), associate for communications (1988-1990), and manager for promotion and editorial services (1991-1999). She "produced educational tools and slide shows, undergirded refugee sponsorship work of 27 affiliate offices with resource information, and served as convention and editorial manager and presenter." [11] In the latter capacity, Wu "conducted more than 70 custom-designed workshops and presentations in 16 states." [12] Public speaking was hard for her, but she eventually overcame her shyness enough to become a remarkably enthusiastic, eloquent, and thoughtful speaker.

In 1981 Aid Association for Lutherans through LCUSA sponsored the second Transcultural Seminar involving 200 participants from Asian, Hispanic, Native American, and white communities. Wu was invited to assist with communication there. This experience heightened her appreciation for multicultural ministry. She later edited the proceedings volume, *Catching a Star: Transcultural Reflections on a Church for All People*. From this point on, Wu "eventually got involved in multicultural work at all levels—national, regional, and local—as a writer, editor, consultant, workshop leader, speaker, project manager." [13]

Wu is a prolific writer. Her writings have appeared in numerous newsletters and magazines and cover a wide range of issues: for example, racism, identity, and multiculturalism. She has an elegant and engaging literary style in which her language is always direct and simple, inviting her readers to enter into reflection and dialogue with her.

Wu has also served on different boards and committees. Besides the ELCA Church Council, she is on the steering committee of the Asian Lutheran International Conference (ALIC), which planned the second international Asian Lutheran gathering held in Bangkok, Thailand, in 2001.

In February 1998, Wu, along with Paul T. Nakamura, Frederick E. N. Rajan, and this author were among 18 leaders honored by CMM as "Examples of a Living Faith." Banners with our likenesses were designed for use in displays and a booklet was published containing our biographies.

In 1999 LIRS moved its headquarters from New York City to Baltimore, Maryland. Wu decided to remain in New York City where she is doing freelance writing and editing.

J. PAUL RAJASHEKAR

Dr. J. Paul Rajashekar is a world-renowned Asian Lutheran theologian and the first person of Asian heritage to be appointed to the position of academic dean by a Lutheran seminary in North America. Rajashekar, in some ways, is also a world citizen having lived, studied, worked, and taught in three continents before immigrating to the United States in 1991.

Rajashekar was born on June 2, 1948, in Mangalore, India, where he grew up. He was a member of the Ambur Synod of the India Evangelical Lutheran Church (IELC), [14] a church founded by LCMS missionaries, and served as a pastor of this church from 1971 to 1972.

Rajashekar received his undergraduate education in India. He attended St. Philomen's College, University of Mysore, from which he obtained a B.A. degree in 1968. In the fall of the same year he became a student at United Theological College, Bangalore, which awarded him a B.D. degree in 1971. In 1972 he came to the United States to attend Concordia Seminary-Seminex, St. Louis, in the midst of the theological disputes among The LCMS. Undisturbed, he finished his S.T.M. degree in patristics in two years.

Returning to India, he joined the faculty of Gurukul Lutheran Theological College and Research Institute in Madras as a lecturer and program secretary for continuing education. He held the position for two years. In 1976 Rajashekar returned to the United States to pursue the Ph.D. degree in systematic theology and history of religions at the University of Iowa, Iowa

City. During the first three years of his doctoral studies, Rajashekar also served as pastor of Good Shepherd Lutheran Church, Wellman, Iowa.

Having receiving his Ph.D. degree in 1981, Rajashekar once again returned to India to join the faculty of United Theological College, his alma mater, as an assistant professor of theology and ethics. He held the position for the next four years until he was called in 1984 to be executive secretary for dialogue with people of other faiths and ideologies in the Department of Theology and Studies of the LWF in Geneva, Switzerland. In this capacity, Rajashekar coauthored a book, *I Have Heard the Cry of My People*, meditations on the theme of the LWF assembly in 1989. He further edited two books and coedited five others.

As a scholar, Rajashekar is a prolific author. He has published more than 40 essays and articles in books and various journals. In addition, he is also a popular lecturer at seminars and professional gatherings and has served as visiting professor or theologian-in-residence at various educational institutions. His involvement with professional organizations as editor, consultant, advisor, chairperson, and member is also extensive.

Areas of his research include revelation in religions, authority and hermeneutics of Scripture in multiscriptural societies, history of Christian encounters with other faiths, and "'Extra *ecclesiam nulla salus*' and the Protestant Reformers." [15]

In 1991 he was called to Lutheran Theological Seminary at Philadelphia as associate professor of systematic theology. Three years later he was promoted to the rank of professor of systematic theology and concurrently served as director of the Institute for Ecumenical and Interreligious Dialogue. In 1999 he became the occupant of an endowed chair professor: Luther D. Reed Professor—Systematic Theology. In 2000 he was appointed academic dean of the seminary, as well as being the continued occupant of the endowed chair professorship.

In recognition of his academic achievements and services to the worldwide church and society, the Purna Jiwan Abundant Life South Asian Ministries honored Rajashekar on August 15, 2000, with a service of thanksgiving at Norwood Park Lutheran Church, Chicago.

FERN LEE HAGEDORN

Ms. Fern Lee Hagedorn "has more than 20 years of experience as an executive producer, writer, producer, filmmaker, project manager, internet and multimedia creative director, and communicator and advocate for multiculturalism. A founding member of the Asian American Film Festival in New York City, she has also been at the forefront of bringing the Bible to modern day audiences through multimedia. Her films and CD-ROMs have garnered more than 20 international awards; and she has been nationally acclaimed by Multimedia Producer magazine as one of the 'Top Outstanding Producers of 1995.'" [16]

Hagedorn (nee Moy) was born in 1953 in Chicago to immigrant parents from China, a year after her mother and two brothers immigrated to the United States. Her "father had already been in the States and had been back to China twice before the rest of the family came." [17] "My father," Hagedorn continues, "entered the United States illegally under the surname 'Lee' (thus my surname of Lee).... [He] purchased papers attesting that his father was a U.S. citizen thereby making him a citizen as well." [18] That was a common practice for the Chinese who wanted to come to the United States during the enforced Chinese Exclusion Act period.

In her early childhood, her parents worked hard at the laundry they owned in Chicago. Her parents, however, never neglected the family and her mother became a strong influence in Hagedorn's life.

Later the family moved to Chinatown, New York City, where the family lived in a small seven-floor walk-up apartment. Heating was inadequate and "winter was terrible," remembers Hagedorn. She attended public school in the Chinatown area and developed an interest in reading, social studies, and art. Around age nine, she became involved in True Light Lutheran Church, where she met Lily Wu. Becoming involved with this church was a key event in her life. From then on she "felt a better sense of identity and purpose in life." [19] The church was also a safe place for her to spend time through her college years.

As a young adult, Hagedorn showed signs of leadership, a point of contention for her with LCMS tradition, which limits women in leadership positions. Hagedorn questioned this dichotomy, especially why the Sunday school superintendent position was not open to her, since she had been a long-time Sunday school teacher. Her leadership also came through in high school where she became a leader in her honor society and an editor of its literary magazine.

After high school, she attended Hunter College of the City University of New York, from which she obtained a B.A. degree in cinema, magna cum laude, in 1975. From 1975 to 1978, she was a communication assistant in the North American Interpretation Office of the LCA. In 1978, she became the first Asian Lutheran woman to hold an executive position in a Lutheran denomination in North America, serving as an assistant director in the same office. Her responsibilities included organizing national events, writing, and editing "public relations materials and [assisting] in film productions." [20]

Hagedorn was the first Asian Lutheran woman to call attention to the plight of Asian American women within the Lutheran churches. And in insisting that an "Asian American woman is both Asian and American,"

Hagedorn in many ways renders a description of herself. She is professional, articulate, creative, assertive, and filial.

In 1983 she became director of the Office of Communication and Interpretation, LWF/USA. Her responsibilities included the production of print and film materials and supervision of national distribution resource center. She "led [the] production of and produced [an] award-winning documentary 'They Speak of Hope,' on church persecution in El Salvador." [21] Hagedorn also produced a "video for the LWF Seventh Assembly in Budapest in 1983." [22]

From 1989 to 1997, Hagedorn was the founder, director, and project manager of the New Media Translations Program of the American Bible Society. In this capacity, she "originated the pioneering concept of how to translate from original languages of biblical texts to present-day *lingua franca* of cinema and cyberspace." [23] To accomplish her goal, Hagedorn "organized and convened working convocations of biblical scholars, translators, filmmakers, software designers, artists, and musicians." [24] Hagedorn's creativity, imagination, and efforts have won her numerous awards, including the recent Gold Award for "Excellence in New Media: Websites–Educational," and the Gold Special Jury Award in "Experimental Film and Video Category: Dramatic." Hagedorn won these two awards at the 33rd Annual WorldFest-Houston in April 2000. There were more than "12,000 entries in various categories." [25] The Gold Award was for "The Good Samaritan (El Buen Samaritano)," an educational Web site for the biblical parable," and the Gold Special Jury Award for "Resurrection," an 11-minute video translation of the Easter story. [26]

As a writer, Hagedorn's published works appear in books, magazines, and conference volumes. Since 1998 she has been a media consultant, working from her residence in Beach Lake, Pennsylvania.

Hagedorn has also contributed generously of her time in serving the community as leader of Tiger and Cub Scouts and Little League, and in the church internationally, nationally, and locally as a member of boards and committees, as well as a Sunday school teacher, musician, and youth leader.

Hagedorn's achievements are remarkable. And yet as an Asian American woman, her life continues to be a mixture of grace and challenge. One problem is having to cope with racism. "As a child," she recalls, "my sister and I were bullied by white girls in the playground. In the past, I have felt more subtle racism in certain stores and even in certain religious gatherings." [27] Since the family's move to Beach Lake, she and her children are occasional targets of stares and impolite remarks. To her, racism "is a continual learning experience on two levels: how to deal with this racism privately and how to deal with it publicly." [28]

As a media consultant, her current goals are "to maintain a balance of being a mother, wife, and daughter and still pursue [her] interests particularly in the areas of [her] professional work." [29] And as an Asian American woman her current challenge is "to maintain a sense of Asian identity for [herself] and [her] children as part of the Asian diaspora in the United States." [30]

CHARLES MATSUMOTO

Dr. Charles Matsumoto and his wife Mary were among the most active Asian Lutherans in the Redress Movement. [31] He is an advocate of equality and justice, a strong supporter of theological education for Asian Lutheran seminarians, as well as an avid golfer.

Born on March 25, 1932, in San Jose, California, Matsumoto was the tenth child of Mr. and Mrs. Otogoro Matsumoto, who immigrated to the United States during the early twentieth century. His father was a truck gardener. His mother was a busy housewife, helping her husband and rearing their twelve children. He received his "early education in San Jose … and continued [his] education in Ault, Colorado, from 1942 [to] 1945 during the period of forced exclusion from California." [32]

At the end of World War II the family moved back to California where Matsumoto became a student at Santa Clara Union High School. After graduation in 1949, he studied medical technology at San Jose State College from which he received his B.A. degree in 1953. After receiving an M.S. degree in bacteriology from the University of Idaho in 1955, Matsumoto joined the U.S. Army and served for two years before his honorable discharge in 1957. Then he resumed his graduate studies at the University of Washington, from which he received a Ph.D. degree in pharmacology in 1963. He "furthered [his] professional training by taking a postdoctoral research fellowship at the National Heart Institute in Bethesda, Maryland." [33] From 1965 to 1992, he was employed as a research pharmacologist by Eli Lilly and Company in Indianapolis, Indiana. He retired in 1992.

Matsumoto was raised a Buddhist but at the age of 32 became a Christian by adult baptism into the Southern Presbyterian Church in Rockville, Maryland. After he and his family moved to Indianapolis, they joined Bethany Evangelical Lutheran Church in 1966. In 1979 he was elected as a synodical "representative to the board of directors, Wittenberg University, Springfield, Ohio, and served two [three-] year terms." [34] In 1980 he was "elected to serve on the Executive Council of the Lutheran Church in America." [35] Matsumoto held this position for seven years until the birth of the ELCA. He earned the distinction of being the first lay Asian Lutheran male to be elected to such a high position in any Lutheran church in North America.

During his tenure, he became involved with the Asian Lutheran organization. [36] Matsumoto's sense of equality was an asset in the organiza tion's opening its membership to the laity.

After the 1988 merger, Matsumoto continued to be active in the organization and the church-at-large. He served as a member of the board of CMM for four years, with the last two years as chairperson. He was the secretary of the Association of Asian Lutherans—ELCA for four years and is presently serving a six-year term on the ELCA's committee on discipline.

CORAZON GUTIERREZ AGUILAR

Known as Cora to her family and friends, Rev. Corazon Gutierrez Aguilar was the first Filipina to become an ordained clergy through the Alternate Route to Ordained Ministry program of the ELCA. Born on July 23, 1942, in Manila, Philippines, Aguilar felt the call to ministry at age 32 while caring for her dying father. But as a member of the Lutheran Mission, The LCMS in the Philippines then, she had no opportunity to fulfill her call until 18 years later when she became a member of the ELCA. Her faith journey was long, filled with joy, happiness, hardship, and fulfillment.

Aguilar is the oldest of four children born into a family associated with the Philippines military. Her father was a military doctor. Her family belonged to the privileged class. She herself received an excellent higher education at Adamson University, a private university in the Philippines, from which she obtained a B.S. degree in 1964 and then an M.S. degree in 1979 from the University of the Philippines in Quezon City.

After graduation from Adamson University, Aguilar became an assistant technician at the National Institute of Science and Technology, which in 1968 changed its name to the Food and Nutrition Research Institute. She "rose from the ranks until [she] reached the position of science research associate III, a step away from section chief." [37]

In 1979 she was due for a promotion, when family life intervened. Aguilar's husband, a former captain in the Philippine navy, had an assignment in another province and wanted her to join him there. Aguilar chose family over career. From then on she became a volunteer at Immanuel Lutheran Church, her home congregation. She was happy doing volunteer work. But life took a different turn in 1990 when her husband "had to retire" from the navy. The family was "not prepared for this event. It brought a big change in [their] life." [38] At the same time, the family decided to come to the United States to join her husband's family, leaving all their comfort behind. Life in the United States was hard on the family, but Aguilar continued to do volunteer work in the Filipino church and community.

In the spring of 1992, she became a student at Pacific Lutheran Theological Seminary (PLTS), working toward the M.T.S. degree, a two-year program. During her second year at the seminary, she concurrently served as an intern at Holy Trinity Lutheran Church in Alameda, California. Upon completion of this program she was called to Messiah Lutheran Church in Hayward, California, as its part-time then full-time pastor. Her work there includes a creative ministry of outreach and care to students at a campus nearby.

In addition, Aguilar's service to the church goes beyond her congregation. Presently she is a member of the candidacy committee of the Sierra Pacific Synod, the steering committee of CMM, and the ALIC Task Force. She is also a leader of the ELCA's Filipino ministry strategy team.

GEORGE TAN

Dr. George Tan, pastor of St. John Lutheran Church in Cerritos, California, is not a typical Lutheran clergyperson. "When you walk into St. John...on any given Sunday, don't expect to be handed a bulletin. This is a church of tomorrow. Just take a seat, relax and look up on the wall. The show is about to begin." [39] Tan is not typical among pastors in that he makes use of technology to aid him in Sunday worship. The result has been remarkable.

When he was called to St. John in 1995, "the congregation consisted of 45 or 50 members, mostly white Lutherans of German and Scandinavian descent.... Through studying church growth and his experience leading an ethnically diverse congregation in Berkeley, Tan knew it was time to make some changes." [40] Convinced that "many members and visitors are computer-literate," [41] he took a bold step in introducing computer technology into the worship life of the congregation. Within four years, the number of worshipers at St. John increased to about 115 "each Sunday representing 26 countries." [42] Under his leadership, St. John Lutheran Church has become one of the success stories in the ELCA's attempt to do multicultural ministries.

Tan was born on October 13, 1950, in Hong Kong into a Christian family. His association with the Lutheran church began when he was in high school. He was baptized into the Chinese Rhenish Church in 1964. Five years after his baptism, he felt the call to ministry. After high school, he attended Hong Kong University, from which he obtained his B.Soc.Sc. degree in 1974. Two years later he became a student at Luther Theological Seminary in St. Paul, Minnesota. In 1980 he received his M.Div. degree upon completion of internship at the Chinese Rhenish Church in Richmond, California.

He was ordained on June 3, 1984, by the United Church of Christ and became the pastor of the Berkeley Chinese Community Church, UCC, a congregation that consists of American-born Chinese. He was told that he could not lead this congregation with success because he was born overseas. In reality, under his leadership the congregation "grew in strength and matured in the faith." [43]

During his pastorate at Berkeley, he entered into a D. Min. degree program at Golden Gate Baptist Theological Seminary, Mill Valley, California, focusing his studies on outreach ministry, especially to overseas-born Chinese students at the University of California at Berkeley. He implemented his D.Min. project at Berkeley Chinese Community Church, giving birth to an overseas-born Chinese congregation out of an existing American-born Chinese church.

Because of his creativity in bringing the faith to others,Tan is one of the most popular Asian Lutheran speakers and workshops leaders in the ELCA today.

CHERIAN C. PUTHIYOTTIL

Dr. Cherian C. Puthiyottil is known as one of the most socially conscious Asian Lutherans in North America. Since his arrival in the United States via England in 1981, he has been involved with community service agencies and church-related organizations trying to serve others. But he is also a man of prayer; he spends one hour daily in the prayer room.

Puthiyottil was born on May 26, 1946, in Kerala, India. His family belongs to the Syrian Orthodox Church (St.Thomas Christians) in India. He himself was an ordained priest in that tradition. He received his education in India, Britain, Germany, and the United States.

After the completion of preuniversity graduation, Puthiyottil attended the Orthodox Theological College in India from which he graduated in 1967. He received his B.A. degree from Kerala State University of India in 1970. From 1980 to 1981, he did special studies in Germany, Britain, and the United States in the areas of pastoral counseling, writings of Syrian fathers in their original languages, patristic, and liturgy. LS awarded him the D.Min. degree in 1988. Puthiyottil is one of the few international scholars in the Aramaic language.

Puthiyottil was an active and important member of the Orthodox Church in India. From 1970 to 1980, he served as assistant to the bishop of the Orthodox Church of India in Kottayam, India.While serving in this capacity, he also assumed other duties in the church. For example, he was the general secretary and director of the Christian Student Movement of India from 1971 to 1980, vicar and chaplain of the Kottayam Medical College, staff of the Orthodox Theological College, and vicar and administrator of the Thazhathangadi Church. He also served as editor and publisher of a youth magazine and of liturgical and theological books for Orthodox Christian publishers in India. In 1981 he became the vicar and pastoral counselor of the Gregorios Orthodox Church in London, England.

In 1982 Puthiyottil joined as staff Central Lutheran Church, Minneapolis, Minnesota, and in 1990 he was ordained as an ELCA pastor. His primary responsibility was social ministry and neighborhood development. This position gave him the freedom to engage in a wide range of activities, including but not limited to the following:"neighborhood worship services, literacy classes, job counseling and placement services, sewing classes, health classes, and individual and family counseling." [44] He was further "involved in working with [African]-American pastors and youth and Native American adults in [the] community." [45]

During his tenure at Central Lutheran Church, he became the founder and spiritual director of the Skyway Connection Ministries in Minneapolis, part of the Urban Community Association of Minneapolis, and served numerous other community and church-related committees, task forces, associations, and boards, in addition to starting four business corporations. Further, he authored in 1991 a book, *Welcoming Strangers to a New Land: A Model for Successful Refugee Sponsorship*.

On January 6, 2000, Puthiyottil was installed as pastor-director of the Multicultural Mission Center, an AGORA (marketplace) ministry of the Minneapolis Area Synod, intended to strengthen the ministries of existing white and ethnic congregations.

8

A GIANT STEP

TEN YEARS AFTER THE U.S. CONGRESS PASSED THE IMMIGRATION REFORM BILL and a year before Canada closed its door to immigrants, the North American demographic landscape in 1975 shifted rather drastically, even before the arrival of Southeast Asians from the war-torn Indochina region. From 1965 to 1975, the number of Asians from East and South Asia in the United States increased considerably. Concerned with the increase of Asians and other persons of color in their midst, the West Coast Lutheran leaders of the AELC, the ALC, the LCA, and The LCMS organized a Western Regional Lutheranism (WRL) group to strategize ministry possibilities. The WRL group appointed two subcommittees [1]—one in the Northwest, the other in the Southwest—to assist in deliberation.

Meanwhile, as previously mentioned, the ALC and the LCA had also made commitments on the national and some district or synodical levels to address the injustices done to "minorities" and to explore ways and means of ministry with them.

The year 1977 was a significant one for both the LCA and for me. That was the year DMNA decided to appoint me to be a resource developer and consultant for Asian ministry in North America and to contribute part of my time at PLTS as an adjunct member of the faculty. The appointment itself, effective January 1, 1978, which could be termed coincidental or providential, for one church body proved to be an important transitional step in future Lutheran ministries with Asians in North America. It was also the year in which I received my Ph.D. degree from the University of California at Berkeley.

In this chapter I will describe the LCA's work among the Asians in North America and the role I played in it.

INTENTIONAL MINISTRY

Up to the time of my appointment, Lutheran ministry with the Asians in North America was haphazard. The LCMS by now had three congregations total and an equal number of missions under development; the LCA had two, with Paul T. Nakamura independently developing a Japanese ministry in Torrance; and the ALC had one in North America. [2] These congregations were isolated from one another. The larger church had not yet provided systematic ways for the clergy and congregants to come together for support, nurture, and fellowship. But with my appointment soon changes would be made in one church and then another.

Two Pastors from Hong Kong

My first task was to bring into the LCA two Chinese ministries under development by two pastors from Hong Kong. The ministry in San Francisco was under the direction of Rev. Charles Kuo, who had served a two-year term as president of the ELCHK but now was employed as a custodian at St. Mark's Lutheran Church in San Francisco. On the side, however, Kuo had gathered a small Mandarin-speaking group for worship and Bible studies. Earlier Kuo had approached the LCA for ministry opportunity, but he had been turned away.

The ministry in Monterey Park, California, was under the direction of Rev. Andrew Kwok, who had been the pastor of one of the largest Lutheran congregations in Hong Kong before immigrating to the United States to assist Wilson Wu in developing a Cantonese-speaking component at Faith Lutheran Church. This situation posed some problems involving the partnership between Kwok and Wu and the future location of the ministry, which was considered to be too close to the parish Wu served.

By January 1978, the possibility of placing Kwok on the staff of Faith Lutheran Church part-time under DMNA support had begun to be explored. "Strength for Mission" funds might be used to support this ministry. On January 21 of the same year, I paid a visit to Kwok and came away with the feeling that such partnership might not work. [3] Kwok himself had some misgivings about DMNA expectations. Nevertheless, on April 21, 1978, Foster submitted "Strength for Mission Proposal" to Rev. Malcolm L. Minnick Jr., director of the Department for Church Extension, DMNA, outlining the situation and a proposed budget for the ministry.

While negotiations continued on course, Kwok had the first youth gathering on Saturday, September 9, and an informal worship service in his home the following day, with about 50 people present. On September 22, Minnick and I paid Kwok a visit. By then all involved realized that the partnership at Faith would not work.

Where to locate the ministry was yet another thorny issue to be solved. Given the difficulties, we concluded it should not be located too close to Faith or to St. Paul's Lutheran Church, which was again interested in Chinese ministry. Many conversations went on between the synod office and DMNA field and central staff. In the meantime, Kwok continued to hold worship services in his garage and driveway.

In early October, Kwok received an anonymous note, postmarked October 5, 1978, protesting his "illegal assembly every Sunday... [and asking him] to remove [his] assembly to a proper place." [4] The writer promised that if no action were forthcoming, he would report the assembly to the police and to the Immigration and Naturalization Service in Los Angeles. The writer thought the group was "Korean people" who in his opinion "are law abiding citizens." The note ended with a threatening statement, "you may face deportation." The worshiping group moved to a Seventh Day Adventist church for worship and Alhambra became the chosen location for this ministry.

By the end of 1978, both groups were recognized as mission congregations under the development of the Pacific Southwest Synod with program support provided by DMNA.

A Big Gamble

The Presbyterian Church of England had introduced Christianity to Taiwan in 1865. The Lutheran presence on this beautiful island occurred in 1949 with the arrival of political refugees from mainland China. Among them was a C. A. Chin, a medical doctor and lay preacher. Chin carried on his practice in Kaohsiung, a city in southern Taiwan. A year later, two Norwegian nurses arrived to work in a Presbyterian hospital in Taipei. In 1951 two American missionaries came to survey the situation. The Taiwan Lutheran Church was organized in 1954.

The Presbyterian and Lutheran presence in Taiwan somehow contributed to the formation of the first Taiwanese-speaking Lutheran congregation in North America. Mr. and Mrs. William Wei were Presbyterians who moved to San Diego from Taiwan via Canada in 1979. Dr. David Chen, a product of the TLC, was studying at Waterloo Lutheran Seminary and Wilfrid Laurier University in Waterloo, Ontario, and serving as an interim pastor at Formosan Christian Church in Toronto then. The Weis were members of this congregation.

In February 1979 Chen wrote to Dr. Delton Glebe, president of Waterloo Lutheran Seminary, expressing his desire to serve the Taiwanese in San Diego after his graduation in June of that year. In the same letter, he also noted that two families from his parish in Toronto had already moved there. Glebe referred his inquiry to Dr. Walter Wagner, director of theological education, Division of Professional Leadership (DPL), LCA. Wagner forwarded the matter to Minnick, who in turn directed Foster and me to do a feasibility study.

On July 25, 1979, Foster and I went to San Diego. We met with a small group of persons from Taiwan, which included the Weis. The group expressed a desire for spiritual guidance from the Lutheran church.

A demographic study was made. The 1970 census reported 3,259 Chinese persons in San Diego. I considered this figure low. Thus, using this figure as a base (by this time I had acquired some demographic skills from Matsushita), "and adding an annual increase of 7 percent, but excluding the births and deaths rates and a sudden surge of immigration," [5] My own projection for 1978 was 5,594. Within this figure was a small Taiwanese presence—177 to be exact—throughout San Diego County. There were three Chinese Protestant churches, plus two Bible study and fellowship groups serving the Chinese, but the Taiwanese dialect was not used by any of them.

After the study was made, Foster and I recommended that DMNA enter the field, confident that the population would increase due to "(1) continued in-migration; (2) the change of emigration policy by the Taiwanese government." [6] But in my memorandum to Minnick, I also cautioned "that [for the present] a ministry exclusively with the Taiwanese has limited potential." [7] Under normal conditions, no one probably would have recommended to DMNA to enter the field. But in this case both Foster and I decided to gamble and won.

Mrs. Trudy Wei had a lot to do with the success of this ministry. She was and is not only a generous supporter of the congregation, but she also spends her time and talents serving the congregation as vice president of the congregation council, deaconess, and elder of the church. Wei also served a term as a board member of CMM. Presently she is one of the directors of the Center for Chinese Ministries, located in San Diego.

Wei is the fourth child born in Taiwan into a Presbyterian family of seven—five sons and two daughters. Her father, a medical doctor, was strongly influenced by Presbyterian missionaries and "encouraged his children to be healers of bodies and souls." [8] The children heeded their father's encouragement. Her oldest brother is a medical doctor practicing his profession in Singapore. The other three "are ministers in Taiwan, Brazil, and the United States... [her] younger sister is married to a missionary." [9] She and her husband are successful businesspeople.

Her journey toward Lutheranism started "when [she was living] in Canada with [her] husband and children," [10] and through her association with Chen, her interim pastor. After they moved to San Diego and felt the need for a church home, they, together with a few others, invited Chen to come to serve them. Chen agreed to come but did not want to change his denominational affiliation. In fact Chen "insisted [that] the Taiwanese church, to be organized in San Diego, be associated with the Lutheran Church." [11] Wei was instrumental in securing the first property for the congregation in Carmel Valley and the property in Rancho Pensquitos, the future site of the congregation. As of this writing, she has spent one third of her life "as a Lutheran in [her] Christian faith journey." What reflection might she have to share? "I have enjoyed being a Lutheran, and working with Pastor Chen and other leaders of the Taiwanese Lutheran Church and national organizations," Wei reflects. "I thank God for his grace and goodness to my family." [12] She and her husband are blessed with two sons who are endodontists in San Diego and a daughter who is married to a physician in Chicago.

Oversight or Intentional Oppression

A little more than a year into my job, I accidentally discovered that the compensations for Kuo, Kwok, and myself were considerably lower than that of white colleagues doing comparable work for the church. I raised the issue with DMNA officials regarding compensations for Kuo and Kwok. DMNA subsequently raised their salaries somewhat, but mine remained unchanged other than the usual cost-of-living increase.

When Matsushita realized how low my compensation was, he took up the matter with the DMNA officials. He was told that for my position I was adequately compensated. Unsatisfied, Matsushita raised the issue repeatedly, and again he got nowhere other than becoming a "nail in the eye," as the Chinese saying goes, to DMNA officials.

After my two-year term was up, I was offered a one-year renewal contract. I was reluctant to accept the offer. I raised the question with my superior as to why there was not an increase of compensation for me when I requested an increase for Kuo and Kwok. I was told the reason was because I did not ask for an increase for myself. In turn I indicated that I was asking for it now. I was offered an additional one thousand dollars. I refused to accept it. Subsequently another two thousand dollars were added to the compensation package.

From that point on, I decided that I would be involved in setting compensation for Asian clergy. David Chen was the first beneficiary of my action, followed by Rev. Paul Hsu.

CLERGY FROM OVERSEAS

Asian emigration to North America was not only in response to a more liberal immigration policy, but it was also due to the social, political, and economic instability in the various homelands. Hong Kong, with its imminent return to China, was particularly vulnerable. Among the immigrants in 1970s and 1980s, there was a good number of clergy belonging to various denominations.

The more entrepreneurial ones would quickly develop a following. Yet most of the groups were not large enough to provide a decent income.

Others would quickly change to other professions or look for a denomination with which to affiliate. Because its geographical proximity to Asia and heavy concentration of Asians, the Pacific Southwest Synod attracted a large number of Asian clergy seeking affiliation. I was often called upon to assist synodical officials in interviewing them.

The top officials of the church themselves realized the situation needed to be dealt with. Accordingly, in 1979 DPL, DWME, and DMNA produced a document, "Immigrating Pastors and the Lutheran Church in America," [13] that gave guidelines and procedures for "missionaries sent by overseas churches for ministry in the LCA, Lutheran pastors immigrating to the United States or Canada," and "guidelines for acceptance into the ordained ministry of the Lutheran Church in America for Lutheran pastors immigrating to the United States or Canada." [14] (The ALC had similar guidelines.)

The obvious problem with this document was that it dealt only with Lutherans. The less manifest issue was, in my opinion, that it was too European and too middle class in orientation to be applicable in some, if any at all, of the "minority" settings. In 1982 when the matter of receiving clergy from Asia (Lutheran and other-than-Lutheran) was under intense discussion, Minnick sent me a copy of the guidelines, requesting me to review them and to share my reflection with him. I reviewed the document and sent my reactions to Minnick. At one point, I even went so far as to say that "using the institutional expectations and requirements to determine who should be allowed to become a member of the ministerium has its own merit as well as liability." [15] To me, the institutional expectations and requirements, as they were stated in the document, were too theoretical and rigid. Thus, using them as criteria might eliminate the less traditional but otherwise creative and talented individuals from the institution. I went on to argue that "function should be the determining factor," especially in the Asian North American context, for inclusion. [16]

Another issue regarding overseas clergy was the matter of placement after they had been received in the ministerium. Rev. Chin Tao Sum, a clergyperson from the Lutheran Church—Malaysia and Singapore Synod who applied for admission and was received into the ministerium in 1983, provided an occasion for discourse. Chin immigrated to the United States under the auspices of a fundamentalist congregation in Modesto, California. After working with that congregation for a time, he decided to return to the Lutheran church. His English was elementary and his mobility was limited to the Modesto-Stockton area, because he had purchased a home in Modesto. The central question was who had the responsibility to place him—DMNA or the synod, which had accepted him into the ministerium?

Rev. Stanley E. Olson, now bishop of the Pacific Southwest Synod, and Minnick exchanged a number of letters on this matter. To complicate the situation further, on February 21, 1983, Chin sent a letter to Ms. Connie Reece, assistant to the bishop, indicating that he would begin a ministry in Modesto. Minnick sent me a note, asking me about this ministry, since he knew "absolutely nothing of any plan to start ministry in Modesto, California." [17] Minnick was concerned about Chin and made every honest effort to place him, but to no avail.

Partly due to the placement issue, another round of debates on guidelines flared up, culminating with a letter from Olson addressed to Massie Kennard, director for minority concerns, DMNA; Minnick; Dr. Kenneth C. Senft, executive director of DMNA; Wagner; Foster; and me. [18] In this letter, Olson called attention to a recapitulated policy statement by Minnick as a point of departure. He also acknowledged that "any one of us" could have written such a statement. Then Olson went on to say, "I must live and work with that policy. I find it to be both a racist and grossly insensitive policy. It is the kind of policy one would expect of church bureaucrats who go about their work in a cold and impersonal way never wondering about what those policies do to those who must abide by them." [19] Olson continued by saying he could no longer live with "the system much longer and will once again serve notice that [he] both desire[s] a revision of the policy or must speak out against the grandiose proclamations and reports of the LCA on inclusive ministry." [20]

Olson's letter elicited a sympathetic response from Wagner. He suggested that Olson and Dr. Nelson Trout, president of the South Pacific District, ALC, host "an intense weekend experience in Los Angeles" [21] to explore the issue. As a suggestion, Wagner further offered a course of action for Olson to consider. Nothing came about.

On June 1, 1984, Wagner sent a copy of "Guidelines Related to the Acceptance of Pastor from Overseas, Draft #3" to Olson for his review. This document included two sections: (1) "Ordained Persons Immigrating to North America," including Lutheran clergy and clergy of other churches; (2) "Persons Resident in Canada and the United States Ordained by Overseas Churches," including again Lutheran clergy and clergy of other churches. This document was less rigid and more applicable to "minority" situations.

One other issue regarding clergy from overseas was who was to say "no" to them when they were not qualified for admission into the ministerium. When it came to Asian clergy, the synodical officials and chairs of commissions and committees usually looked to me for help, putting me in an unenviable position. Thus, I wrote to Minnick for guidance, which generated a flurry of correspondence among the officials. On June 8, 1984, instructions came from Minnick, directing me as he had previously, to put a stop to the person's process should the person's English be deficient. However, once a person had entered into the process and there was a sense that the person "should not pursue [his or her] application any further, that it should come from an official source." [22] such as the bishop or the committee chair. Be that as it may, I continued to be under pressure to assume the responsibility of saying "no" to my own kind.

COOPERATIVE MINISTRY

The purpose of LCA guidelines concerning overseas clergy was twofold: first, the clergy's ever growing presence in North America; second, the church's need for qualified workers. In the case of Asian ministries, there were simply not enough clergy around, even though by 1978 the church had already produced a few native and foreign-born ones. Accordingly the LCA, during the decade of 1978 to 1987, received a fair number of Asian clergy, including clergy transferring from other-than-Lutheran churches and from Hong Kong, Taiwan, Korea, and Singapore. Still, the demand exceeded the supply in terms of quality but not quantity. [23]

In 1980, as previously mentioned, Foster made a trip to Asia to become familiar with ministries there. In February 1981, I spent three weeks traveling in East Asia, meeting with church officials, introducing Asian ministries in North America to them, and learning about church life in East Asia from them. Our presence in Asia might have planted the seed for creative specialized ministries in North American ministry.

Cooperation between the LCA and the ELCHK

By 1980 there was a good number of Lutheran laity immigrating to North America, particularly from Hong Kong. Not unlike the concerns expressed by the JELC earlier, the ELCHK expressed concern, through DWME officials, for the spiritual well being of these new immigrants and urged the LCA to minister with them. [24]

In May 1981, President John Tse and Vice President Gai Yingkui of the ELCHK visited North America to discuss cooperative ministry possibilities. Tse and Gai met with Minnick and me in New York. Both sides agreed that if such a cooperative ministry should take place, it should be the new ministry under consideration in Toronto, Ontario, where a large group of Lutherans from Hong Kong now settled. Shortly after the meeting, Rev. Lam Tak Ho, executive secretary of the ELCHK, sent a list of Chinese Lutherans in Toronto to me.

In a September 17, 1981, letter to Minnick, Tse informed him that the ELCHK had decided to cooperate with DMNA in the Toronto ministry. Further the ELCHK would provide a pastor for the ministry and a financial contribution in the amount of U.S. $5,000 a year. In his letter to Tse, Minnick stated that the ministry would begin on February 1, 1982, and that Rev. Wing

Fai Tsang had been selected to be the pastor-developer.[25] The agreement also included sharing with Tse periodic monthly reports from the pastor-developer. This was the first joint venture between these two churches.

Missionary from Japan

The Japan Evangelical Lutheran Church (JELC) is a missionary-minded institution that is at the same time concerned about the spiritual welfare of the Japanese in diaspora, as chapter 4 describes. Thus, "since 1965 the JELC has had [a] missionary pastor serving with the Igreja Evangelica de Confissao Lutherana no Brasil in Japanese language ministry."[26] In 1975 the JELC sent its first pastor to Germany to serve in the Evangelical-Lutheran Church of Wurttemberg. In April 1976, the JELC through DWMIC of the ALC sent the first missionary, Rev. Ikuo Takatsuka, to the United States for a three-year term. Takatsuka was called to Holy Trinity Lutheran Church in Ankeny, Iowa. [27] Rev. Yutaka Toda followed him in the fall of 1977. Toda "became one of the three pastors for ministry at St. Paul Lutheran Church in Clearwater, Florida."[28] In 1981 DWMIC called Rev. Akihiko Tominaga to serve "as an associate pastor in Elk Horn Lutheran Church, Elk Horn, Iowa."[29]

The first three missionaries to America served in white congregations. Following in their footsteps, Dr. Fumio (Stephen) Tani, the fourth missionary, arrived in Los Angeles in December 1977 to serve as a self-supporting missionary to the Japanese-speaking persons in that area.

Tani received his theological education at both Taiwan Theological College and Concordia Seminary in Taiwan. After his ordination in 1955 he was sent to Japan to be a missionary. In 1961 he entered Kansai Medical University. He was awarded a doctor of medicine degree in 1965 and a Ph.D. in 1976. He also did specialized training at the Osaka City University Graduate School.

By the time he arrived in Los Angeles, Tani was a successful physician in Japan. It was his intention to build a church-motel-restaurant complex in Los Angeles for his ministry and to work with Paul T. Nakamura in Torrance. He was to commence his ministry in January 1978. An orientation was given to him by DMNA staff in New York and by the Pacific Southwest Synod in Los Angeles in January. But soon misunderstanding developed and Tani returned to Japan six months later to continue "his medical practice which included the building of a clinic and a hospital."[30]

DMNA staff felt the need for Japanese language ministry in Southern California. Thus, after Toda concluded his first term as missionary in the Florida Synod, he was invited to continue his work in America. He was assigned to Our Redeemer Lutheran Church, Garden Grove, California."[31] Using this congregation as a base "Toda developed the first Japanese language ministry on behalf of the LCA."[32] In the opinion of the DMNA staff, "this was a constructive experience even though there was some frustration." [33]

After completing his second term as missionary to the United States, Toda returned to Japan. Rev. Mikio Noguchi was called by DMNA in April 1984 to replace Toda. In the meantime, "plans were to change the location of the ministry from Garden Grove in order to be more accessible to a greater number of Japanese speaking persons." [34] Orientation for Noguchi and his family was entrusted to Rev. Everett Nielsen, a shared DMNA and synod staff person, and me. Unfortunately there was no time "for language training or culturalization," [35] before Noguchi was thrust into the ministry. The Japanese-speaking group, which was grieving the departure of Toda, rejected Noguchi, [36] resulting in "a lot of learnings... but also a lot of hurt." Noguchi and his family returned to Japan after one year of service.

At this point, officials of the ALC, the JELC, and the LCA felt the need for a three-way consultation before proceding further. Thus a "Consultation between Japan Evangelical Lutheran Church, The Lutheran Church in America, The American Lutheran Church [was] held at the Hyatt Airport Hotel, Los Angeles, California, on March 5-7, 1986." [37] Representatives from the three churches were "President K. Sato, Rev. H. Machino, Rev. I. Takatsuka, Rev. J. Livingston [JELC]; Dr. James Bergquist, Rev. Warren Sorteberg, Dr. Mark Thomsen, Rev. Douglas Swendseid [ALC]; Dr. Kenneth Senft, Rev. Malcom Minnick, Dr. Edmond Yee, Dr. W. Currens, Rev. Norman Nuding, Rev. D. Anderson [LCA]," [38] plus three guests from Japan and two from America.

At the end of the consultation, the group named the cooperative program Japan-America Cooperative Evangelism Program (JACEP). This was "a partnership effort in mission between the JELC, The LCA, The ALC, and the successor church, the ELCA." [39] The group also reached agreement on mission priorities, responsibilities, logistics, and other matters. The LCA identified Torrance, California, and Princeton, New Jersey, as possible project sites. The ALC identified Honolulu, Hawaii. [40]

As a result of this consultation, Ikuo Takatsuka, who had previously served a term as a missionary in Iowa, "was sent by JELC to the LCA in April 1987" [41] to serve the Japanese-speaking population in Southern California, using the Lutheran Church of the Resurrection in Huntington Beach, California, as a base.

After a year of mentoring by Foster, pastor of Lutheran Church of the Resurrection, Takatsuka began his ministry. The ELCA affirmed the agreements worked out in 1986 and continued (and still continues) JACEP. Takatsuka's ministry has several facets. (1) He was to be "involved in pioneer outreach evangelism to Japanese people in seven or eight communities that are within 45 minutes driving time of Huntington Beach....(2) He would develop house churches in each of these communities....(3) He [would] also serve as pastor to Japanese students attending colleges and universities in the Orange County...and Los Angeles...area. (4) He [would] be the coordinator of various services that will be helpful to Japanese persons immigrating to the United States or on assignment....(5) [He would] continue to serve as a liaison with JELC as it pertains to Christians who are returning to Japan and who need to become related to congregations in Japan...[and would] receive information from JELC about Christians coming to southern California and will seek to help them to identify with a Christian congregation in the community where they live."[42] Minnick, who was then director of the Department for Mission Development, Division for Outreach (DO), ELCA, considered the last facet as "membership conservation."[43]

Ordained in 1969, Takatsuka is the longest serving missionary from JELC to the Lutheran churches in North America.

SHARING, LEARNING, SUPPORT, AND FELLOWSHIP

Another aspect of my work was to provide occasions for sharing, learning, support, and fellowship for Asian clergy and laity alike. Through DPL and the Division for Theological Education and Ministry (DTEM), ALC, I was able to bring the Asian clergy and some laity together at PLTS from time to time for a few days. The agenda at such gatherings always included continuing education and much time for sharing and fellowship, a critical need at the time. The seminary under the leadership of Dr. Walter M. Stuhr, president, was always open to hosting such gatherings. In 1985 Asian clergy from both the LCA and the ALC had a joint conference in Los Angeles.

I provided leadership not only to North American Asian clergy, but clergy from Asia as well. In the summer of 1980, the continuing education office at PLTS and I jointly hosted a group of clergy from Japan. In the summer of 1985, I directed the Asian Program for the Advancement of Training and Studies of the Hong Kong and Taiwan Lutheran churches. The event was held in Berkeley, California.

A DMNA Spy

One of the most agonizing aspects of my ten years with DMNA was how to preserve my own integrity without being disloyal to the institution and without subjecting Asian clergy to be overly exposed to undue institutional scrutiny. On the one hand, the LCA's management style was "management by objective"—a practice not easy for Asian clerics to understand. Before immigrating to North America they had been trained by and served in a different system. On the other hand, the bureaucrats did not always appreciate the Asian clerics' operative value system and expectations of the institution, because they did not always coincide with that of the LCA. In addition, my own social, religious, and political articulations and positions often differed from both groups', to the annoyance of bureaucrats and Asian clerics alike.

Therefore, I was often caught in between. Because of its management style and attitude on race, the institution often expected me to act like
an indigenous employee of the "colonial society"—that is, someone hired
to work on behalf of the colonizers to control other indigenous people.
Because of my employment by the institution as a functionary, thereby performing duties between the group, the synodical officials, and the central
office staff, Asian clerics considered me a DMNA spy. When one of the clerics told me what this group thought of me, I did not know whether to laugh
or to cry.

To preserve my own integrity under these circumstances and to promote bridge building between the LCA and the Asian clerics, I resorted to my
Confucian sense of history. I adopted a strategy of gentle remonstration with
the bureaucrats when it seemed they were too strong from an Asian point of
view and a style of circuitous reporting with the Asian clerics when it
seemed that the unvarnished truth would do more harm than good. Minnick,
the ever-perceptive bureaucrat, always discerned the "real McCoy" in my
words and deeds.

My relationship with this group of clerics was not unique, however.
When Rev. William E. Wong came on the scene in 1988, he too faced problems with the group, as chapter 12 describes.

MISSION POSSIBLE

DMNA's commitment to Asian ministries in North America was real,
though not always fair (the LCA was hardly unique in the regard). But commitment to mission and ministry was one thing, providing language-specific
and culturally-sensitive written materials to nurture Asian Lutherans to grow
in faith was something else. DMNA officials were not unaware of this problem. Yet, due to the compartmentalization of the church bureaucracy, there
was not much that the officials could have done, so it seemed. I on occasions was given the task of persuading Division for Parish Services (DPS) to
give consideration to producing spiritually nurturing materials for congregations. The process was cumbersome. The result was unsatisfactory. Besides,
there was no one on the DPS staff who could undertake the task of writing
and editing such materials, as chapter 10 details.

These circumstances along with funding cuts beginning in the early
1980s were among the many challenges I faced. But by the end of my decade
of work in DMNA, 19 Asian congregations and ministries were added to the
LCA and subsequently to the ELCA. One exception was the ministry in
Federal Way, Washington, which had started without my knowledge. In the
end it had to be closed. The task of closure was assigned to James Moy, assistant to the bishop of the Pacific Northwest Synod, and me. After many ago-

nizing conversations, the ministry was terminated.

In many ways, I was a transitional figure who happened to be on the scene at the right moment. With the help of so many others, I, more or less, guided one of the predecessor bodies of the ELCA into ministry with Asians. With the birth of the ELCA, Asian ministry in America became a permanent feature in the church, with constitutional support, giving rise to an even more intentional ministry with Asians, which chapter 12 explores.

"IN INSTRUCTION THERE IS NO GRADING INTO CATEGORIES"

By the time I arrived at PLTS as an adjunct professor of Asian studies on January 1, 1978, the seminary had already adopted "a statement of purpose which sees the seminary as a theological center for all the Lutheran churches in the western United States... [and] a 'rationale' for the M.Div. curriculum which underscores the need to prepare persons to minister to the particularities of the place, persons, and time." [44] It had also appointed Will Herzfeld, pastor of Bethlehem Lutheran Church, Oakland, California, as adjunct professor of urban ministry.

My own role at PLTS was modest and limited, yet demanding in that I was essentially performing two distinct jobs—one for PLTS and the other for DMNA. Below is a description of involvement at the seminary.

Center for Multi-Cultural Ministry

On September 11, 1978, the southwest Inter-Lutheran Coordinating Committee on Theological Education and Leadership Development for Minority Ministries met in Los Angeles and accepted the concept paper, "A Minority Study Program at PLTS: A Preliminary Thought," written by me. The committee asked Rev. John A. Nasstrom, regional mission planning director, LCUSA, to present it to the WRL group for consideration. On September 14, 1978, Nasstrom, along with Paul T. Nakamura and Phil Molnar, met with the group. "The synod and district presidents and others present endorsed your (committee's) recommendations," wrote Nasstrom to the members of the Inter-Lutheran Coordinating Committee, "and asked the Pacific Lutheran Theological Seminary to elaborate further the proposal for a Minority Ministries Study Center, spelling out program, budget, and suggestions for implementation." [45] The seminary was asked to report back to WRL on February 7, 1979.

In his capacity as president, Stuhr responded to WRL and proposed a two-phase program: Phase I—research and planning, Phase II—multiracial, multicultural ministries center. He also submitted a two-phase budget. [46] The WRL group accepted the proposal and instructed the seminary to implement it. However, there was no funding forthcoming from WRL. The seminary was unable to implement the proposal in full.

I was asked to oversee the development of the center. DMNA officials realized the importance and the vitality of the center and provided supplementary budgetary assistance for its development and maintenance for nine years following its inception in 1979.

Through the Center for Multi-Cultural Ministry, I offered the first course on multicultural ministry studies among all Lutheran seminaries and member schools of the Graduate Theological Union (GTU), and one of the first, if not the first, among the member schools of the Association of Theological Schools in North America. I also provided support and guidance to the students of color and other students interested in multicultural ministries as well as to congregations and interested clergy from near and far.

A Slight Shift

As my work at the seminary continued to increase, the board of directors at its November 20, 1982, meeting approved, with faculty concurrence, the recommendation for appointing me to the regular faculty. At the same meeting the Board passed the following motion: "MSC to request from the Division for Mission in North America, LCA, continued additional support for the Multi-Cultural Ministries Studies program."

DMNA accepted the request. In 1983, I was made associate professor. From this point on, my time with DMNA was decreased annually.

In addition to my current responsibilities at PLTS, I am also a member of the core doctoral faculty for the GTU.

9

Right Direction

"ASIAN-AMERICAN MINISTRY IS ALSO A CONCERN OF OUR DISTRICT," FRED Wimberly, South Pacific District staff, stated in his report to the district's Nineteenth Annual Convention. "Pastor Joseph Wong is a consultant for our District in Asian-American ministry....Pastor Wong attended a seminar on Asian-American Ministry in the Lutheran Church with the purpose of discovering new ways in which we as Lutherans can be more effective in ministry in the Asian-American community." [1]

By the time the Nineteenth Annual Convention of the South Pacific District was held in 1979, the ALC had one congregational ministry in Honolulu and a community service ministry in Los Angeles's Chinatown. The AELC had no ministry with Asians up to this point. This chapter describes the ministry with Asians of these two church bodies from 1978 to 1996.

THE BISHOPS' COMMISSION ON ASIAN MINISTRIES [2] OF THE ALC

Approximately 23 months after the Wimberly report to the Nineteenth Annual Convention, the district reported to the Twenty-first Annual Convention that "the Bishops' Commission on Hispanic Ministries has been an effective unit and this has encouraged the District Council now to form a similar Commission for Asian Ministries." [3]

The newly organized Commission for Asian ministries at its March 9, 1982, meeting adopted a "Revised Preamble," which consists of "Statement of Purpose," "Appointment of Members," "Term of Office," and "Number of Meetings" per year. This preamble became the guiding document for the commission's operation for the next six years until the birth of the ELCA in 1988. Wong chaired the commission for the first three years. Rev. Benjamin Shum became the chair in 1985.

Shum was born in Hong Kong and received most of his secondary education there. He obtained his B.A. degree from Wartburg College in

Waverly, Iowa, in 1973 and his M.Div. degree from Wartburg Seminary in Dubuque, Iowa, in 1977. After his seminary graduation, he spent one full year in CPE before returning to Hong Kong where he served as an assistant director for Lutheran Social Ministry, LCHKS. While in Hong Kong, he also taught at Concordia Seminary for one year. Later he and his family returned to the United States. In October 1980 he was called to be an associate pastor by Good Shepherd Lutheran Church in San Francisco to develop a Chinese congregation.

Grace Lutheran Church in Palo Alto originally supported Shum's ministry. Later DSMA provided program support. Shum's ministry in San Francisco was creative. The group organized a Chinese language school, provided a tutorial after-school program for a large number of neighborhood children, in addition to offering the more traditional evangelism programs of Word and Sacrament ministry. And Shum himself was deeply involved in community service. He was also a commissioned chaplain in the U.S. Army's reserve unit.

Under the guidance of the commission, the South Pacific District by March 9, 1982, had expanded its ministry with Asians, including the following ministries under development: Truth Lutheran Church, Los Angeles, a Chinese ministry, a "Korean ministry at Long Beach" under the leadership of Rev. David Kang, and "Chinese Mission Outreach of the Lutheran Church of the Good Shepherd, San Francisco" under the leadership of Shum.

It also appeared that DSMA was planning a joint project with the ELCHK. It was reported that at the same meeting Wong "shared with the Committee that DSMA is enthused about the project but he is not." [4] Wong's lack of enthusiasm for this potential joint project appeared to have something to do with "the role that the Consultant of Asian-American ministry has to play in this project ... [as well as with] who will get the blame ... if the project failed in the future." [5] Wong's concern may or may not be justified, but within three months Rev. Lester Hoffmann, service mission director, DSMA, announced the postponement of this project because "the candidate chosen by Evangelical Lutheran Church of Hong Kong is doubtful in terms of gifts." [6]

In 1982 David Kang, a member of the commission, offered a set of strategies for Korean ministries, including a request to Lutheran congregations in the district not to rent their facilities to other-than-Lutheran groups and the appointment of "a person in-charge of the Korean ministry." [7] Kang was eventually appointed to be that person. But Louis Shim, a part-time pastor of a Korean group in Garden Grove, California, later challenged his appointment. The commission arrived at a compromise by alternating the position between Kang and Shim every other year. And the matter of Kang's strategies was referred to the district staff for consideration.

By the end of 1982, Shum presented a paper on "Strategies on Asian

Ministries in South Pacific District, TALC" to the commission for consideration. It was decided that the Shum paper "should be sent to Dr. James A.
Bergquist, National Director of DSMA and Rev. Phil Wahl, Director of Urban
and Ethnic Ministries for reference." [8]

A little more than nine months into the life of the newly organized
commission, Wong raised the issue regarding the role of the consultant in
Asian ministries. The members of the commission "suggested that Dr. Wong
put in writing the role he sees fit with his ministry and the Committee [com-
mission?] will analyze it and then go from there." [9] Apparently Wong did not
put it in writing.

In 1983 Wong's title was changed from consultant to director, which
eventually raised more confusion within the commission and beyond. [10] In
the spring of the same year, the commission authorized Rev. Jerry Borgie to
write to Rev. Philip Wahl, asking him for clarification regarding Wong's job
description. Borgie wrote to Wahl on May 24, 1983. But Wahl, for one reason
or another, had not responded to Borgie's inquiry in an expeditious way. The
commission at its October 4, 1983, meeting once again passed a formal
motion requesting Borgie to write a second letter to Wahl, "urging him for
immediate response to the 05/24/83 letter." Again Wahl did not respond
immediately. The delay seemed to have increased Wong's frustration. Thus, at
the commission's December 1 meeting, Wong "pointed out that his 'call' to
serve in Los Angeles ten years ago was 'metro' ministry. With requirements of
his increasing participation and involvement in developing more new Asian
ministries, he questioned...what really were his job descriptions and responsibilities of his 'call.'" [11] Wong further admitted that he was confused and questioned on "what level he should be functioning. District? National? Or
both?" [12] It seems that Wahl never responded to the inquiries.

In the same year, the official report to the district convention indicated that "Joe [Wong] identified six new Asian ministries that have been
developed in the district. He anticipates that four or five new Asian ministries
will be started in the district each year." [13]

One of the goals of the commission was to recruit Asians for
Lutheran ministries, initially focusing on Koreans and Chinese. The recruits
were to be given an orientation regarding Lutheran theology and liturgical
practices as well as the structure and polities of the ALC so that they might
have a better idea what the institution was all about prior to their decision
whether or not to request admission into the ministerium. I was asked to
organize the orientation program to be held at Faith Lutheran Church in
Monterey Park on May 23-25, 1984. [14] The participants comprised four Korean
and three Chinese pastors from the other-than-Lutheran traditions. Presenters
at the orientation included seminary faculty and national and district staff.
Wong and Kang served as resource persons and Wi Jo Kang was present as

an observer. The district provided the budget for the orientation.

At the end of the orientation, participants gave the program a favorable evaluation, but declined to take further steps in joining the ALC.

In the following year, both Kang and Shim left their respective ministries. Kang subsequently resigned from the ALC clergy roster altogether. In the same year, Mr. James L. Sims, service mission director, DSMA, reported that "Truth Chinese congregation (now Gloria Dei) has relocated from Los Angeles to Monterey Park, Calif." [15] Sims further reported that Good Shepherd Lutheran Church in San Francisco had given the building to the Chinese group's exclusive use.

It was also in 1985 that the Bishops' Commission on Asian Ministries was reconstituted and Shum became its director. Under his leadership the commission "continue[d] to provide input for the ongoing ministries and [had] lifted up eight possible opportunities for new Asian work." [16] In addition, in 1985 Shum teamed up with me to organize an Asian pastors conference in Los Angeles for clergy of the ALC and the LCA. Shum carried on the work of the commission and of his ministry in San Francisco for the next two years until the birth of the ELCA. By the end of 1987, the ALC had gained a total of 10 ministries in the Asian community, including a joint Chinese ministry with the LCA, a joint Korean ministry with the AELC, a seafarers ministry, a Vietnamese ministry, a Hmong ministry, and five new Chinese ministries.

ASIAN MINISTRIES OF THE ASSOCIATION OF EVANGELICAL LUTHERAN CHURCHES

The AELC was a group of more than four hundred congregations that broke away from The LCMS in the 1970s over theological issues. The association was loosely structured and had limited resources for new mission development.

Korean Ministry

St. Jacobus Lutheran Church, Woodside, Long Island, New York, however, had a Korean ministry formally related to the congregation. The Korean group was led by Rev. Hun Reo. Reo was born on March 3, 1928, in Pyungyang, North Korea. He received his B.A. degree from Kweng-Hee University in Seoul, South Korea, in 1960 and his M.Div. degree in 1978 from Sao Paulo Presbyterian Theological Seminary in Sao Paulo, Brazil. He was ordained into the Presbyterian church in the same year. Later he immigrated to the United States, where he attended New York Theological Seminary, from which he obtained his STM degree in 1982. He was received into the ALC ministerium in 1985 and was called to St. Jacobus Lutheran Church as an assistant pastor. Reo's pastorate at St. Jacobus was a joint ministry of the ALC and the AELC.

Chinese Ministry

Rev. Paul Chang, as mentioned in chapter 2, resigned from True Light Lutheran Church, New York City, in 1959 to pursue graduate studies. By the late 1970s or early 1980s Chang was in the real estate business and had settled in Naperville, Illinois. Chang was successful in this business. Thus in the early 1980s he had an idea of building a brand new Chinese retirement community in Florida. The architectural plans show a community with modern buildings accented with a touch of Chinese style, a hotel, schools, and a church situated along the waterways of Florida, reminiscent somehow of Suzhou, China.

It was Chang's hope to donate the land set aside for a church to the LCA. Malcolm L. Minnick assigned Rev. W. Baxter Weant, deployed staff, and me to confer with Chang on the transfer of the land. However, before any negotiation could begin, Chang's dream fell through. Yet his heart and his faith never left the church. At this point, he wanted to contribute $20,000 toward a ministry with the Chinese living in and around Naperville. I visited with Chang in the fall of 1983 to explore ministry possibilities.

A year earlier Rev. Bill Danker of Seminex had called Rev. Delbert E. Anderson, secretary for East Asia, DWME, LCA, to inquire about the possibility of placing one of his students, Far-Dung Tong, "in a mission assignment in East Asia." [17] While feeling positive about Tong, Anderson was reluctant to assign him to East Asia due to a certain "incident" that occurred in the Basel Christian Church of Malaysia when Tong was a pastor of that church. After the incident, Tong was forced to leave the church.

Meanwhile, Tong and his family settled in Naperville in 1983. Toward the end of August of the same year, "with the encouragement of Paul Chang, a Chinese member of St. Timothy, Naperville," [18] Tong and his wife, Ming Ming, approached the bishop of the Illinois Synod, LCA with a proposal to do ministry with the Chinese in and around Naperville.

Minnick subsequently encouraged the synod to get in touch with me, should Tong be interested in applying for admission into the ministerium. I visited with both Chang and Tong in the fall of 1983, and on January 10, 1984, I revisited Naperville and met with both Chang and Tong again. During this visit, I learned that the situation had changed quite a bit. In the first place, the ministry had already "begun under the leadership of Far-Dung Tong" [19] financed by Paul Chang. The first "informal gathering took place on December 4, 1983, at the apartment of Pastor Far-Dung Tong." [20] Second, it was Tong's intention now to seek admission into the AELC, because the admission procedures were "more expeditious than that of the LCA's ... [as well as] a matter of expedience, due to his immigration status." [21] I went on to state in my memorandum to Minnick that "both Mr. Tong and Mr. Chang expressed the hope that the ministry would eventually become LCA sponsored." [22]

In February 1984 "Tong was called by Grace Lutheran Church, Glen Ellyn, as Missionary-at-large in Dupage County and was installed by the Bishop of the English Synod of the AELC." [23] In the following years, the congregation, called Truth Lutheran Church, worshiped first at St. Timothy's Lutheran Church and then at Trinity Lutheran Church, Warrenville.

After 1988 the congregation became part of the ELCA. Tong resigned as pastor in August 1991. Two years later the congregation called Peter Wang, a new seminary graduate to be its pastor. In 1996 the congregation bought the old Nichols Library as a place for worship and for programs.

Even though the ministries were separated according to denominational boundaries, the Asian clergy and some key lay leaders never quite considered that they belonged to separate institutions. They occasionally would come together for fellowship, support, and continuing education. And yet they as a group were never of one mind, as the next chapter reveals.

10

COMMUNITY IN ACTION

BEFORE MY APPOINTMENT TO THE DMNA STAFF, NO MECHANISM EXISTED TO bring the Asian Lutheran clergy in North America together for fellowship, sharing, learning, and support. But commencing in 1978 an organization began to take root in the community and in the church. It would not only bring clergy and laity together but would also provide them with a forum with which they could be creative and through which they could demand justice and participate in a wider circle that embraced different communities.

This chapter traces the development of the Association of Asians and Pacific Islanders–Evangelical Lutheran Church in America (AAPI–ELCA); the history of the Matsushita Scholarship; production of Asian-appropriate materials; and Asian participation in and contributions to trans-Lutheran events such as the Transcultural Seminars, the Consultation on Preparation for Ministry in an Inclusive Church, and redress as well as human rights.

ASSOCIATION OF ASIANS AND PACIFIC ISLANDERS—ELCA

The development of this association can be traced back to 1977 when Lloyd Burke, bishop of the Pacific Southwest Synod, asked me to go to Los Angeles to meet with Asian clergy in the greater Los Angeles area. This group eventually formed the nucleus of the first caucus meeting that took place on September 19-21, 1978, at Faith Lutheran Church in Monterey Park, California.

The months preceding that first meeting seemed to be a frustrating time for both Malcolm Minnick and me. To begin with, William Lesher and I thought it might be a good idea to gather the Asian clergy for a conference preceding my installation in April 1978. While agreeing to the idea, Eiichi Matsushita thought my installation should be an academic affair, an idea that Minnick opposed. The clash of ideas, perhaps, was what prompted Minnick to write to Lesher stating that I should not be installed as an adjunct professor of PLTS.

Furthermore, Minnick's opposition was because of my ignorance of what DMNA, through Massie Kennard's office, was trying to do with the "minority" communities within the LCA. For me it was more than just my unawareness of ecclesiastic practice, it was also my ignorance with regard to what this caucus meeting was supposed to be about. After a number of telephone calls, one of which was quite heated, between Minnick and me, it was decided that the meeting would be held in the fall.

It was also decided that the conference should involve only the West Coast LCA Asian clergy. The question regarding Joseph Wong's participation was raised, however. The Asians wanted him to be part of the conference, based on the Asian sense of propriety. The DMNA officials' objection to his participation was grounded on ecclesiastical boundaries—this was to be an LCA event. The DMNA officials won the battle but not the war, as is illustrated below.

This conference brought together both DMNA officials and Asians for the first time. DMNA officials gave eloquent speeches on the mission of the church and listened to Asians talk about their ministries and what needed to be done in their community. Although I did not want to make a formal speech, I was asked to do so. I, too, spoke of a vision of ministry with the Asian community, and concluded my speech with the story of Mencius's first encounter with King Hui of Liang.[1] The king asked Mencius, the philosopher-politician, how he could benefit his kingdom. Mencius advised the king not to speak of benefit or profit but of humaneness and rightness. I used this story implicitly to serve notice that in the past the church had not been just regarding Asians. Under the veil of this tale, I pledged that in my work I intended to uphold the principles of humaneness and rightness. From this point on I provided staff support to this group until the birth of the ELCA. Then Bill Wong became the consultant to the association.

The second conference, billed as the Asian Lutheran Pastors Conference, was held on September 13-14, 1979, in Tacoma, Washington, and involved most of the Asian pastors in North America. At this conference, the group made a series of recommendations urging the church to do ministry with Asians in North America as well as exhorting the church to make inclusivity a reality. The Asians were in essence demanding inclusion in the life of the institution.

The participants elected James Y. K. Moy as the chair of the conference. Under Moy's leadership, the conference advisory committee developed a governance structure and a set of bylaws, which were adopted by the 1981 conference.

Shortly after the 1979 conference, the so-called Kaohsiung incident occurred in Taiwan. The Nationalist government cracked down on a Taiwanese organization that advocated political freedom for the people living on the island. The head of the Presbyterian church on the island was arrested and jailed. Members of the mission congregation in San Diego, under the leadership of David Chen, were deeply concerned about the violation of human rights of their compatriots in Taiwan.

On Sunday, January 20, 1980, a meeting was held at the church to discuss the issues. I went to San Diego to give the congregation moral support. Those who were present "expressed hopes that the LCA would do something on their behalf." [2] I took the occasion "to introduce the LCA's structure to the group and to inform the people that if they wished the church to consider taking action on their behalf, it [was] necessary for them to channel their wishes through the structure." [3]

Later, Chen wrote to the advisory committee requesting the committee to channel the congregation's concern to the church. When this matter was brought up at the advisory committee meeting, Charles Kuo, who was a committee member, became upset. In his mind, politics and the church did not mix. Afterwards he submitted his resignation to me, and I forwarded it to Moy. In turn Moy forwarded it to Kennard, who wrote Kuo a long letter reasoning with him, but to no avail. [4]

The 1981 conference was held on October 14-16 at Our Redeemer Lutheran Church, Garden Grove, California. Participants at the conference, now called Biennial Asian Pastors and Professional Workers Conference, included churchwide officials, one synodical bishop, synod staff, Asian clergy of the LCA and the ALC, lay associates, one layperson, who was on the Executive Council of the LCA, as well as seminarians of both churches. The ALC clergy present were given voice but no vote at this conference.

There were considerable tensions at this conference over two issues. First, there was a presentation by a representative of the National Coalition of Redress and Reparation on the matter of redressing the ills done to Japanese-Americans during World War II. The discussion angered the older generation of Chinese pastors who remembered the atrocities the Japanese soldiers committed in China and to the Chinese during the war. Second, there was the question on membership in the conference. The title of the conference itself suggested that it was an organization for clergy and professional workers. Dr. Charles Matsumoto, a layperson and a member of the Executive Council of the LCA, objected to the exclusive nature of the organization. The conferees overruled Matsumoto's objection. But this was not the end of the matter. Matsumoto persisted at the next conference until the group decided to admit laypersons as members.

After the 1981 conference, a newsletter was published. Fern Lee Hagedorn and I were responsible for the project. But soon problems occurred. Lee Hagedorn resigned from LCA central staff and the Chinese-speaking community expressed a lack of interest in the project. The latter was not too surprising, since the newsletter was in English.The tension at the 1981 conference may have led to what developed among some Chinese pastors.

Apparently there was a group of Chinese pastors who did not think the organization served their interests well.Without informing the officers of the executive committee and the staff who had been providing support to the organization, this group of clergy had a meeting by themselves on June 22-24, 1982, in San Francisco, and organized themselves as the *xinyizong beimei huaren shenggongrenyuan lianhui* (Association of Chinese Lutheran Ministerial Workers in North America).The following persons were elected as officers: Daniel Chu, chair; Joseph Wong, vice-chair; Isaiah Chow, Chinese secretary; Hoy-san Loke, English secretary; Charles Kuo, treasurer; Wilson Wu, liaison; and Paul Hsu, publicity.

The organization was governed by a set of bylaws [5] and the annual membership fee was $60. In a November 2, 1982, communication under the signatures of Chu and Chow, the members were informed that the next meeting would take place before Christmas. They were further notified that the minutes in Chinese and English were being put in order and would be sent out, along with the bylaws, soon. [6]

At the August 5-6, 1982, Asian Pastors and Professional Workers' Executive Committee [7] meeting a fear was raised in a letter by Paul Nakamura [8] addressed to the Asian Advisory Committee "that there seems to be a splintering and disintegration among the members of the Asian American caucus and the need to strengthen the unity of the Asian American caucus is essential." [9] Nakamura's letter elicited the following response:"Daniel Chu and Wilson Wu, [both were members of this executive committee], have organized some of the Asian (Chinese) pastors for mutual support.The pastors don't speak English well so they say nothing and feel left out, stated Wilson Wu." [10] Chu also took the occasion to assure "the group that the new Asian pastors association will not fracture the Asian American Caucus." [11]

After the initial meeting it appears that this new organization, due to internal problems, never met again. But the mere existence of this association pointed out some significant language, ideological, and cultural differences within the larger group itself.

After the 1981 conference, the organization's name was changed to Asian American Caucus. In part this was in keeping with what other ethnic groups in the church called their organizations. Further, the conferees were also heeding Matsumoto's plea for inclusiveness. The advisory committee was renamed "Executive Committee."

At the 1983 conference, the conferees passed a number of resolutions, including a resolution urging DMNA, DSMA, the AELC, and the Chinese Rhenish Church, Hong Kong Synod [12] to inform congregations about violence against Asians and to develop ways and means to combat the same. They also passed a resolution reaffirming an earlier one that urged the churches to hire "ethnic minority professors in all Lutheran seminaries by the Fall of 1985." [13]

After the 1985 conference, the name of the organization was once again changed to Asian Lutherans in North America. Now Asians, clergy and lay, from the AELC, the ALC, and the LCA all could be part of the organization. The organization, however, decided to have two executive boards, one LCA and one ALC.

The 1985 conference devoted considerable energy to the "new Lutheran church," parish education, stewardship, and evangelism. A motion was passed "to authorize the executive boards of the Asian Lutherans in North America to have power to appoint or recommend names of Asians for the New Lutheran Church." [14]

In the same year, the organization published a new newsletter under the leadership of Fred Rajan, Kwang Ja Yu, and Lily Wu. This was "a product of our joint ALC-LCA Asian Caucus conference held in November 1985 in Los Angeles," [15] stated the editors. "The primary purpose of this newsletter is to be a channel of communication within our community." [16] The first issue was published in November 1985.

The last conference of the Asian Lutherans in North America was held May 6-8, 1987, in San Francisco. Much time at this gathering was spent discussing the new Lutheran church, transitional matters, and nominations to various positions in the ELCA.

With the birth of the ELCA in 1988, the organization's name was once again changed—it was called the Association of Asians—ELCA. This association, like other ethnic associations in the ELCA, has an informal structural relationship with CMM and receives funding from the commission. The association also introduced membership fees for the first time. On October 10, 1991, the association adopted a set of new bylaws that spelled out its purpose, membership and benefits, structure and function, included its relationship to the ELCA, and so forth. The association continues to sponsor a biennial assembly for both clergy and laity and to publish a newsletter.

Finally at the 1997 assembly at the Marriott Hotel in Los Angeles, the association adopted its current name—Association of Asians and Pacific Islanders—ELCA, in order to reflect the reality of its membership.

EIICHI MATSUSHITA MEMORIAL SCHOLARSHIP

"H" (what everyone called him) Matsushita died on August 2, 1984, the very same day I returned to the United States after a long trip to Asia. Heartbroken, I called all Asian clergy and workers to notify them of H's death.

The following spring, bluebonnets—the state flower of Texas—

accented only by patches of red earth here and there blanketed the Texas countryside. A pattern was formed, resembling an Oriental rug. The sky above was clear and the air was scented with a mild sweet fragrance. The road from Austin to Houston was straight, smooth, and devoid of traffic. On this road, on April 11, 1985, a yellow Toyota Celica was speeding toward its destination—Houston. The driver and a passenger were chatting amiably on subjects other than the work they had just completed in Austin and were supposed to do in Houston the next day. Suddenly the conversation stopped. The driver and passenger—Martin L. Yonts and myself—turned, looked at each other, and almost simultaneously said, "H is here."

We fell silent, each of us thinking his own thoughts. Matsushita had accompanied us on this drive on a number of occasions before. He was there to mentor me on-site and to suggest where ministries should be located. He was Yonts's and my dear friend, whose voice we always heeded. On that drive to Houston, we strongly felt his presence.

After a long silence the conversation resumed. We talked about how to perpetuate the memory of our friend. We finally decided that a scholarship for Asian seminary students studying in American Lutheran seminaries ought to be established in his name. We decided, too, to take up the matter with Yutaka Kishino, a pastor-developer in Plano, Texas. Kishino readily agreed.

The matter was brought to the LCA Asian Caucus executive committee meeting at the Hyatt Hotel, LAX, on May 15-16, 1985 (there were also two ALC representatives present at this meeting). The executive committee approved the proposal by Yonts, Kishino, and me and decided to bring the matter "to the Fall conference" for consideration. [17]

When the matter was presented to the general conference, the idea of establishing a scholarship was well received. But the matter of naming it after Matsushita, a Japanese, caused considerable debate. The older Chinese pastors who still remembered the pains of World War II objected to naming the scholarship after him. After the matter was settled, a few of the older pastors walked out.

I was charged to raise funds for a brochure, which the group would use to launch a fund-drive. I secured $500 each from DMNA and DSMA for the brochure, which was designed by Linnea Wong. The officials of the two divisions, however, suggested that the scholarship fund be lodged at PLTS and that the seminary be asked to invest the funds on behalf of the caucus. The caucus agreed, but the administration of the scholarship remained the sole responsibility of the executive committee of the caucus. Further, Kishino, Bill Wong, and I were charged to spearhead the fund-raising efforts. The caucus also spelled out a set of eligibility criteria and application procedures.

On November 3, 1986, I reported to the executive committee of the

Asian Lutherans in North America that a sum of $1,500 had been received. The first two scholarships in the amount of $500 each were awarded to two Asian students attending PLTS in 1989.

From this humble beginning, the scholarship fund has accumulated close to $90,000 in principal and interest, as of April 2000.

BILINGUAL MATERIALS AND RESOURCES

At the August 5-6, 1982, meeting of the Asian Pastors and Professional Workers' executive committee, I reported that Asian ministries in the LCA included 12 Chinese, two Japanese, and one Hmong. On June 26, 1985, Rev. Warren Sorteberg, director for urban and ethnic ministries, DSMA, sent a letter to all service and mission directors, indicating that there were a total of 16 Asian ministries in the ALC. With the exception of one LCA Japanese ministry, which used English on Sunday worship and had monthly worship in the Japanese language, all other congregations and ministries used predominantly Asian languages in worship and in education.

The need for language and culturally appropriate materials for worship, education, and nurture was acutely felt by Asian clergy and workers. Both the ALC and the LCA mission executives were sympathetic and decided to explore the possibility of producing bilingual materials for Sunday school. In addition, DMNA also decided to translate a number of social statements into Chinese.

On October 14, 1981, at the Asian Pastors and Professional Workers Conference, I announced that the social statements would be available sometime in 1982, but the bilingual Sunday school materials were in limbo. However, conversations on such materials continued between the ALC and the LCA officials. A number of social statements did come out in the following year, but the Sunday school materials were never produced, despite the series of conversations held between the officials of both churches.

The Asians, on the other hand, continued to voice their needs and served notice that the church itself should do something about the Euro-American-centric materials in general. On September 20, 1983, Ms. Carolyn Green of DPS, LCA, reported "that several settings of the *LBW* have been translated into Spanish, as has the Word and Witness program; that work on a new curriculum for the larger church will be guided by consultants to insure that DPS editors and artists eliminate racism in all church materials; that a multicultural hymnal is being developed." [18] But Green said nothing about the Asian language-specific Sunday school materials.

By this time, the two churches had discontinued the conversations. LWF somehow at that moment also got involved with the matter and offered to provide $40,000 as a one-time grant so that a Chinese staff could be placed at Fortress Press to assist the publisher in obtaining materials from

Taosheng Publishing House, a Lutheran press in Hong Kong and Taiwan, or to help to produce the much needed materials. LWF also had someone in mind for the position. After much negotiation involving not only Fortress staff, but DMNA staff as well, it was decided that the LCA could not accept LWF's offer.

Fortress Press then proposed to Taosheng that it was willing to purchase and sell the Chinese materials on a consignment basis—an idea the Taosheng officials rejected.

In the meantime the Asians continued to press for parish education materials. Thus, at their 1985 joint conference, the conferees sought action on the following recommendations:

1. Strong and urgent need for bilingual worship materials.... Also needed with worship materials [was] a handbook on how to conduct a bilingual service.
2. Develop adult Bible study material and or curriculum in Asian languages.
3. Strong need for translators of Asian languages and proofreaders of translated materials. Also adequate funding needed for translating materials.
4. Materials containing stories of the Asian Christian mission field...and the history of the beginnings of Asian churches to be included in various educational publications of the three church bodies. [19]

By this time, the merger of the three church bodies was but two years away. Little attention was paid to these recommendations. At the same time, a group of people of color under the auspices of DPS was working on a series of culturally sensitive resources for the four ethnic communities. The resources were called Living Waters of Faith Series. "Each resource is written uniquely from the perspectives of a particular racial/ethnic group....The entire series is dedicated to four late racial/ethnic leaders: Carlos Benito, Eugene Crawford, Massie Kennard, [Eiichi] Matsushita." [20]

The Asian series called *Eternal River: An Asian Cultural Awareness Resource* was primarily written by Lily Wu with the help of Fred Rajan and myself. I also served as series editor.

The Asians' press for material also resulted in the translation of three confirmation booklets—the "Fast Facts" series. I served as editor of these as well.

TRANSCULTURAL SEMINARS

The concept of Transcultural Seminars was deeply rooted in the African-American community. [21] The initial focus was on the black church, but it quickly developed into a gathering of five ethnic groups—Asian, African-American, Hispanic American, Native American, and white from the AELC, the ALC and the LCA—under the auspices of LCUSA. [22]

The seminars' aim was to make the Lutheran church inclusive by 1990. The first seminar was held May 7-9, 1981, in Cincinnati, Ohio. The second was held on October 21-24, 1981, in Chicago. These two seminars' impact on the planners of the new Lutheran church was considerable. Joseph Wong and I served on the steering committee for both seminars. At the first seminar, eight Asians were present and at the second the number was 20.[23] At the first seminar, Fern Lee Hagedorn presented a paper on "The Asian American Woman: A Case of Mistaken Identity." I also presented a paper on "The Asian Americans: Their History, Community and Culture."

The Asian Caucus's contributions to both seminars went beyond these two papers and Wong's and my participation on the steering committee, because the participants themselves at both seminars contributed richly to the whole.[24]

At the end of the second seminar, all participants signed the document "Our Word to Our Church for Our Church," in which the participants affirmed the needs of inclusion and authorized Will Herzfeld to represent them at the Commission for a New Lutheran Church (CNLC). Through Herzfeld this group issued a call for a quota system and the establishment of the Commission for Women (CW) and CMM.

These two seminars provided the first opportunity for Asian Lutherans in North America to interact with other persons of color, and vice versa, in a formal setting. The next opportunity came at the Consultation on Preparation for Ministry in an Inclusive Church. Six Asians participated in this gathering held June 24-27, 1982, in Chicago. This consultation was sponsored by the Consultation on Theological Education.[25]

JUSTICE DEMANDED: THE CHIN CASE AND REDRESS

Toward the end of the 1970s, the economy in the United States began to spiral downward. Asia, and Japan in particular, was the target of blame. Meanwhile, Southeast Asian refugees continued to arrive. From Los Angeles to Boston and places in-between, violence against Asians in America took a sudden surge. White Americans once again perceived Asians as the "New Yellow Peril." Matsushita, myself, and other Asians who traveled frequently on business for the church often encountered overt racism and physical threats.

The Vincent Chin Case

No case, however, galvanized Asian and other ethnic communities more than the Vincent Chin case. In 1982 on the night before his wedding, Chin, a Chinese-American, was killed by two white unemployed Detroit autoworkers, Ronald Ebens and his stepson Michael Nitz, who mistook him for a Japanese.[26] The judge sentenced the two killers to a three-year probation and a $3,000 fine each, which outraged not only Asians but persons of color from other communities as well. When the judge was confronted by the news media, he said that, "Asian-Americans owe him gratitude, because he gave them unity." [27]

Outraged, community activist Helen Zia, from Detroit, Michigan, and others organized protests and demanded justice. I was part of the protest movement. On September 22, 1986, I wrote to Attorney General Edwin Meese, asking him "to (1) file a motion with the Sixth Circuit Court of Appeals to rehear the matter, or (2) file a petition with the U.S. Supreme Court to reverse the Sixth Circuit Court of Appeal's decision." [28] On October 10, 1986, I received a personal response [29] from Linda K. Davis, Chief, Criminal Section, U.S. Department of Justice, assuring me that "the Department of Justice has announced that Mr. Ebens will be reprosecuted." [30]

Asian Lutherans too were alarmed by the killing and violence against their own people and repeatedly submitted resolutions and recommendations to Lutheran churches, requesting the churches to advocate on their behalf and to educate the rest of the church regarding Asians and violence against them. The churches took no particular action, excepting in the case of redress. But even in this case, Asians took the lead.

Redress

On February 19, 1942, President Franklin D. Roosevelt signed Executive Order 9066, which authorized the internment of 120,000 people of Japanese ancestry during World War II. "President Gerald R. Ford rescinded Executive Order 9066 on February 19, 1976, ... and stated: 'An honest reckoning must include a recognition of our national mistakes as well as our national achievements. Learning from our mistakes is not pleasant, but as a great philosopher once admonished, we must do so if we want to avoid repeating them.'" [31] In 1988 President Ronald Reagan signed the Civil Rights Act passed by the Congress. This act awarded $20,000 to all persons affected by the internment. Reagan also apologized to the internees. Moreover, the act likewise established an educational fund. Thus, "in the late 1970s, there was a surge of interest among many Japanese Americans in seeking legal redress for what they saw as a grievous abridgement of their constitutional rights justified in the name of national security but at its base motivated by racism. Redress for the internees meant not just an acknowledgement of the wrong that had been done, and not just an apology from the government...redress also meant monetary compensation for loss of their freedom." [32]

Asian Lutherans in America also played a role in lending moral support for the redress. Charles and Mary Matsumoto were members of the Indiana-Kentucky Synod and active at the synodical level. At their prodding, the synod at its 1980 convention passed a resolution memorializing "the LCA to support the passage of Senate Bill 1647 and House of Representatives Bill 5499 for the creation of a Presidential Study Commission on Wartime Relocation and Internment of Civilians Act." [33] The memorial further called on the LCA to communicate this support to other government officials and to call on member synods to support these bills. The Committee on Memorials from Synods recommended "that the response to the memorial from the Indiana-Kentucky Synod be referred to the Division for Mission in North America for transmittal to the Lutheran Council USA's Office for Governmental Affairs." [34]

The 1980 LCA convention was held in Seattle, Washington. Present at the convention were a number of Asians, including Charles Matsumoto and Bill Wong as delegates and Lee Hagedorn, Matsushita, and me as staff. This group did not like the idea of referral and transmittal. The group wanted the convention itself to take an action on the memorial and decided to challenge the recommendation by the Committee on Memorials from Synods. On the last day of the convention, Bill Wong, on behalf of the group, "moved to amend the recommendation…by addition: 'Be It Resolved that the LCA through this convention goes on record to support the passage of Senate bill 1647 and House bill 5499 for the creation of a Presidential Study Commission on Wartime Relocation and Internment of Civilians. Therefore the DMNA will communicate our support of these bills to LCUSA's Office for Governmental Affairs….' The Rev. Stanley E. Olson moved to amend the amendment by inserting the word 'intent' in place of the word 'passage.' Wong moved to postpone action until 9:00 a.m. The Motion to postpone was adopted." [35]

The Asians regrouped to strategize what to do next. I contacted Robert Brorby, an attorney and a member of the Executive Council, LCA, for advice. Olson joined the group discussion. With the help of Brorby and Olson, the group came up with a substitute amendment, which was presented to the convention by Olson at 9:00 a.m. The substitute reads: "Be It Resolved that the Lutheran Church in America through this convention records its support of the creation of a presidential study commission on wartime relocation and internment of civilians during the Second World War and that this support be conveyed by the Division for Mission in North America to the Lutheran Council in the U.S.A.'s Office for Governmental Affairs." [36] Both this text and the substituted motion were adopted.

The Asian Caucus meeting in 1981 in Garden Grove endorsed the Redress Movement of Japanese Americans, but not without heated debates and hurt feelings. The painful memories of World War II prevented the older Chinese pastors from making a distinction between the Japanese soldiers who caused havoc in China and Japanese Americans who were interned in America during the war. When the motion to endorse the movement was adopted, they walked out of the room.

The Pacific Southwest Synod at its 1982 convention adopted a reso-lution in support of "the efforts of the National Coalition for Redress and Reparations, the Japanese American Citizens' League, and other groups to obtain from the government reparations for victims of the evacuation," [37] including monetary compensation, education for the public, and so forth. In addition the synod was to memorialize the LCA "to endorse this vital issue that affects the life of our country." [38]

The Eleventh Biennial Convention of the LCA held September 3-19, 1982, in Louisville, Kentucky, did not have time to consider the memorial submitted by the Pacific Southwest Synod. It was referred to the June 1983 meeting of the Executive Council of the LCA.

At the June 1983 Executive Council meeting, many debates ensued. In the end the Executive Council voted to approve the memorial from the synod. Matsumoto recalled, "the approval did not come easily. In fact, one Bishop, [who was also a member of the council], indicated to me that the memorial would not have been approved if I were not present at the meet-ing." [39] The Executive Council also "request[ed] the Division for Mission in North America to prepare appropriate material for use in the congregations of this church on Sunday, February 19, 1984, which is the 42nd anniversary of Executive Order Numbered 9066." [40]

On August 8, 1983, I was informed about the council action by Elna Solvang, administrative assistant to the executive director, DMNA. In the same letter, Solvang asked for guidance as DMNA prepared to develop the materi-al. In the end, the task was assigned to Lee Hagedorn, who in consultation with Nakamura and me, produced the following: "February 19, 1942—February 19, 1984: The 42nd Anniversary of Executive Order 9066: Detention and Relocation of 120,000 West Coast Japanese," a two-page document.

This document gives a summary of the internment and what the church has spoken about it. Then it calls on congregations to set aside February 19, 1984, to commemorate the injustice that Japanese Americans had received. Further, it calls members to action by searching their own atti-tudes and following "the example of the bishop of our church in writing to the highest officials of our nation and to our own members of Congress... to assure that the suffering inflicted on one segment of American society not so long ago, will not be repeated." The document ends with a prayer. It also lists Nakamura and me as contact persons for more information.

The Asian community and some Asian Lutherans did not rest until the drive for redress became a reality. Lutheran Oriental Church and its pas-tor, Nakamura, continued to perform some significant functions in the move-ment after 1984. In July 2000 "both houses of Congress... approved spending $4.2 million to construct a visitors center and museum at the Manzanar [41]

National Historic Site in the Owens Valley." [42]

Did the Asian Lutherans' efforts in the Redress Movement have anything to do with the construction of a visitors center and museum at Manzanar? It is not easy to measure. But it is undeniable that it was through the hard work and persistence of the Asians that the LCA acted on the matter of redress the way it did.

11

A Different Landscape

After immigrating, the great majority of traditional Asians stayed in Hawaii, on the East and West Coasts, or in big cities like Chicago in mainland America. But this demographic landscape changed drastically after 1975 with the arrival of refugees from Indochina. Asians began to be seen in cities, big and small, all across the United States. Southeast Asian refugees had no choice. They went where their sponsors were, adding yet another slightly different-colored thread to the tapestry of American multiculturalism.

Some refugees accepted baptism offered by the sponsoring congregations as a gesture of gratitude but not as a spiritual commitment to the faith. After they had settled in a given place for a period of time, some found it necessary to move closer to their relatives or friends. Others moved for climatic reasons. Thus began an "in-migration" movement within the Indochinese community.

By the end of 1985, Lutheran Immigration and Refugee Service (LIRS),[1] an agency originally founded to handle European refugees and immigrants, had resettled 14,382 of Indochina's refugees. Some of them were placed in Lutheran congregations,[2] giving these churches an excellent opportunity to minister with the resettled persons. But ministry has many facets. In its broadest sense, it includes everything we do in our daily life. In this chapter, however, ministry is defined in terms of Word and Sacrament outreach. Attention is focused here on ministry with these refugees among the major Lutheran denominations in the United States only.

Which one of these congregations that had received the resettled persons was the first to provide Word and Sacrament ministry with them is difficult to determine, without making a detailed inventory of each congregation's record. Such a step, however, has not been taken, due to time constraints and the unevenness of congregational recordkeeping.

However, it is possible to describe the beginning of four Southeast

Asian ministries [3] in three different Lutheran denominations, showing how local congregations, clergy, and national church bodies had responded to the presence of these refugees. [4]

VIETNAMESE LUTHERAN CHURCH, GARDEN GROVE, CALIFORNIA

The LCMS initially had no overall national mission strategy to minister with the Indochinese refugees. However, one of its former clergy does have the distinction of being the first to play an important role in assisting the Vietnamese themselves to organize the first Vietnamese congregation among the Lutheran denominations. In the process, this very person also incurred the displeasure of his superiors. Donald Moorman is his name.

Rev. Donald Moorman was born on August 18, 1943, in Indianapolis, Indiana. Moorman came from a working class family. At age five he felt the call to ministry, as he "heard about the work of foreign missionaries." [5] Even at that young age Moorman "equated...ministry with mission work." This equation would be significant in his ministry with the Vietnamese. After completing his college education, he attended CS, St. Louis, obtaining his M.Div. degree in 1969. After graduation he served two parishes in Arizona before accepting a call to St. Paul's Lutheran Church, Garden Grove, California, where he served from 1977 to 1987. In 1992 Moorman transferred his roster membership to the ELCA. He is presently serving King of Glory Lutheran Church, Newbury Park, California.

Garden Grove was where Moorman imprinted his mark on Vietnamese ministry. St. Paul's Lutheran Church is located in a neighborhood with many apartments. Two years after his arrival at St. Paul's, Moorman "began noticing a decided upswing in the number of Vietnamese people in the apartments around...[the] church." At about the same time, Moorman started to receive "referrals from Lutheran churches in the Midwest concerning Vietnamese families they had sponsored who had moved to Orange County," in which St. Paul's Lutheran Church was located.

Moorman, the ever-faithful "missionary," visited everyone who was referred to him by the churches in the Midwest. To his amazement, he found every one of them was baptized but no one was willing to join his congregation. This discovery gave him an insight into the nature of the Vietnamese community and culture—the Vietnamese accepted baptism as "a gesture of respect not [as] a spiritual commitment, something those churches [in the Midwest] didn't understand."

Though feeling helpless, Moorman was determined to do something. He made contact with the Indochinese Refugee Center in Garden Grove and its director to offer his help and that of the congregation's. The director recognized the good work of LIRS in resettling the Vietnamese as well as the possibility that Lutherans may "have a significant spiritual ministry among the Vietnamese." With that encouragement from the director and the realization that The LCMS had no plan to begin work among the Vietnamese in Orange County, Moorman knew that if this ministry with the Vietnamese was to take place, it had to come from the local level. He began to immerse himself in the Vietnamese community—Little Saigon—which is about three miles from St. Paul's.

In late 1979, Moorman's work seemed to have borne fruit. A certain young man came to see him, indicating that he felt the call to ministry and that he was willing to do what was required to prepare himself to become a pastor, without questioning the Lutheran faith at all. Moorman became suspicious. Later he discovered that the young man "was...sent from Hanoi to infiltrate the Vietnamese community in America."

In early 1980 another Vietnamese man, an active member of the Christian Alliance Church, felt the call to ministry. But he wanted to be affiliated with "a church that had a national identity in the U.S. This was so that as Vietnamese moved out into the wider culture, they could always find a church that could minister to them." He was interested in the Lutheran church, "because of its excellent record in settling Vietnamese refugees."

This man and Moorman met and instantly discovered that they "were kindred spirits who had a deep commitment to mission work and a common understanding of how we could work together in ministry." Moorman gave him and his family instruction in the Lutheran faith and made arrangements for him to go to a seminary that was willing to establish "a special educational track in order to graduate the first Vietnamese Lutheran pastor." He had no luck with the first seminary he approached, but the second accepted his proposal. Life at the seminary was hard on this man due to educational differences and financial needs, though he received some support from the Lutheran Women Missionary League (LWML) and from some individuals from the churches. This man and his family also worked hard to support themselves and his education.

After graduation from the seminary in 1983, he was assigned to Garden Grove. In the meantime, Moorman had secured "$50,000 seed money to begin the work from a churchwide offering called 'Forward in Remembrance.'" The district office also promised further support should this ministry prove to be "a viable outreach."

By now Moorman had learned that in the Vietnamese culture, ceremonies, rituals, titles, and human relationships are important and that events are not taken lightly. With this awareness in mind, Moorman ignored the advice of his superiors and created "a major community event out of the beginning of this new ministry and [called] the man 'pastor' even though he did not have that title yet according to denominational rules." [6]

The event "drew community and political leaders from all over

Orange County and official letters of congratulations from state and national leaders....Many plaques and certificates of recognition were given to Vietnamese Lutheran Church as it began its ministry. The local media gave it great coverage. No LCMS official was present." They were angry at Moorman's calling a vicar "pastor."

The first worship service was held on August 7, 1983. "The ministry was an immediate spiritual and numerical success." But not all was well. While Moorman adopted a hands-off position regarding the operation and decision-making processes of the Vietnamese ministry, there were a number of individuals who, he said, insisted on interfering. New to The LCMS, the Vietnamese did not always understand how the policies and polities of the church work, in practical terms. They had to depend on Moorman, who on occasion "functioned as an 'angry pit bull'... and had to bare [his] teeth a number of times."

Even though Moorman did not want to admit it, this congregation's success, in addition to the efforts of Vietnamese members, had a lot to do with his commitment to the people and his understanding of ministry. For example, to facilitate communication and to give the new arrivals a sense of welcome, he took a college level course in the Vietnamese language. He often accompanied representatives of the Vietnamese church to the airport to meet new arrivals. Further, to bring himself up to speed in cross-cultural ministry, he began reading "many books on foreign mission strategies, sociology, anthropology and ethnic history," culminating with the publication of his own book on Vietnamese ministry, *Harvest Waiting.* [7]

Moorman, however, was a reluctant author. At first his resisted the publication of the materials he had collected. Later he consented to do so only after he had received numerous requests for information from others and to protect his materials from being twisted "to fit their [church officials'] preconceived ideas about cross-cultural ministry."

Because of the vitality and success of this ministry, The LCMS developed a strategy for Vietnamese ministry nearly a decade later, as chapter 15 describes.

SOUTHEAST ASIAN MINISTRY IN MINNEAPOLIS

The LCA was the first church body to ordain a Southeast Asian into ministry. Rev. Sunthi Paul Chookiatsirichai was ordained in 1982 as an associate pastor at Bethlehem Lutheran Church in Minneapolis, Minnesota. Part of his responsibility was ministry with Southeast Asian refugees and to develop and implement an effective ministry to these refugees through Lutheran Social Service and the Minnesota Synod.

A man of many talents, Chookiatsirichai was born in Bangkok, Thailand, on April 22, 1945. He began his higher education in 1964 at the

Tharmarsart University, Bangkok, studying political science, law, and business management. In 1968 he was a student at Lutheran Bible Institute in Issaquash, Washington. While he was at the Bible institute, he also studied English and philosophy at two nearby institutions of higher learning. He obtained his B.A. degree from Bethel College and Seminary, Arden Hills, Minnesota, in 1973, and his M.Div. degree from Luther Northwestern Theological Seminary, St. Paul, Minnesota, in 1975.

From 1972 to 1982, he worked as a warehouseman (Teamsters Union) part-time and then full-time after his graduation from seminary. In the meantime, he founded the China Projects, "a cooperative ministry with Lutheran Campus Ministry at the University of Minnesota." [8]

By 1982, the year he was ordained, the Minneapolis and St. Paul area had become a major center for Indochinese refugees, whose needs were beyond any congregation's ability to meet. Chookiatsirichai worked tirelessly. Yet his ministry at Bethlehem Lutheran Church did not go well, resulting in his resignation without call in December 1984.

In the meantime, a Concerned Group for East Asian Ministries met in January and February 1985 to discuss plans for the future and to attempt to provide support and work for Chookiatsirichai. The group at its February meeting "suggested that he could start the survey work [on the Southeast Asian situation]...during his two months severance pay period and in connection with part time interim work." [9] At the same meeting Chookiatsirichai reported my impending visit.

I arrived in Minneapolis on April 3 "to assess ministry possibilities among the Southeast Asians." [10] I spent the next three days in Minneapolis meeting with a large number of Southeast Asian leaders and synod staff. "The Southeast Asian leaders identified [six] areas in which the Lutheran church may be of assistance to them and their community," [11] ranging from job training programs and employment, to providing funds for the United Southeast Asian Mutual Association. But they mentioned nothing about ministry needs.

On this same visit, I also realized the explosive relationship between some blacks and some Southeast Asians and predicted that "unless something is done, there could be a repeat of the Philadelphia situation in Minneapolis." [12] I subsequently proposed a multifaceted model for ministry in Minneapolis, [13] but nothing came about. Sunthi Paul Chookiatsirichai resigned from the ELCA roster in 1994.

Bethlehem Lutheran Church was not the only congregation that was engaged in Southeast Asian ministry in that city. There were a number of congregations of the ALC and the LCA that provided ministries with them as well. Later in this chapter a cooperative model of an ALC congregation that attempted ministry with the Hmong is described. The second example of early LCA ministry with Indochinese refugees is the Hmong community in Philadelphia.

HMONG MINISTRY IN PHILADELPHIA

St. Simeon's Lutheran Church, an LCA congregation, was located in a rather quiet neighborhood in North Philadelphia called Hunting Park, a community in a transition that began in the early 1970s. In 1978 the congregation was approached by LIRS as to the possibility of sponsoring a refugee family. In November the Kues, a family of eight, arrived in Hunting Park to begin a new life in a strange land. "The Rev. Rinda Rogers of Lutheran Children and Family Service assisted the congregation step by step as they learned how to make a family feel at home in a new neighborhood." [14] The initial experience proved to be positive. In March 1979, the Hang family of eight arrived, under the sponsorship of the church. Two more families came in May the following year.

Rev. Edwin Miller, pastor of the congregation, and Rogers did what they could to provide the daily necessities to these families. The congregation also began teaching basic English and linking these families to essential social services. "The number of families increased as word got around that Hunting Park and St. Simeon's provided a welcome, a home, and ample help in getting settled." [15]

As their numbers increased, the Hmong felt the need for a central place for them to carry on their culture and tradition. They approached Miller to see if the church would let them house a culture center in the church basement. With encouragement from me, the congregation consented. Soon thereafter the Hmong wanted Miller to teach them the faith of the church. Miller gladly obliged. On Sunday, May 3, 1981, 53 people were baptized into the faith and the membership of St. Simeon's Lutheran Church.

The Hmong now felt that they needed a leader from their own ranks to lead the group, noting that it was not because Miller was not doing the job, but the job had grown to the point where additional staff was needed. A series of conversations took place between Miller, Rev. John R. Cochran, assistant to the bishop of the Southeastern Pennsylvania Synod, and me as well as other DMNA staff. In December 1981, on behalf of the congregation and the synod, Cochran submitted a proposal for a lay associate to DMNA for consideration. The DMNA cabinet acted favorably on the proposal.

The Hmong recommended that Hang Chay, the head of the second Hmong family to arrive in Hunting Park and St. Simeon's, be the person to be employed as their leader. Hang became one of the three Asian lay associates in the LCA's lay associate program in the early 1980s. [16]

Under Hang's leadership, the group flourished and named itself the Hmong Community Evangelical Church. Hang himself later went through the ELCA's alternate route to ordained service program and became an ordained pastor of the church.

HMONG MINISTRY IN MINNEAPOLIS

As mentioned above, Minneapolis was one of the major Southeast Asian refugee centers in America. Our Saviour's Lutheran Church, an ALC congregation located near Lutheran Social Service of Minnesota and the office of its refugee resettlement, contributed to the growth of the refugee community. Shortly after the refugees began to arrive in that city, Our Saviour's became a sponsor but at that time the congregation provided no outreach ministry to them.

Rev. Donald Rudrud became senior pastor of Our Saviour's in 1978. Rudrud was born on April 10, 1939, in Van Nuys, California. He obtained his B.A. degree from St. Olaf College in 1961 and his B.D. degree from LS in 1965. The ALC ordained him in 1967. He served two parishes before coming to Our Saviour's as its senior pastor.

Being new to Our Saviour's, Rudrud was not aware of the refugees living in the neighborhood. He admitted that he "heard about the Hmong people from another pastor in my part of the city." [17] But soon on one spring day he saw an Asian woman walking down the street, "carrying a huge basket on her head filled with clothing." His encounter with this Hmong woman raised his awareness of their presence in the neighborhood.

Shortly thereafter "a Hmong family appeared at worship…and sat in the back row." The head of this worshiping family told him that they were Lutherans from Spokane, Washington, and that his name was Xai Yang. This second encounter enabled Rudrud to realize how little he knew about his Southeast Asian neighbors. However, Rudrud is not the kind of man who would let his own ignorance stop him from taking further action. He went about asking "others in [their] Minneapolis Lutheran urban committee and in the leadership core of Our Saviour's to consider how [they] could learn more about the people and culture of Southeast Asia."

They decided to contact Ms. Ellen Erickson at the refugee office of Lutheran Social Service of Minnesota. Erickson was both resourceful and helpful to them. Subsequently, a series of learning meetings were organized. They learned about Southeast Asian history, culture, and religion as well as refugee issues from experts and refugees themselves at these meetings. At the end of the series of meetings, the needs of these refugees became apparent. The refugees needed "help in learning English and help in finding jobs," but nothing about wanting "to hear about Jesus" and the Lutheran faith.

Soon a language school was organized and a seminary student was hired to direct and to teach English as a second language. Volunteers initially came from Our Saviour's but soon members from other churches and students from several nearby colleges came to teach and to help out as well. The program expanded to include other classes such as "math, general equivalency diploma (GED), city survival skill assistance, and computers." As the program flourished, a fund-raiser was added to the staff.

The congregation also provided space to the Lao Association. Soon Cambodian and Hmong families joined the congregation. A few members of Our Saviour's learned some elementary Hmong language to facilitate communication. Then some members began to ask when more evangelical work would be done with the Hmong. At about this time, LS offered the service of Rev. Simon Lee, who was spending a year at the seminary as a doctor of ministry student.

Lee proved to be resourceful and caring. With Lee's knowledge of Chinese language and culture, Rudrud and he soon established a worshiping community for the Hmong people—called the Hmong Christian Fellowship Group. After Lee returned to Hawaii, the fellowship was led by a number of Hmong.

In the meantime, Lutheran clergy in Minneapolis also realized the importance of theological education. Thus a Southeast Asian Leadership School was established with students from many denominations attending.

But not all Hmong leaders who had led the fellowship proved to be resourceful. The fellowship never grew to be more than 60 in number, with 10 to 15 at worship on Sundays. In 1993 the fellowship moved to Central Lutheran Church for worship. Prince of Glory Lutheran Church, located among public housing projects in north Minneapolis, ceased to be a congregation in 1995 and its building became available. The fellowship moved to that location and named itself Hmong Evangelical Lutheran Church. But by the summer of 1998, the members of the congregation had scattered. However, efforts are being made by the Division for Outreach (DO) and the Minneapolis Area Synod to regroup the scattered members and to identify new pastoral leadership for them.

In the fall of 2000, new mission outreach with the Hmong people began at Luther Memorial Church in North Minneapolis. This effort has the support of the Minneapolis Area Synod. Moreover, DO is helping to facilitate a Hmong strategy for the Twin Cities.

Will this group, like a fallen phoenix, rise again? No one knows. Besides, historians are not good prophets.

12

SOMETHING NEW

THE EVANGELICAL LUTHERAN CHURCH IN AMERICA FROM CONCEPTION TO BIRTH required lengthy incubation and involved arduous labor.[1] Some Asian Lutherans were involved on all levels in the formative stage of this new Lutheran church body. Mary Matsumoto and Joseph Wong were on the CNLC, the highest deliberative and legislative body in the merger process. Stacy Kitahata was a member of the design committee for Women of the ELCA, and I, having contributed a paper on "Racism in America" to CNLC's discussion on the subject, chaired the design committee for CMM. Other Asians also participated in synodical transition teams.

When this new institution became a reality in 1988, a number of Asians were appointed to churchwide, regional, and synodical positions. Thus the focus of this chapter and the next is on the work of these individuals and the ministries among new Asian ethnic groups initiated by the ELCA. This chapter covers the period from 1988 to 2000 and focuses on the Asians' involvement in the Commission for Multicultural Ministries.

THE ASIAN MINISTRY DESK

"The Commission for a New Lutheran Church established commissions as units to which was assigned the responsibility of providing services, advice, and counsel in the area of the commission's specific function to various parts of the several expressions of the ELCA. Commissions were considered as permanent as any other unit of the churchwide organization."[2] Thus CMM accordingly "shall assist this church in working toward the goal of full partnership of people of color and primary language other than English in the life of this church."[3] In order to achieve this constitutional mandate "this commission shall organize itself into Asian, Black, Hispanic, and Native American communities, each with an executive staff person from that community and each with additional staff adequate to meet needs of the partic-

ular community." [4] The commission's first board meeting was held June 30-
July 1, 1987. At this meeting Rev. Craig Lewis was elected executive director
of this unit.

It was into this commission that two Asians, Rev. William (Bill) E.
Wong and Rev. Frederick E. N. Rajan, were appointed to the staff and I was
retained for the year 1988 as a consultant to the Asian ministry desk.

In 1987 Wong was appointed director for Asian ministries and on
January 4, 1988, he reported to work. "It was a very cold day, a wind-chill factor of minus 40 to 60 degrees. In the midst of the cold [he] wondered why
[he] had decided to move from Tucson, Arizona." [5] On that day, Wong experienced far more than just intemperate Chicago weather and a nearly empty
cubicle that was to be his office for the next eight-plus years. He also faced
monumental challenges. How was he going to "fit into a framework of an
institution that never had such a position before,…to make that position
known to other staff in the ELCA and synods,…to provide information about
Asians and Asian ministries,…to enable the rest of the institution to make
use of the position and the person"? [6] Also unbeknownst to him on that day
was that after the first four years in his churchwide career, he would move
from position to position, making it difficult for him to undertake long-range
planning. Despite all of these challenges, however, Wong in the end became
an accomplished churchwide leader, a steadfast advocate for the Asian community, and a tremendous connector for the geographically scattered Asian
Lutheran community in the United States.

Moreover, Wong's ministry in the Lutheran Center went beyond the
Asian community. In the fall of 1998, he served as interim director for black
ministries. Beginning in 1990, he also served as the CMM staff person who
related to the ELCA Arab and Middle Eastern group. Under his leadership, the
first Arab and Middle Eastern consultation took place at the Lutheran Center
on October 15, 1990, and the second June 25-27, 1992, resulting in the establishment of the Arab and Middle Eastern ministry program. When Rev.
Bassam Abdallah was contracted as the part-time director for that program,
Wong's responsibilities shifted to that of supervising him.

THE MAN AND THE STRATEGY

Wong was born on October 24, 1952, in Los Angeles. His parents,
however, were born an ocean apart—his father in San Francisco and his
mother in China. His father moved to China as a child and returned to the
U.S. following World War II. His mother immigrated to the United States in
1949 and met his father in San Francisco. Interestingly, she was far more
acculturated to the American way of life than his U.S.-born father. His mother is the one who encouraged him to become conversant with both cultures.
His father was a partner-owner of a fish and poultry business on Spring Street

in Los Angeles's Chinatown and his parents' early life, Wong recalled, "was rough." Yet they never neglected to educate their four children—three boys and a girl—among whom Wong is the eldest.

When Wong was in his early teens, his parents sent him to a Chinese language school sponsored by what later became Faith Lutheran Church in Monterey Park, California. After graduation from high school, he went to the University of Southern California in Los Angeles to prepare for an anticipated career in dentistry. After obtaining his B.A. degree in psychology in 1974, Wong did not enter dental school. Instead, he spent two-and-a-half years serving as a junior administrative assistant in the finance department of the City of Monterey Park. In the fall of 1977, he became a student at PLTS, Berkeley.

During his seminary years, he was active in the church on all levels. On campus, he was also instrumental in bringing students of color together for support and fellowship. He obtained his M.Div. degree in 1981. In the same year, he was ordained after receiving a call to be the pastor-developer of Faith-Evergreen Lutheran Church, which eventually became Grace Lutheran Church, San Jose, California. He served that congregation from October 1981 to May 1984. Subsequently, he served as the first associate pastor at Tanque Verde Lutheran Church in Tucson, Arizona, until his appointment to the churchwide staff in 1987.

From January 1988 to February 1, 1992, he was the director for Asian ministries in CMM. Because this position was unprecedented in the history of Lutheranism in North America, Wong initially was unrecognized and underused. "Part of the struggle," Wong remembered, "was to convince staff members that if they had anything related to Asians, and especially if it had Asian ministry implications, to be sure to consult with me or with a group of Asians that I [would] organize.... [We would] provide them with appropriate advice and counsel that would help them to decide on or develop Asian ministry." [7] Another initial problem Wong and other commission staff faced was "trying to feel out what was [their] responsibility and how active [they could] be [in pursuing the responsibility]," [8] and how the ELCA constitution should or could be interpreted.

As the executive director, Lewis took a strict interpretation of the constitution. It was his position that "if there were items covered by another unit [Wong's] job was not to do that unit's work. [His] job was to make sure that the unit did the work that it was supposed to do." [9] The frustration for Wong, however, was that "units were not fulfilling everything under constitutional mandate that came under multicultural ministry." [10] To remedy the situation, Wong pursued a strategy, outlined by Lewis, of "relationships and interdependent partnerships" with the staff of other units and key people in the church. He spent much time meeting with staff of other units, in addition to "parish pastors, synod staff, shared staff, deployed staff,...regional staff,...church councils, concerned people, and congregational leaders." [11] Wong was able to make this strategy work, especially with staff interested in joint projects. Before long, he was involved in finishing projects left uncompleted by the predecessor church bodies and participating in new initiatives.

Projects from the Predecessor Churches

One of the first leftover projects in which Wong was involved was an inter-Lutheran (LCMS and ELCA) evangelism project. The subcommittee on evangelism of the Cooperative Parish Projects Committee asked Wong to join it and work on a project formerly known as "The Transcultural Outreach Pilot Project...Beginning in August of 1985, [this project] sought to respond to a need in southern California to reach out to the growing number of people of different races and cultures." [12] The project was redefined and eventually became an Asian evangelism project with the hope of producing Asian-specific materials for evangelization. Wong and Rev. James Capers, director for witness evangelism in the Division for Congregational Life (DCL) were the two project managers. [13] Their responsibilities included convening the design team; preparing and managing the project budget; and coordinating the development of various resources.

The design team initially met May 4-5, 1989, at PLTS. The project resulted in an inter-Lutheran Asian evangelism consultation, which also served as a continuing education event for all participants. This consultation provided information that resulted in producing a Japanese language evangelism audiotape, Southeast Asian language brochures, and a Chinese evangelism event.

Wong's next project was to follow-up on long-range plans for Korean ministry. Wong's involvement in this project led to joint planning with DO for developing "a strategy with the Korean community for ELCA outreach in the U.S.A." [14] in 1992. However, due to budget cuts within the ELCA and Wong's change of position, this project was aborted. A Korean ministries gathering was convened January 18-20, 1996, when Wong resumed the position of director for Asian ministries.

The purposes of this gathering included discussion on "topics of concern,...information about the ELCA and the Korean community,...updates about Korean ministries,...nurture and support for participants,...relationships [building] and networking among the participants." [15]

Wong also completed a number of ABHNA (Asian, Black, Hispanic and Native American) projects sponsored by the former DPS, LCA. It was under his guidance, for example, that the confirmation materials—the Fast Facts series, which was translated into Chinese—and *Eternal River: An Asian Cultural Awareness Resource* were published.

Learning and Caring

In addition to project managing, Wong was constantly on the road visiting Asian seminary students and Asian ministries. He sought to learn from his colleagues, provide care to them and the parsonage families when needed, as well as give encouragement to seminarians. In turn, his colleagues shared their concerns, desires, and needs with him. [16]

Wong was generally well received. He provided a link between Asian clergy and the rest of the ELCA synod staff who usually "did not know how to care for them." [17] At first, the older generation of immigrant Chinese clergy was skeptical about him because he was American-born. In their opinion, Wong was nothing more than a "hollow bamboo," a designation referring to those North American-born Chinese who possess little knowledge of traditional Chinese culture. According to Wong, the relationship between him and this group improved when in 1990 he financially supported its desire to have a Chinese language newsletter, called "ELCA Chinese Ministry Newsletter." [18]

Consultation, Education, and Resources

In his early years as director for Asian ministries, to implement CMM's strategy of interdependent partnerships Wong held two significant consultations in partnership with other units of the church. The Japanese ministry consultation was held July 1, 1990, and the Southeast Asian Ministries Consultation took place January 9-12, 1992. For the latter consultation Wong teamed up with DM, DO, and the Division for Congregational Ministries (DCM). He also made use of focus groups, enlisting the services of Department for Research and Evaluation staff and Stacy Kitahata, DGM, as resource persons. These consultations surfaced a number of needs, such as resources for ministry and theological education for Southeast Asians. After these consultations, Wong began to lay groundwork for theological education for Southeast Asians and others, as well as to explore possibilities to develop resources for ministry.

Wong's efforts to provide continuing education for Asian pastors and workers led him to confer with James Moy and Rev. Bill Behrens, project manager, of the Growth in Excellence in Ministry (GEM) program. He was successful in obtaining GEM funds for continuing education programs for Asian clergy. But realizing that the ELCA itself would probably not be able to produce resources for ministry, Wong supported and became active in the Pacific Asian American Christian Education (PAACE) project. "This is an ecumenical effort focused on developing and producing Asian Pacific American-specific English-language Christian education resources." [19]

As for Asian-specific language resources, he focused his efforts on encouraging DCM to translate some existing English language resources into different Asian languages and to produce others. The result was the translation of several short resource pieces into Asian languages.

Position Shifted

In the fall of 1991, Lewis resigned as executive director of CMM to become an assistant to Presiding Bishop Herbert Chilstrom. While maintaining his own position, Wong simultaneously served as interim executive director of CMM from December 1991 to January 1992. At the October 18-20, 1991, steering committee meeting, I was elected chair. At a subsequent steering committee meeting held January 11-12, 1992, "a motion was presented by DeAne Lagerquist, 'to concur with the Bishop in the nomination of the Reverend Frederick E. N. Rajan for election by the Church Council to a four year term as the Executive Director of the Commission for Multicultural Ministries.'" [20] The motion was seconded and "was adopted unanimously." [21]

With the election of Rajan as executive director, Wong became the coordinating director for the Multicultural Mission Strategy, from February 1, 1992, to February 1, 1993. Meanwhile, Paul T. Nakamura served as interim director for Asian ministries from April 15, 1992, to January 31, 1993.

Back at the Helm

From February 1, 1993, to April 1, 1994, Wong was back at the helm assuming a dual position as director for Asian ministries and director for the Multicultural Mission Strategy. In his capacity as director for Asian ministries, Wong set an impressive list of goals for the remaining eleven months in 1993,[22] and accomplished everything he set out to do.

In addition, he "worked with Ms. Candace Kamper of Augsburg Fortress, Publishers in convening a Taosheng Publishing House [23] Resources Advisory Group meeting, July 8-9, 1993, [24] at the Augsburg Fortress store in Mountlake Terrace, Washington." [25] The purpose of this meeting was "to share, evaluate, and offer suggestions for Chinese language resources." [26] Similar to my earlier experience, Wong, as hard as he tried, could not garner the desired response from the publishing houses. From their perspective, the market and sales potential for such material was not large enough to cover publishing or handling costs.

Other consultations were more successful. Together with Moy of DM, Wong conducted a successful Southeast Asian Theological Education Seminar, October 1-3, 1993, at LS. In the meantime, Rev. Robert Hoyt, DO, initiated a Chinese Ministry Consultation scheduled for May 23-27, 1994, at Chinese Life Lutheran Church, Alhambra, California, and invited Wong to participate in developing and organizing it with him.

Another shift

Little did Wong know that within months after the October 1993 steering committee meeting, another round of reconfiguration would take place within CMM and the director for Asian ministries position would be eliminated all together. Wong remained as the director for the Multicultural Mission Strategy, beginning on April 1, 1994. He was also responsible for the Anti-Racism Training Institute, a program to train a cadre of people to do antiracism workshops in synods.

In the absence of an Asian ministries director, Nakamura, who once served as interim director, was contracted as a consultant for Asian ministries.

The staff reconfiguration was less than satisfactory. Thus, in the following year another round of restructuring occurred after the February steering committee meeting. Wong reported to the committee at its October meeting, "This year is the fourth consecutive year that my position description has changed. I am again serving as the Director for Asian Ministries. I am again redeveloping the CMM Asian ministries program." [27] He continued to serve as the director for the Multicultural Mission Strategy as well. In the latter capacity, he was responsible for the Multicultural Mission Institute and oversaw the implementation of the Multicultural Mission Strategy.

Once again Wong had to reconnect with the Asian ministries, workers, pastors, and leaders. Within a short period he made 22 visits. In addition, he also formed a partnership with Moy "in developing the following leadership projects: Southeast Asian Theological Education Seminar, Asian Leaders Advisory Group, and a Chinese pastors gathering." [28]

The topic of Asian-specific resources had been under discussion for quite some time, even before the birth of the ELCA. Wong was very much mindful of the need for such tools and the time and energy that had gone into the discussion over the years. After he resumed his position as the director for Asian ministries, he began working with Ms. Evelyn Soto, director for multilingual ministries resources, DCM, in developing such resources. The process was painful for Wong and his efforts did not result in the production of many Asian-specific publications.

Both developing and implementing ministry strategies were also very much on Wong's mind. Accordingly, he once again became a partner in DO's effort to develop a strategy for South Asian outreach, leading eventually to the development of the first South Asian ministry in Illinois. Wong also worked with DO in developing its strategies for Chinese and Korean ministries to the point where they reached the implementation stage. Concerned with the mission of the church, Wong assisted DO in implementing these strategies.

After 1995 the CMM staff configuration was mostly in place, with Wong being the only staff holding two positions.

Mission Accomplished

The constant shifting of his position during the last four plus years of his ministry in CMM, coupled with the challenge of dealing with the ambiguity, resistance, and hostility on part of some people toward multicultural ministries, Wong's ability to develop continuity in Asian ministries clearly was limited and his efforts to recruit candidates for ministry was hampered as well. Yet under Wong's leadership 16 Asian ministries were added to the ELCA.

As the first director for Asian ministries, Wong plowed new furrows. He paved the way for subsequent development in Asian work through the various ministry strategies and softened the ground within churchwide offices and synods. His presence in the churchwide office also enabled various staff to become more aware of the Asian presence in America.

Return to the Parish

On August 9, 1996, Wong resigned. He left CMM shortly thereafter to become pastor of the Lutheran Church of the Incarnation in Davis, California, on October 6. CMM's announcement of his resignation reads in part:"Bill Wong has been a faithful partner with us....His departure will truly be a great loss for the commission. His departure also leaves me [Director Rajan] with the loss of a personal confidant and friend." [29]

In the meantime, I served as interim director for Asian ministries from October 1, 1996, to February 28, 1997.

NEW MAN AT THE HELM

On March 1, 1997, Rev. Pongsak Limthongviratn assumed the directorship for Asian ministries. Within a year his title was changed from director for Asian ministries to director for Asian and Pacific Islander ministries to reflect the current reality of membership.

Limthongviratn, whose grandparents went to Thailand in 1930 from Southern China, was born on November 16, 1955, in Piehit, Thailand, into a third generation Christian family. His grandfather owned a small business and his father was in the auto body and mechanic business. His father was also a lay evangelist who, together with his eight brothers and three sisters, started four congregations in different parts of Thailand. Two of these congregations eventually joined the Church of Christ in Thailand, while the other two became members of the Evangelical Fellowship of Thailand. His mother was a native Thai whose family was torn apart during World War II. A member of the Chinese church in Bangkok later adopted her. He is a third-generation Christian. Limthongviratn joined the Lutheran church in 1977 after the first two Lutheran missionaries came to Thailand from Norway.

Before coming to the United States in 1989 for further education,

Limthongviratn himself was an evangelist, church planter, theological educator, author, editor, and translator. His first exposure to higher education was at St. Louis Commercial College in Bangkok from which he received a Dip. in Commerce in 1974. His heart, however, was not in the business world. Thus, he decided to pursue theological studies. First he went to the Bangkok Institute of Theology from which he received a Dip.Th. in 1977. From there he continued his theological education at the Lutheran Theological Seminary in Hong Kong from which he obtained the B.Th. degree in 1981 and the M.Div. degree in 1983.

Returning to Thailand after graduation, Limthongviratn started Hua Mark Lutheran Church in 1983. In 1985 he started the Laksi Lutheran Church and worked there until 1989. At the same time, he served two theological educational institutions. He was on the faculty of the Bangkok Institute of Theology from 1983 to 1989 and on the staff of the Lutheran Institute of Theological Education from 1984 to 1988. He also served as dean at the latter institution for the academic year 1986 to 1987.

Limthongviratn is prolific in the area of Christian literature. He authored *A Dictionary of Theological Terminology* (1989) and translated into Thai the following works: *Christian Stewardship* (1986), *Augsburg Confessions* (1987) and *Law and Gospel* by C. W. Walther (1989), and *Fundamental Christian Beliefs* (1990) and *The Life of St. Paul* (1992) by William Arndt. In 1984 he was the editor of Martin Luther's Small Catechism and in 1985 he served as a coeditor of Luther's Large Catechism when these two works were translated into Thai.

In the fall of 1989, he became a student at the Lutheran School of Theology at Chicago (LSTC) from which he obtained a Th.M. degree in 1991 and a Ph.D. degree in 2000. While he was studying at LSTC, he also began a ministry with Thais in the Chicago area. This congregation, Thai Community Church of Chicago, is the first in the history of the ELCA and its predecessor bodies. It joined the ELCA in 1993.

Continuation and Expansion

In his present capacity, Limthongviratn continues the work of the "Yee and Wong eras." [30] He has expanded our work as well. Under his leadership, the number of ministries has increased from 55 to 75 and the percentage of congregations becoming self-supporting has jumped from 25 to 35 percent. He has brought in 25 new leaders in Asian ministries. During his tenure, a Center for Chinese Ministry was established and the Chinese ministry study program at LS and PLTS, initiated before his time, also came to fruition. In addition, he paved and guided the way for U.S. Asian Lutherans and the Lutherans in Asia to form, for the first time ever, an official international network.

Joy and Sorrow

His present position has brought him both joy and sorrow. The maturity and growth as well as the occasional gatherings of the Asian-Pacific Islander Lutheran community bring Limthongviratn a sense of joy and satisfaction. Adequate funds to expand the mission of the church are lacking, however, because CMM is not a program unit. This disturbs him. Though he feels that he is well respected, he has observed that sometimes others treat the commissions in the ELCA structure as second-class units and do not take them seriously. That saddens him.

Limthongviratn, however, is a man who welcomes challenges. And as the first Protestant Thai trained in systematic theology, he shoulders heavy burdens and faces immense ministry opportunities in the United States and in Thailand.

FROM RELUCTANT PREACHER TO EXECUTIVE DIRECTOR

Rajan's first position in CMM was that of associate director for advocacy, a position he held for one year. His responsibilities included advocacy for the four communities and working with the Lutheran Office for Governmental Affairs (LOGA). Rajan's position changed three times within his first four years in the unit.

Rajan was born on October 15, 1949, in Tamil Nadu, India, when his native land was in the process of nation building. This place was "blessed with heavy winds coming from the Indian Ocean and the high mountains that surround the inland." [31] Childhood for Rajan was typical. He was raised in the Arcot Lutheran Church, "organized in 1913, 50 years after the Danish Missionary Society began work in North Arcot." [32] After high school, he attended Annamalai University and in 1971 received his B.A. degree in economics and statistics-political science. In 1975 he received his M.A. degree in economics from Madras University. Both institutions are in Tamil Nadu. Within a year after graduation, he married and moved to the United States for future studies and employment. He and his wife, Sheila, intended to make a new life for themselves and to earn some money to support their families in India.

They settled in Tacoma, Washington, in 1977. His wife found employment as a nurse while he became a student at Faith Evangelical Lutheran Seminary (FELS) in Tacoma, [33] from which he obtained an M.Div. degree in 1980 and a Th.M. degree in 1981. After he completed his theological education, he felt reluctant to enter into the ordained ministry. He did not find the theology presented by FELS faculty to coincide with his personal understanding of what Lutheran theology was all about.

In the following year, the Rajans moved to Houston, Texas, where he spent three years in CPE at Herman Hospital. His plan was to become a clinical pastoral educator. During his residency at Herman Hospital he was intro-duced to this author who, together with Martin L. Yonts, tried to persuade him to become an ordained pastor, but to no avail.

A Reluctant Preacher

Rev. Philip Wahlberg, bishop of the Texas-Louisiana Synod, however, succeeded in persuading him to change his mind. Rajan was ordained in 1985, after receiving a call from Holy Trinity Lutheran Church, Irving, Texas, where he served as pastor for two-and-a-half years before his appointment to CMM.

During his pastorate in Irving, Rajan served the church in a variety of capacities. He wrote the Asian section of *Living Waters of Faith Cultural Awareness Series* and was the recorder for the Cultural Awareness Series Steering Committee. He was president of the Association of Asian Lutherans in North America and edited the association's newsletter. For the synod, he chaired the multicultural ministries committee and the cross-cul-tural ministry committee. He served as the secretary of the synod's mission committee.

A Step Closer to the Top

"The Evangelical Lutheran Church in America at the Constituting Convention in 1987 adopted the following goals: It shall be a goal of this church that within 10 years of its establishment its membership shall include at least 10 percent people of color and/or primary language other than English (5.10.A87.)." [34]

In the following year, in response to this goal, the Multicultural Mission Strategy Task Force (MMSTF) was established. It "was made up of rep-resentatives from the African American, Asian, [35] Hispanic, and Native American communities; the Conference of Bishops and the Church Council; executive directors of the DO, DM, DCL, Commission for Communication, and CMM; executive assistant to the bishop of the church; and the bishop of this church who chaired the task force." [36] MMSTF was in need of a staff to coor-dinate its work.

Lewis promised to provide a person from his staff to coordinate the work and appointed Rajan to be the director for the Multicultural Mission Strategy in 1989. He was to coordinate the activities of the six working groups and the task force itself. Rajan did an impressive job in coordination.

The task force completed its work in 1991. The ELCA churchwide assembly in the same year adopted the strategy. Now Rajan's job was to over-see its implementation by various groups within the church. But before he had a chance to work with the different units in the church to implement the strategy, Lewis resigned. Rajan was elected to take his place in 1992.

The Shape of CMM

Under the able leadership of Lewis, CMM staff in the first few years of the unit's existence had to develop directions, guidelines, and relationships with other churchwide units. In addition, CMM faced intra-ethnic rivalries, rapid staff turnover, as well as racism, "resistance and hostility toward the full participation of African American, Asian, Hispanic, and Native American peoples in the life of this church." [37]

Furthermore, three years or so into the life of the ELCA, "under Focusing for Mission," a program of restructuring the churchwide units, commissions were established "to address specific tasks of particular urgency for the church." [38] However, "neither the governing documents [nor] Church Council actions... defined the particular urgency for which the CMM has been commissioned." [39] Under this new rubric, steering committees rather than boards governed commissions.

Though observers agreed that the ELCA by then had "changed—a little," [40] it was not enough to prevent Lewis from letting out some anguished cries before he joined the presiding bishop's staff:

> Genuine commitment to justice on [the] part of some in our church has disguised or obscured a strong neoconservative mentality among some members which gravitates away from true justice and equality as we understand it. These neoconservatives claim dedication to equality and justice for all, but are strongly opposed to any specific measures to achieve those objectives. They fail to see that noncooperation with evil is as essential as cooperation with good. Racism and malevolent ethnocentrism are among the principalities and powers with which we must contend. These threats take us by way of the cross, and cause us to ask are we worthy of our calling. [41]

Then he turned his attention to the ethnic communities. "The African American, Asian, Hispanic, and Native American membership is called from the periphery of the church to prophesy," he maintained, but "the silence of African American, Asian, Hispanic, and Native American prophecy is deafening!" [42] Others experienced the pain and anguish Lewis felt as well.

By the time Rajan took over the position of executive director, the ELCA had experienced a series of budget cuts, staff reductions, unit reconfigurations, and low morale in the churchwide office. CMM was no exception. In addition to the lack of genuine commitment to justice, the resurgence of neoconservative mentality, and the silence of the ethnic communities in face of increasing oppression described by Lewis, CMM also had to deal with its "ambiguous, if not ambivalent," [43] role and function. CMM was in search of an identity and a course for action. The unit itself further experienced rapid staff change along with increased expectations and workload.

CMM was not in good shape. Observers further agreed, though there might not be any fault on part of the staff, that the CMM staff was not very effective in dealing with the "principalities and powers."

Challenges and Opportunities

Thus far in the history of any Lutheran church in North America, Rajan is the only Asian to hold such a high-level position. In his first report to the steering committee at its March 1992 meeting, he spoke of challenges and opportunities. In actuality he faced more challenges than opportunities. In his first month as executive director, for example, he had to deal with the staffing needs of the commission. He assigned Wong to take over the position vacated by him; promoted Maria Suarez, a senior secretary, to be an assistant director for administration when Martin Smith was transferred to another department; and appointed Carmen Rabell, a senior secretary, to be interim director for Hispanic ministries when "Tito Moreno resigned due to failing health." [44] As for the position vacated by Wong, he appointed Nakamura as interim director for Asian ministries. He intended to begin a search for a permanent director for Hispanic ministries in May.

In the meantime, he faced another round of budget cuts, which left him with no choice but to reduce funding for the advisory group meeting and for racial justice work. He also had to leave the associate director for racial justice advocacy position unfilled.

In view of the staff changes and vacancies, he decided that the unit's program priorities needed to be reviewed and promised the steering committee that he would give the members a report to consider at the fall 1992 meeting. In the midst budget cuts and staff reconfigurations, Rajan also had to finish three major projects under his direction as the director for the Multicultural Mission Strategy. [45]

Though the tone of his first report was optimistic, Rajan knew that there were further challenges ahead. Sooner or later he had to make CMM more effective in dealing with the "principalities and powers."

Merger, Quotas, and Budget Cuts

Before Rajan had a chance to review the unit's program priorities, he faced another round of budget cuts, which, all things considered, was not as serious as the fate of CMM and the challenge to the representational principles. It appears that during his first years as the presiding bishop of the church, Dr. Herbert W. Chilstrom visited a large number of clergy and listened to their concerns, one of which was CMM within the structure of the church. Accordingly "in his report to the Church Council at its Spring 1992 meeting," [46] Chilstrom raised the matter of revisiting the structural changes made under

"Focusing for Mission." The intent was another round of restructuring, "including merging the Commission for Women and the Commission for Multicultural Ministries with other churchwide units." [47]

Merging CMM with another unit would end the existence of the commission. It would also violate the intent of the people who advocated its inclusion into the structure as an independent unit. Its function was to enable the church to increase the membership of people of color by 10 percent within the first 10 years of the ELCA and to ensure justice for all. Chilstrom sent a letter to some key people in the church for advice. He received a number of letters, including my response, against the merger. Chilstrom's top staff and Rajan threatened to resign if the merger took place. Chilstrom dropped the matter.

The issue of the representational principles came from participants at the Call to Faithfulness conference. This event brought together self-identified "evangelical Catholics" to discuss the newly emerging ELCA. This group and some theologians began to challenge the principles from theological and confessional perspectives. Rajan was concerned and, in a characteristic understatement, he stated "we need to pay close attention to this trend." [48]

Subsequently the issue was referred to the administrative subcommittee of the Church Council for consideration. The subcommittee later "recommended a process by which the commission would study and report to the ELCA Church Council." [49] CMM studied the issue and recommended that the representational principles be retained as they were. The 1995 churchwide assembly reaffirmed the principles.

Though under pressure from within and without, Rajan was determined to move ahead with the extension of ministry and relationship building. He took steps to strengthen the relationship with synods by changing Ms. Tammy Jackson's title from associate director for synodical ministries to director and by providing "leadership training and support to the synod multicultural ministry leadership" [50] and other churchwide units. Thus, in June 1992, for example, CMM teamed up with DO to organize a consultation on Arab and Middle Eastern ministry, eventually resulting in the creation of the CMM Arab and Middle Eastern ministry program in 1995.

New Projects

In his efforts to extend the ministry of church, Rajan realized that ministry must come from within the community. It was important to strengthen the communities and the individuals engaged in multicultural ministries. It was equally important that he listen to and learn from the people. Accordingly, he took further steps to strengthen the partnership with synods and associations as well as to hold town meetings at different locations throughout the church.

Leadership preparation was another area to which Rajan turned his attention. He initiated a leadership development program to enhance the skills of the ethnic leaders holding positions in the church. He also realized that effective ministry could not be done in the ethnic communities without culturally- and theologically-appropriate resources. Furthermore, the root cause of injustice must be addressed. The program he proposed to deal with injustice was the establishment of the Anti-Racism Training Institute. "The goal of this project is to train four individuals from each of seven synods [initially] to conduct anti-racism training and education in their own synods and to provide them with resources to do so effectively." [51] The training and education was to be held annually. The first resource was "a user-friendly videotape with a study guide, to sensitize youth to the effects of racism on individuals and society and share ways in which youth can become active partners in dismantling racism." [52]

In the meantime, the CMM budget was cut by $60,000.

Forging Ahead

As the ELCA continued to establish and shape itself, each church-wide unit was expected to develop program directions for the coming years. In October 1993, Rajan presented to the steering committee his version of Major Program Directions for 1995-1997, [53] along with a concept paper on ethnic ministry programs. [54] Both of these papers were predicated on the assumption that the steering committee, of which I was chair, would approve the new mission statement for CMM. In both of these papers, Rajan showed boldness in his commitment to multicultural ministry and his maturity in the work. The steering committee approved his program directions and adopted the mission statement.

Faced with budget cuts and realizing perhaps that staff effectiveness needed to be better utilized, Rajan at the March 1994 steering committee meeting presented a plan for restructuring and staff reduction. The steering committee gave its tentative approval, provided that Rajan's consultation with Rev. Robert N. Bacher, executive for administration, and Chris Stein, director for human resources, was successful.

On March 15, 1994, Rajan had a telephone conference call with four executive committee members. [55] (As chair I would have been part of this discussion, but I was out of the country.) Rajan informed them that he had consulted with both Bacher and Stein and that "the implementation plans for staff reduction are within the policies and procedures of the ELCA." [56] Then he outlined his plans. The date for implementation would be April 1, 1994. The two directorships to be terminated would be those of Rev. Jerome Dorsey and Rev. Gordon Straw.

On March 28, 1994, Rajan had another telephone conference call with the four members of the executive committee. It was obvious that by this time, some problems had surfaced. Rev. Callon Holloway, vice chair, raised concerns expressed by several members of the steering committee. After considerable discussion, it was agreed "that the implementation plan presented by Pastor Rajan at the Steering Committee meeting March 11-12, 1994, was intended to be a proactive one as a result of the Zero-Base Budget process and was to become effective at the direction of the Executive Director." [57]

On April 1, 1994, Rajan implemented the plan. Ministry consultants replaced the ethnic ministry directors. [58] Paul Nakamura was appointed Asian ministry consultant.

Turbulent Year

Rajan's plan was not popular and came under intense fire from three ethnic communities. [59] On April 3, Rajan flew to Oakland, California. The next day he met with me at an airport hotel. Together we tried to come up with a plan to respond to the criticisms and misinformation, but to no avail.

On May 9, 1994, I convened a teleconference meeting with the members of the executive committee and Rajan. He reported "an enormous amount of misinformation and discussion" [60] on his April 29 memorandum regarding reorganization of CMM. He further reported that there seemed "to be concern that the ELCA [was] backing away from its commitment to mul-ticultural ministry...[there was also] a perception that the elimination of the Ethnic Ministry directors positions occurred without input from the steering committee." [61]

Rajan further announced that there would be a summit of associa-tion presidents in June to discuss unit reorganization, funding to the associ-ations, and leadership development.

As a result of the June meeting, a multicultural summit with Chilstrom, CMM staff, and members of the steering committee was scheduled for October 13-15 at a conference center outside Chicago. Chilstrom himself presided over this stormy and emotionally-charged meeting. At the end of the gathering, the decision to restore the positions of ethnic ministry direc-tors was reached. Rajan accepted the decision and proceeded to restore those positions immediately. It was further agreed that beginning with the next steering committee meeting, association presidents would attend all subsequent meetings with voice but no vote.

A Splendid Idea

In the Multicultural Mission Strategy a goal was set that by the year 1998, 500,000 of the ELCA members would be African American, Asian, Hispanic, and Native American. In 1994 this category of membership stood at 106,000. The strategy was not working.

Rajan was obviously disturbed about this. "Our beginning was an Easter event!" he asserted in his report to the steering committee. "We should not forget our freedom is in the resurrection. We should not forget that out of darkness comes light, out of hopelessness comes hope, out of pain comes joy, out of emptiness comes fulfillment." [62] Then he let out his rallying cry, "Let us keep on moving, moving with our eyes set on Jesus." [63]

In the back of his mind, Rajan was trying to discern how to keep on moving. An idea came in 1996. Viewing the statistical report on ethnic membership, he realized that there was something seriously wrong. Instead of growing, African American and Hispanic congregations were experiencing a membership decline while Asian and Native American membership remained unchanged. Rajan knew what was wrong. The question in his mind was how to reverse to trend and enable the congregations to grow.

He realized that "three things are essential for the effective work of ethnic ministries:…, accountability, responsibility, and urgency," [64] which were [and still are] absent from the present structure of the ELCA. To remedy the situation, he proposed an idea of having nongeographical ethnic synods. [65]

The steering committee debated, at length, the merit of such an idea, but in the end felt that it was "unprepared at this time to affirm or negate the idea." [66] The committee encouraged its members to consult with their respective communities and report their findings at the next steering committee meeting. It further asked the executive director "to consult with other churchwide units and executive staff regarding the creation and viability of nongeographical synods." [67]

The idea eventually reached the Conference of Bishops. A sense spirit prevailed that the time had not yet come to implement such a splendid idea.

A House in Order

Beginning in 1996, CMM finally reached a point of stability in staffing, operation, and financial support. Rajan turned his attention to expanding CMM's connection with other denominations and the international scene. Its anti-racism program was copied by other denominations. The Arab and Middle Eastern ministry was firmly in place. Rajan himself began to venture out into the global scene, making connections and forming partnerships.

But as he surveyed the scene within the ELCA, Rajan encountered a dream still unrealized. Ten years into the life of the ELCA, the goal of 10 percent membership of people of color was nowhere in sight, though his staff in partnership with other units had devised various ethnic-specific strategies for mission. The number of seminarians of color was fewer than before. The few faculty of color at different seminaries were aging rapidly, without replacements coming up through the pipeline.

On the other hand, membership in ethnic congregations had grown somewhat. The anti-racism program drew greater attention and support. The associations were becoming stronger. The Chinese ministry study program was established at LS and PLTS. [68] Multicultural ministry seemed to have arrived at a crossroads. Rajan interpreted these challenges as a sign of opportunity. He was determined to make the most out of the situation.

Eight Windmills

In the spring of 1999, Rajan began circulating a few ideas among his friends and confidants. He was once again wondering how to make the system more responsive to the ethnic communities and how to enable the ELCA to be truly multicultural. His friends encouraged him to develop his ideas further, resulting in a concept paper entitled "Windmills." [69] The steering committee enthusiastically approved the eight "windmills," and expected progress reports at future meetings.

The eight windmills he offered in this paper were: (1) the gift of the churchwide staff, (2) scholar-in-residence program, (3) seminary-college partnership, (4) teaching churches, (5) ethnic ministry centers, (6) mission to the USA, (7) internship, and (8) mega-multicultural education events. Under each heading, he laid out his arguments and detailed a program in response to the need. In the scholar-in-residence program, for example, he pointed out the present ethnic seminary faculty situation and future needs. Then he proposed "that all eight seminaries set aside funds each year beginning with the year 2000 for a person of color ELCA member to receive a Ph.D. degree in theology." [70] The seminary presidents welcomed this idea. Rajan further acknowledged that this was not a new idea. LSTC already had such a program.

The eight windmills were well received by others also, because they fit into the existing structure and could be implemented.

At the March 3-4, 2000, steering committee meeting, Rajan reported, "Since the last steering committee meeting, I [have] shared the 'windmills' with many people. I am pleased with the affirmation and support that I received for these ideas. ... Currently, this director is putting together a consultation on implementing this plan." [71]

Moving On

CMM today is a different commission from the day Rajan took over as its executive director. It has found its identity and a niche in mission. The ELCA too has changed—a little more! Rajan the preacher was right when he cried, "Let us keep on moving, moving with our eyes set on Jesus."

13

ON THE MOVE

AFTER THE BIRTH OF THE ELCA, A NUMBER OF ASIANS WERE ON THE MOVE within the churchwide, synodical, and regional expressions of this church. This chapter describes the ministry of these Asian leaders in the new church and two Asian ministries initiated by the ELCA.

JAMES MOY: FROM SOCIAL MINISTRY TO THEOLOGICAL EDUCATION

By the time Dr. James Y. K. Moy joined the churchwide staff in 1988 as a director for program development in the Division for Social Ministry Organizations (DSMO) in Chicago, he had served the church as a pastor, college administrator, program development specialist, director for a Lutheran Social Services agency, and an assistant to a bishop. His intellectual curiosity, professional competence, and skills provide him with a well-supplied toolbox for ministry. He does not give people the impression of self-importance nor has he displayed an air of arrogance. He is an excellent storyteller; he knows how to engage a listener's attention.

Early Years

Moy was born at home on March 15, 1934, in New York City's Chinatown. His father, a Confucian, immigrated to the United States at an early age. His mother, from a wealthy Christian family in Hong Kong, came to America after her arranged marriage to his father. This arrangement—although common—was not a compatible one. His father was in the restaurant business and became prosperous during Word War II. His mother stayed home to care for the family and never learned English. The Moys lived in an apartment at 33-37 Mott St., commonly known as *sun lau* (new building), where many prosperous families resided. The building was "a vertical Chinese village. All the doors were always open, and everyone moved freely from apartment to apartment. The women could have a social life without leaving the building, while the children actually had dozens of mothers and fathers... they would invariably address as 'Auntie' or 'Uncles.'" [1]

When Moy was in the third grade, the family moved to Brooklyn where his father had a restaurant. This move caused Moy to lose a year at school, as his English was weak. His family decided to move back to Chinatown.

After their move back to Manhattan, Moy resumed his friendships and began going to True Light Lutheran Church to join his friends. True Light was a supportive community. One of the anecdotes Moy tells was that of a Sunday school teacher, a white woman, who told her class that the world was coming to an end. "We are in the eleventh hour," [2] she said. This was quite frightening. The most significant person in Moy's life at that point was Helen Wu, a Sunday school teacher who befriended him in those early years. She supported him and became almost a surrogate parent.

Sports and church activities became a major part of his life. Another significant person in his early life was Calvin Gum, who taught Moy how to box and play the piano. Gum also became his Cub Scout master; he would take the children hiking and camping. Moy was active in the congregation's youth and scouting programs; he played basketball on the church's team. He was happy to go anywhere with an adult who would pay attention to him.

Moy was greatly influenced by these individuals and church activities. After a year of confirmation instruction, he was confirmed. He said he liked the class so much he decided to repeat it! Moy may be the only person in North America to have done so.

At one point in his teenage years, Kunsch, his pastor, loaned him Kretzam's Commentary on the Book of Luke. Moy read it thoroughly. "In fact, that's when I think I probably became a Christian," he reflected. After reading the story account of the crucifixion, Moy recalled an emotional experience when he decided to "give [his] life to Christ." He was baptized on May 11, 1944, and, though his parents never joined the congregation, church life and his growing interest in faith studies had a major impact on his life. By the time he went to Valparaiso University, from which he obtained a B.A. degree in 1956, his spiritual foundation had been laid. While Moy was in college, Helen Wu continued to write long letters to him, giving him encouragement and support. "Oh, another epistle from Helen!" his roommate would quip.

Cultural Transition

Moy had grown up in two worlds torn with cultural and value conflicts—Chinatown and the Western world. When he arrived at Valparaiso University in the fall of 1952, he decided to take advantage of this new world and severed his relationship in Chinatown. It also became clear to him that he had to learn proper English in order to survive freshman composition! He even had to learn how to use a knife and fork in the cafeteria.

Life at Valparaiso was filled with new friendships and academic success. Those years helped him to relate to whites and find his own identity. The most significant faculty member he had was Dr. Elsa Dronberger, a sociology professor who taught him the value of being a "marginal person." The concept of marginality influenced him greatly.

Moy was introduced to Mabel L.Y. Chin in the summer of 1956. He was a student at CTS in Springfield, Illinois, while Chin studied at BS in New York City. The two corresponded with each other extensively, became engaged in June of 1957, and were married in December of that year.

Discovery and Higher Education

After a year at CTS, Moy decided that The LCMS theologically was not the right institution for him. The espoused theology differed significantly from his experience at True Light. He learned there were great differences in theology in the English District and the rest of The LCMS. So he transferred to BS and eventually joined a ULCA church in Brooklyn. He spent two years at BS before transferring to Gettysburg Seminary, Gettysburg, Pennsylvania, for his Lutheran year, and received his B.D. degree in 1960. He was ordained in the same year after receiving a call to Christ Lutheran Church, Germantown, New York, as its pastor. By his own admission, Moy "did a good job" at Christ. But he was also interested in campus ministry. Dr. Henry Hetland, executive director for campus ministry, LCUSA, suggested that he pursue graduate work, and Dr. Alfred Beck, president of New York and New England Synod, ULCA, suggested that he apply for a synod fellowship.

In the winter of 1962, armed with a Samuel Trexler Foundation Fellowship, he went to Columbia University, New York City, to study guidance counseling and student services in higher education on a part-time basis, while serving the parish. In 1963 he was awarded an M.A. degree and accepted a position at Macalester College, St. Paul, Minnesota, as dean of men, assistant dean of students.

In August 1966, he was awarded a Bush Leadership Fellowship and took courses at the business school and the divinity school at Harvard University and the Episcopal Theological Seminary in Cambridge, Massachusetts. The program included an internship, which he did in the office of the vice president for development at Ohio University. He remained on campus from 1968 to 1971 and continued to work and study.

He served as supply preacher at St. Paul Lutheran Church, New Haven, West Virginia, from 1968 to 1969, and accepted a call to be its pastor in 1969.

A Critical Lesson

In 1971 he accepted an appointment at Wartburg College, an ALC institution in Waverly, Iowa, as director for student affairs (dean of students). By this time, Moy saw the value in working as a layperson at a Lutheran institution and when confronted with an LCA polity that would drop him from the clerical roster, he accepted that decision. The president of the college offered to write a supporting letter that would enable him to serve on the clerical roster of the ALC, but he declined that offer. He felt that this ministry as a layperson was valid and did not need ordained status. At that time, Moy was the only senior administrative staff person who was a person of color. This proved to be a great benefit to the college when a racial incident occurred just a few days into the fall semester of 1971. He devoted an enormous number of hours relating to students, listening to their grievances, attending rallies, and soliciting assistance from faculty members to calm the campus from tension that the incident had provoked. His experience at Ohio University during the Kent State University shooting and campus riots and demonstrations in the late 1960s proved invaluable. It was apparent that the college was unprepared to meet the needs of African American students who had been recruited. Moy today feels that "Lutheran colleges and seminaries will not change or respond to the needs of students of color on campus until there is a critical mass of such students who can voice their feelings honestly and critically."

He completed his Ph.D. degree in guidance counseling and student services in higher education in 1972.

Return to the Roster

In 1976 Moy and his family left Iowa and moved to Seattle. He and his spouse had agreed that whoever took the first job would encourage the other to pursue the next job. They also agreed to seek employment in a more cosmopolitan environment when their older son approached high school. So when there was a presidential change at Wartburg, the timing for their next move was ripe. His spouse was offered a position at the University of Washington in Seattle, so the family made its move. From 1976 to 1977 he was a program development specialist at Seattle Opportunity Industrialization Center, an African American organization. His chief responsibility was grant writing. Moy attended grantsmanship workshops and discovered that he enjoyed writing and was good at it. From 1977 to 1983, he served as executive director at Lutheran Community Services and then as area director at Lutheran Social Services (LSS) of Washington and Idaho in Tacoma, Washington. In 1977 he also returned to the clergy roster of the LCA.

In the following year, I met Moy in Tacoma at the Asian caucus meeting where he was elected president of the Asian organization of the LCA.

Assistant to the Bishop—Round One

In 1983, Rev. Thomas Blevins, an assistant to the bishop, was elected bishop of the Pacific Northwest Synod. Shortly after he took office, he decided to assemble a new staff to work with him. Moy was appointed to serve simultaneously as assistant to the bishop and DMNA deployed staff. In this position, he was able to utilize the full range of his training and skills in working with congregations and with synod and churchwide staff. He guided and counseled both established congregations and missions under development with skills, knowledge, and enthusiasm.

During his years in Washington, Moy also taught courses in communication to first-line supervisors in the Air Force at McChord Air Force Base in Tacoma, Washington, through the University of Eastern Washington and subsequently through Chapman College. Teaching assignments took him to the following places: Elmendorf AFB, Alaska; Anderson AFB, Guam; Hickam AFB, Hawaii; and Wright Patterson AFB, Ohio. "It was always a challenge to teach men and women whose Commanding Officers 'ordered' them to take that class." Moy was up to the challenge and received consistent outstanding evaluations from his students.

A Move to the Churchwide Office

Moy's first position in the churchwide office was that of director for program development in DSMO. He worked with program directors of LSS agencies across the ELCA, assisted in the development of a grants process for the division, and focused on the need to serve the poor by encouraging agencies to evaluate their program and how they could improve the delivery of services. His special interest included the development of a "Request for Proposal" to LSS agencies interested in training pastors to work with victims of domestic violence and sexual abuse.

When Rev. Joseph Wagner, executive director of DM, asked him to consider joining the staff as director for inclusive leadership development in 1989, Moy gladly accepted the position. His responsibilities included implementation of the Alternate Route for Admission to the Roster of Ordained Ministry policy, recruitment of candidates of color for ordained ministry, distribution of financial assistance to multicultural seminary students, and development of theological education programs for Southeast Asian candidates on the alternate route. He served as advisor to alternate route committees at various seminaries and found special satisfaction in working with multicultural faculty of the ELCA seminaries.

Moy enjoyed working with his supervisor, Dr. Phyllis Anderson, director for theological education. They had a good relationship built on mutual trust and respect. In this position too Moy teamed up with the staff of CMM in delivering theological education to the ethnic communities in the ELCA as well as providing counsel on recruitment matters. He recognized the limited number of candidates within the church. His plans were to go beyond the church in the United States to recruit qualified persons for ministry, but these plans became entangled in the web of interchurch relations.

Moy faced a further problem—budget reduction—in the early days of the ELCA. His budget had been reduced from $250,000 to $30,000, but this did not discourage him. He put his grant-writing skills to work and obtained funding for many programs through Lutheran Brotherhood fraternal insurance company.

Moy has consistently tried to find ways to improve himself and to increase his skills and knowledge through continuing education and workshops. One of the workshops that impacted him significantly was the SRI organization in Lincoln, Nebraska. SRI is a "head hunting" firm. Its staff developed a structural interview process they found helpful in selecting top executives across the country. Moy attended a workshop in 1990.

Several months later, Moy went to Fuller Theological Seminary to meet Dr. Charles Ridley to talk to him about "culturally biased testing instruments." During the conversation, he discovered that Ridley had independently developed a process similar to SRI's and written a manual about it. Moy's curiosity was totally aroused and bought a Ridley manual, which he immediately passed on to Malcolm L. Minnick, DO. Subsequently, Ridley was contracted as a consultant to assist DO in developing an instrument for selecting pastor-developers. This resulted in DO's adoption of a "Behavior Structured Interview Process." Moy is rather proud to have discovered Ridley and considers this one of his major contributions to the ELCA.

Assistant to Bishop—Round Two: Honor, Reflection and Retirement

In 1996 Moy returned to Seattle, Washington, to serve as assistant to the bishop of the Northwestern Washington Synod. The transition back to Seattle was an interesting one. Significant changes had occurred in his eight-year absence. When asked about it, Moy noted that "before the merger the attitude [of LCA clergy and parishioners] towards LS was 'keep out,' this was LCA territory. Now, the atmosphere has completely changed. The spirit of cooperation between our educational institutions such as Pacific Lutheran University, Trinity Lutheran College, and the Western Seminary Cluster consisting of PLTS and Luther was much more noticeable than before. It was change for the better." The big shock was his discovery of former ALC congregations' reaction to the office of synod bishop. The ALC polity had been significantly different, so it was an adjustment to be aware that his presence at some churches was not always welcome. "There seems to be more suspicion,... more distrust,... and less of a sense of church in its broader sense. I am sorry to see that," Moy lamented.

His service to the church and the academic community spans forty years. In recognition of his service, Valparaiso University in 1989 honored him with an award. The citation reads in part: "The Valparaiso University Alumni Achievement Award is designed to honor alumni who have been widely recognized for outstanding achievement in their chosen career or area of professional life. James Y. K. Moy has demonstrated strong Christian leadership, integrity, and character. His skills, initiative, and dedication have reflected great credit on his alma mater."

Scheduled to retire in the spring of 2001, Moy reflects on his life, his career, and the church. On his life, "Well... it's been a long journey,... a long process of growth.... I was fortunate to have people who cared and sustained me through those early difficult years.... I am especially grateful for my spouse's love.... I thank God for bringing significant people into my life. I'm still growing." On his career, "I've always loved challenge, variety, and change. I'd hate to get bored in a job. There are not enough lifetimes to do all the things I would like to do,... but for this life the Lord has taken care of that." On the church, "the Lutheran church is a cultural church; that European cultural memory still sits smack in the middle of everything it does. I don't thing it can get out of its history. What is emerging is a rejection of that state church mentality from Europe. I think the sooner we recognize that, the sooner we can become a truly multicultural church."

In retirement, no one should expect Moy to be inactive. He is open to the possibility of serving as a consultant for congregational "revisioning." He plans on taking courses on Geographical Information Systems, horticulture, and commodities in the futures market and to work on projects on his Washington farm.

DIVISION FOR GLOBAL MISSION

As of this writing, there have been four appointments of Asian leaders to DGM staff. They include Stacy Kitahata, Franklin Ishida, Margrethe Kleiber, and Royan Yuen.

Stacy Kitahata: From Associate Director to LSTC Dean

Dean Stacy D. Kitahata is the first Asian Lutheran woman to be appointed to an administrative and faculty position among all Lutheran seminaries in North America. But before she was appointed to this position, Kitahta was on the staff of DGM. Kitahata, a *Sansei* (third generation) Japanese-American, was born in Los Angeles, California, and grew up in the city's South Central district. Both her paternal and maternal grandparents were immigrants from Japan. Her paternal grandparents, Buddhist by faith, operated a hog ranch in Artesia, California. Her maternal grandparents owned a laundry and dry cleaning business in Los Angeles. There her mother, Naoye, attended the Maryknoll mission school. Both families were doing well until World War II.

In 1942 both families were uprooted and sent to concentration camps. Kitahata's paternal family was sent to Arkansas, first to Jerome and later to Rohwer. Her maternal family was sent to Heart Mountain, Wyoming. "When the camps closed, each family lived in Chicago for several years waiting for a safe time to return to California,"[3] recalled Kitahata. While the families were in Chicago, Kitahata's mother and aunt attended Holy Names Catholic parish. One day the two sisters ventured to the church to see the priest for baptism, but the priest had no time for them. The two young women left hurt and disappointed. They never returned to Holy Names, nor sought baptism again.

Her mother's experience had an impact on Kitahata. "I grew up on this story," recalled Kitahata. "In many more ways than I realize it has shaped my own faith and ministry." Indeed, instead of the Roman Catholic faith that her mother had sought, young Kitahata attended a Lutheran Sunday school at Christ the King Lutheran Church in Torrance, California, and was baptized on July 17, 1977.

She was an active member of the church, becoming a member of the board of Christian education shortly after her baptism. This was the beginning of her service on numerous boards and committees throughout her professional life. Her congregational experience was supplemented by service projects, youth events, and local Christian music and worship activities.

After high school, Kitahata went to UCLA, from which she obtained a B.A. degree in psychology. When she graduated she had no idea what to do with such a degree. Her mother wanted her to pursue an M.B.A. degree but Kitahata was not sure. At the same time, LSS had an opening for a position as director of the Emergency Assistance Center in Los Angeles. Kitahata was hired and served as employment development counselor and emergency assistance coordinator from May 1984 to June 1986. From June 1986 to December 1987, she was the program director of the ALC's South Pacific District Hunger Program.

In the meantime, CNLC was busily at work, designing a new structure for the three merging Lutheran churches. Kitahata was appointed to a task force, which looked at the needs and interests of women and how they might be addressed in the new church. The task force recommended the establishment of the Commission for Women (CW) and a women's organization. Kitahata subsequently served on the design committee for Women of the ELCA at the constituting convention. She was the first person elected to the Women of the ELCA board.

With the establishment of the ELCA, Kitahata took a position as associate director for global mission education in DGM, with weighty responsibilities. Kitahata felt that "it was an exciting time to be involved with a church coming into being." Be that as it may, Kitahata as a young woman of color in the "new church" also had a role of embodying the representational principles and now faced the familiar Asian admonition to act and achieve in order to be a credit to family and culture. In addition, there were pressures to demonstrate that new leaders could also excel and were not only filling slots to project an image of diversity. Kitahata certainly fulfilled expectations and excelled in everything she did.

Despite her broad responsibilities, Kitahata found time to pursue her interest in theology. She attended LSTC part-time from 1993 to 1996 and McCormick Theological Seminary, Chicago, full-time from 1996 to 1997. She obtained her M.Div. degree in May 1997. In July 1997 she was appointed dean of the community and member of the faculty at LSTC.

Directors and Missionary Educator

On May 20, 1996, DGM announced "Rev. Franklin Y. Ishida has been appointed... Director for International Scholarships and International Communication." [4] Ishida assumed the office on July 1. Son of a Japanese missionary, Ishida is a man with global exposure before joining the staff of DGM.

He was born in Japan and received his education in Switzerland, Japan, the United States, and the United Kingdom. His B.A. degree is from St. Olaf College, Northfield, Minnesota, and his M.A. in international relations is from Lancaster University, U.K. Following graduate school, he served for two years in the Department of Communications of the World Council of Churches (WCC). On the side he "also assisted with editing *Laudamus*, the LWF worship book." [5]

"Following his service at WCC, he entered Luther Seminary, was ordained, and served two congregations in the Metro Chicago Synod." [6] While he was still a student at the seminary, Ishida became a member of the first Multicultural Writers Workshop sponsored by CMM. Since then he has written extensively for the ELCA and Augsburg Fortress. [7]

The DGM announcement of his appointment concludes with the following statement: "Pastor Ishida's knowledge of the global church, global issues, and the issues of international students... promise[s] great contributions to the ministry of DGM." [8]

On September 16, 1998, Rev. Margrethe Shizuko Chinen Kleiber became program director for South Asia. She is the first Asian Lutheran to hold such a position in the history of Lutheranism in North America. In this position, "Kleiber oversee[s] ministries and relationships in India, Indonesia, Nepal, Thailand, and Bangladesh." [9]

Kleiber was born and grew up in Hawaii. She received her B.A.

degree from Yale University, her master's degree in social work from the University of Hawaii, and her M.Div. degree from PLTS.

Before joining DGM, Kleiber served as a social worker in child protection services in Honolulu, Hawaii, and did "counseling and case work with runaway youth in Seattle, Washington." [10] She also spent three years in the "U.S. Peace Corps in the lowlands of Ecuador," [11] with her husband. She was ordained in 1993 and served as associate pastor of Tierrasanta Lutheran Church, San Diego, California, for five years.

Kleiber was the past chair of the AAPI—ELCA and was actively participating in planning the first ALIC conference when she joined DGM.

The fourth Asian to join DGM was Dr. Royan Yuen, who in 2000 became the first Asian to be sent as missionary-educator to his country of origin. Yuen was born and grew up in Hong Kong when it was still a British colony. There he received most of his higher education. In 1988 he came to GTU, Berkeley, California, for his Ph.D. degree in Old Testament studies. He was awarded the degree in 1996. DO subsequently appointed him as pastor-developer of Life Lutheran Church, Pinole, California. After the congregation was organized in 2000, Yuen accepted a position from DGM as missionary-educator assigned to Lutheran Theological Seminary of Hong Kong, where he teaches courses in Christian education and Old Testament.

JOB EBENEZER: DIVISION FOR CHURCH IN SOCIETY

Dr. Job S. Ebenezer joined the staff of Division for Church in Society (DCS) in January 1988 as an associate director for the world hunger program. He was responsible for "designing and implementing the hunger education program for the newly formed ELCA ... [and] initiated sustainable agricultural and... development programs at ELCA's outdoor ministry facilities, colleges, and universities" [12]

Before he joined DCS staff, Ebenezer had taught at a college and two universities as well as served as program director in various institutions in both India and the United States.

Ebenezer was born on October 10, 1941, in Vellore, India, where he grew up. He received both his B.Sc. (1960) and M.Sc. (1962) degrees in mathematics from the University of Madras, Madras, India, and M.Sc. (1967) in Aeronautical Engineering from the India Institute of Science, Bangalore, India. Later he came to the United States for his Ph.D. degree in mechanical engineering at the Stevens Institute of Technology, Hoboken, New Jersey. He was awarded the degree in 1973.

A year before he received his degree, he joined the faculty of New York Institute of Technology, Old Westbury. After four years there, he was appointed to the faculty of the University of New Mexico, Albuquerque. In 1980 he returned to his native India to assume the directorship of the Rural

Appropriate Technology Center, Madras, India. Returning to the United States in July 1981, he became an associate director of the Technical Vocational Division of the University of New Mexico-Valencia Campus, Belen. From 1983 until he joined the ELCA staff, he was the director of education at the Los Lunas Correctional Center, Los Lunas, New Mexico.

In 1992 he became director of environmental stewardship and hunger education. Since assuming the position, Ebenezer has developed numerous programs in environmental stewardship and hunger education, including a course on "Global Sustainability and the Churches' Role," a nine-hour seminar for fourth-year seminary students and pastors participating in continuing education.

Ebenezer became a Lutheran in 1981, because he "liked the social justice and hunger program of the Lutheran church...[and he thought he could] influence the hunger program of the Lutherans." [13] He strongly feels "that the churches in general and Lutherans in particular have not done enough in the area of environmental degradation...[which is] one of the major root causes of hunger."

One of Ebenezer's most innovative projects is a "roof-top garden on the seventh floor of the garage of the churchwide offices in Chicago." This project was featured in the *Chicago Tribune*, the *Christian Science Monitor*, and other newspapers, journals, and magazines. "This project has been replicated by Cook County Public Health [and] several churches in inner city neighborhoods." Moreover, "The Johns Hopkins School of Public Health, Boston University Medical Center, UCLA School of Public Health, and several institutions in Africa, Central America, and Asia have made inquiries about this project and are planning to replicate [it] for their public health projects."

The Environmental Protection Agency awarded him "a grant of $52,000 for establishing a program called 'Energy Star Congregation.'" Ebenezer plans "to recruit 15,000 congregations belonging to NCCC to reduce their energy consumption."

Ebenezer is also keenly aware of the rural crisis in the Midwest. Thus "with the cooperation of the South Central Wisconsin Synod, [he is] addressing the rural crisis through establishing a symbiotic community between rural churches and urban and suburban churches."

Ebenezer is not only an environmental steward, he is also a steward of the resources of the church. In his frequent travels, he often chooses to stay at the homes of friends or members of different parishes to save money on lodging. As a rule, he seldom rents a car. And yet for all his efforts at conservation and preservation, as well as contributions to the church and society, he says he receives "very little appreciation or support" from churchwide executives. He is convinced that racism is strong in the Lutheran Center and he fights "racism in [his] unit almost single-handedly." This is a painful experience for him. Ebenezer, however, is determined to "continue this fight no matter what it may cost. [He does] hope that this point of view is put forth to the Lutheran [people] of color community…[because some] feel that the human resources department has not treated the [people] of color fairly in their determination of [their] grades and salary."

DEPLOYED AND REGIONAL STAFF

In July 1989 DO appointed Rev. Yutaka Kishino to be a mission director. His territory covers both Southern California West and Pacifica synods.

Kishino, a descendant of a *samurai* family, was the first Asian Lutheran to be appointed as a deployed mission director. Born on January 3, 1952, into a Christian family in post-war Tokyo, the immediate Kishino family also observed some Buddhist rituals. This was done out of respect for the extended family, which is not Christian. Such practice did not pose a problem for the Kishinos because the rituals were so natural—being part of life itself. At school Kishino was the only Christian, but he encountered no difficulties. Kishino attributes this to the Japanese acceptance of other faiths.

After graduating from St. Paul's Episcopal High School in 1970, Kishino spent the following academic year in Redding, California, as a high school exchange student through the International Christian Youth Exchange program. He was a student at Enterprise High School. From there he went to the LCA's youth ministry camp in Great Barrington, Massachusetts, in the summer of 1971. Here Kishino sensed his call to enter into ordained ministry. However, before his camp experience, Kishino had been influenced by missionaries who encouraged him to inquire about ministerial studies and to come to the United States as an exchange student.

Returning to Japan after a summer at camp, Kishino enrolled at St. Paul's Episcopal University from which he obtained his B.A. degree in 1975. In the fall of the same year he became a student at Gettysburg Lutheran Seminary, Gettysburg, Pennsylvania, from which he received his M.Div. degree in 1979.

While he was a student at the seminary, Eiichi Matsushita took him under his wing. Matsushita guided him through the maze of institutional politics, shared insights on different bureaucratic personalities, and taught him gardening, an activity which Matsushita was fond of. Though a generation apart, the two had a close relationship. Kishino appreciated Matsushita's honesty, intellectual capacity, commitment to Christianity, and at the same time genuine openness to other religions.

After graduation from Gettysburg, he and Nancy Daufert of Lebanon, Pennsylvania, were united in marriage. The Kishinos have a daughter and a son.

Kishino was ordained in 1979 when he was called to serve as assistant pastor of Zion Lutheran Church in Philadelphia. In September 1983, he resigned his position at Zion and became an associate pastor of Resurrection Lutheran Church, Plano, Texas, where he served until May 1987. He was then called to be a mission-developer by DMNA. In that capacity, Kishino has the distinction of being the first Asian Lutheran to develop a non-Asian congregation in the Lutheran churches in North America. Within a year and half, he organized the congregation, which he continued to serve for another six months.

In his capacity as mission director, Kishino enjoys working with others to develop new ministries, with multicultural congregations, and with persons of color. But he also states that the lack of hospitality and the resistance to reach out to ethnic people by white English-speaking congregations are the major concerns for the ELCA's future. In this respect, what Kishino experiences in professional life mirrors what happens in his own life. Kishino has repeatedly experienced both affirmation and rejection in American society and in the church. He attributes this to racial and cultural conflicts and misunderstanding. But he is hopeful that his own Japanese-American children will have a better future.

Kishino also served the church in other capacities. He was a member of the management committee of DWME, LCA, chaired the multicultural commission of the Northern Texas-Northern Louisiana Synod, and served as a member of the Asian advisory committee of CMM.

After the establishment of the ELCA, the Conference of Bishops and DM appointed Dr. Asha Mary George-Guiser as deployed staff. Her territory covered Regions 7 and 8. George-Guiser was responsible for overseeing candidates for ordained and certified ministry in the candidacy process for 15 synods, coordinating mobility for pastors across the regions, assisting in continuing education and leadership support, setting up multidisciplinary diagnostic evaluation teams, and more. This was a challenging and fulfilling position for her but it also gave her "an opportunity to bring color and texture to the whole church." [14]

George-Guiser is a dynamic and engaging preacher and keynote speaker, a graceful liturgical dancer, and a caring but no-nonsense bureaucrat who demands high standards of performance for herself and for others. As a member of the Syrian Orthodox Church turned Lutheran, George-Guiser has the distinction in being the first in a number of areas of achievement. She was the first Asian Lutheran woman of Indian parentage to be ordained in the church; the first to serve on synod staff; and the first Asian Lutheran of either gender to preach at a churchwide assembly.

George-Guiser was born in Ahmadi, Kuwait, on September 9, 1957, and grew up in South India. Her early spiritual life was nourished by and nurtured in the Marthoma Church, a congregation of the Syrian Orthodox tradition. She never heard of the Lutheran church until Elizabeth Waid, a lay associate of the LCA, sponsored her to come to the United States in 1973. From that point on she "lived the church's teachings and core values to reach out to all persons in the name of Jesus."

After graduation in 1977 from Neuman College, Aston, Pennsylvania, with a B.S. degree, George-Guiser attended Lutheran Theological Seminary at Philadelphia. She obtained her M.Div. degree in 1982. The same year she received a call to be an associate pastor of St. James Lutheran Church, Coopersburg, Pennsylvania, where she served until 1984. This period was not a happy time in George-Guiser's life, but the learning experience was invaluable. "My first parish was an eye-opener," she recalled. "The people were ready for my 'otherness,' but the senior pastor and the synod were not."

In 1984 she married Rev. Kim Guiser and accepted a call as an assistant pastor at Christ Lutheran Church, Kulpsville, Pennsylvania, where she served until 1988. This was a constructive and healing period in her life. This call gave her time "to recover and heal from the first call's disillusionment."

In 1993 George-Guiser preached at the festival Eucharist at the ELCA churchwide assembly in Kansas City, Kansas. Wearing a colorful *sari*, a traditional dress of her native land, George-Guiser electrified the assembly with a sermon entitled, "ELCA—A New Jerusalem or a Jurassic Park?" She preached inclusiveness in the church as a way of the future. Her attire and her sermon content also drew a number of detractors who criticized her for not wearing proper ecclesiastical vestments on such an occasion and despised her sermon title. But on the whole, the experience was incredible for her and for the assembly. The listeners applauded repeatedly during her sermon and rose to their feet shouting and clapping at the end of her delivery. The assembly was nourished and moved by her message. George-Guiser was affirmed personally and theologically.

George-Guiser takes education seriously. So despite her heavy workload and demanding schedule, she began a D.Min. degree program in marriage and family ministry and family systems at the Eastern Baptist Seminary in Philadelphia from which she received her degree in 1994.

In the same year, she was appointed as an assistant to the bishop of the Southeastern Pennsylvania Synod with responsibility for mission leadership, including candidacy, mobility, leadership support and for two conferences of the synod. This position has been exciting and challenging to her. But as a caring but no-nonsense staff person, it has not been easy for "non-Asians and whites...to deal with an Asian woman in leadership," George-Guiser wrote. "Requiring high standards and excellence in leadership have been either wholeheartedly welcomed or highly criticized," she recalled with a sense of disappointment. But George-Guiser is convinced that God has placed her "in peculiar places to lift up the name of Jesus with joy and boldness."

In 1998 Rev. Peter Yung-ming Lai was appointed to a position as congregation ministry coordinator of multicultural ministry and evangelism in Region I of the ELCA. His responsibilities include "coordinating workshops and retreats, training local evangelists, visiting and evaluating congregation ministry through working with the bishops, assistants to the bishops, synodical evangelism and multicultural ministry committees." [15]

Before responding to the call to enter ordained ministry in 1981, Lai had a rich background in music, in the restaurant business, and in the teaching profession. Born on December 2, 1947, into a Christian family in Hualien, Taiwan, Lai received his secondary Christian and music education at a Christian school in Taipei. He furthered his education in music at Taiwan Theological College in Taipei.

In 1974 he received a B.A. degree in philosophy from National Cheng Chi University in Taipei. In the same year, he came to the United States to study music at the University of Minnesota. Later he attended Northwest Institute of Medical Laboratory Technique from which he obtained a diploma in 1978. He was certified as a medical technician in the same year. However, Lai did not enter into the medical profession. Instead, from 1978 to 1981, he owned and operated the Formosa Restaurant in Anoka, Minnesota. While he was in school in Taiwan and in the United States, Lai also worked as a private piano teacher.

In the fall of 1981, he entered Luther Northwestern Lutheran Theological Seminary in St. Paul, Minnesota, and he obtained the M.Div. degree in 1985. Following his graduation, Lai served three parishes in Southern California before accepting a faculty position at the Lutheran Bible Institute in Issaquah, Washington.

While he was a parish pastor in Southern California, Lai continued his education at Fuller Theological Seminary, receiving an M.Th. degree in missiology in 1992.

On October 1, 2000, Lai accepted a call to be the mission developer in Federal Way, Washington.

WOMEN OF THE ELCA

Women of the Evangelical Lutheran Church in America is an independent organization from the ELCA, but it came into existence at the same time. The purpose of this organization is to serve the women of the church. On January 1, 1988, this organization appointed Rev. Kwang Ja Yu to the position of director for ecumenical and cross-cultural programming. She held the position until March 5, 1993.

A Korean American woman, Yu was born on February 4, 1946, in Kirin, China, but received her higher education at the Ewha Women's

University in Seoul, South Korea. She received an M.Div. degree from LS in 1984. In the following year, she was ordained upon accepting a call to serve as associate pastor at King of Glory Lutheran Church, Dallas, Texas. In 1986 she was called to Mayfair Lutheran Church, Chicago, as its pastor.

Yu was active in the Asian Lutheran organization, serving as one of the editors of its newsletter. Presently Yu serves as pastor of University Lutheran Church of Hope, Minneapolis, Minnesota.

LUTHERAN WORLD FEDERATION

Rev. Teresita (Tita) C. Valeriano is the first Asian Lutheran in North America to be appointed to LWF, Geneva, Switzerland. Her appointment as director of youth took place in 2000.

An excellent musician, Valeriano was born on October 31, 1965, in Malabon, Philippines, where she grew up. She received her higher education from the University of the East and the Asian Institute for Liturgy and Music. Both institutions are in Manila. In 1994 she became a student at PLTS where she received her M.Div. degree. She was ordained in 1998 after she was called to be the pastor of First Lutheran Church, Tulare, California. In her present position she is responsible for work with Lutheran youth worldwide.

MINISTRY WITH ASIANS

The ELCA follows its predecessor bodies and continues to develop ministries in various Asian communities. Being aware of the increasing presence of South and Southeast Asians in America, however, the ELCA has also actively and intentionally initiated ministries among them. As previously mentioned, a Thai ministry was brought into the ELCA when Limthongviratn became the director of Asian-Pacific Islander ministries. Here, attention is turned to the Filipino ministry in Daly City, California, and the South Asian ministry in Chicago.

Filipino Ministry in Daly City

On June 3, 1987, Malcolm L. Minnick Jr. sent a memorandum to Rev. Michael Cooper-White, pastor-director of the San Francisco-East Bay Urban Coalition, inquiring about the possibility of a Filipino ministry in Daly City, California. Minnick made this inquiry "at the request of the AELC bishop." [16] In this memorandum, Minnick also reminded Cooper-White "that the AELC interest centered around the availability of a [Filipino] pastor." [17] On August 28, 1987, Cooper-White in his memorandum to Minnick stated that he intended to send the ministry profile to him by October 1. I was part of the discussion. I favored the ministry but questioned the site analysis report and the strategy.

This ministry, however, was not an AELC ministry alone. It was a joint effort of the three merging churches. After the ELCA was born, it was "grandfathered in" to DO's program support. Rev. Richard Bowley and Rev. Alexia Bowley staffed this ministry. Though the pastors worked hard, the result was less than satisfactory. The ministry was discontinued within three years.

South Asian Ministry in Chicago

Purna Jiwan: Abundant Life South Asian Ministries is the first ministry among South Asians in the ELCA and its predecessor bodies. This ministry began in September 1997 when Dr. Eardley Mendis was appointed pastor-developer by DO. The first worship service took place November 16, 1997. This ministry does not have a building of its own. It worships in the evenings at Norwood Park Lutheran Church, Chicago.

Mendis was born on October 2, 1945, into an interdenominational family in Sri Lanka. His father was a Roman Catholic, his mother an Anglican. His father died when Mendis was eight years old, but his father's death was also a turning point in young Mendis's life. His mother encouraged him to attend the Anglican church where young Mendis experienced the "love of the priests and fellow Christians." [18] He subsequently became an Anglican.

After high school, Mendis worked for a newspaper company for two years before becoming a student at the Theological College of Lanka in 1966 in preparation for ordained ministry in the Anglican Church in Sri Lanka. He was "ordained a deacon in June 1969, and was appointed as an assistant curate at St. Paul's Church, Milagiriya, an affluent church in Colombo." [19] Ten months later the East Asia Christian Conference (now called Christian Conference of Asia) offered him a scholarship to study at United Theological College in Bangalore, India, from which he received his B.D. degree in 1972.

Returning to Sri Lanka, Mendis was ordained a priest in May 1972. From 1972 to 1985 he remained in Sri Lanka, serving several parishes as well as being a hospital and a university chaplain. He also organized a children's home in 1980.

In 1985 he returned to United Theological College to get a master's degree in Christian ministry. He completed the program in two years. In September 1987, he came to LSTC for a D.Min. degree in pastoral care and counseling. He was awarded the degree in 1990. In the same year he was admitted into the Ph.D. program to study world mission. As preparation for the program, he first completed a Th.M. degree in world mission followed by his Ph.D. program in 1997.

While he was a student at LSTC he became acquainted with Rev. Ruben Duran and Fred Rajan, who encouraged him "to consider an ethnic ministry to South Asians in Chicago." [20] After much prayerful consideration, Mendis accepted the appointment to serve South Asians through the ELCA.

When he was asked how he would describe this first South Asian ministry in the ELCA, Mendis maintained that it is a challenging and rewarding ministry. Apart from the established South Asian churches, there are about 35 churches in Chicago with a membership varying anywhere from 15 to 75. The majority of these churches are organized on ethnic lines and worship in their respective languages. However, even within these homogeneous groups, tensions are not uncommon and as a result a new church comes into existence every now and then. Mendis maintained that belonging to the ELCA and worshiping in English from the beginning would not give any opportunity for such divisions among the members of his congregation. In fact, he believes the congregation will one day be a force that will unite South Asian Christians in the Chicago area, especially the second generation.

Another challenge that the congregation faces in its witness and outreach is the deep religiosity of South Asians who are primarily Buddhists, Hindus, and Muslims. The adherents of these religions become more devoted once in the United States than they were in their own countries. One reason for this is they believe that Western culture has a negative impact on their children and therefore they should be exposed more and more to their religious and cultural heritage. As a result, these South Asian religions are well organized and the places of worship are rapidly increasing.

However, Abundant Life has not failed in its witness to people of other faiths. The weekly Bible study in Devon (the commercial and residential hub of the South Asian community) in Chicago has brought together not only Christians from different denominational and ethnic backgrounds but also a few Hindus and Muslims. A striking thing at Abundant Life services is the presence of Hindus, Buddhists, and Muslims, particularly at special services. On many occasions they have requested prayers for special needs.

Abundant Life members have a vision of serving South Asians around the Devon area through a gathering place for senior citizens with a midday hot meal, English-as-a-second language classes, a computer learning center, immigration counseling, citizenship classes, health care awareness, programs for children including after-school activities, free access to Internet and e-mail facilities, and a clothing center.

The congregation has earned a reputation for great singing. The choir is known as "Purna Jiwan Singers." On many occasions, the choir has made a deep impact through the professional quality of the singing. In addition to English, the choir sings in several South Asian languages. Both Mendis and the congregants believe that one day the church will be a self-propagating and self-supporting congregation of the ELCA in the Chicago area.

14

ASIAN LUTHERANISM—WHICH WAY?

BY THE MID-1990s, ASIAN LUTHERAN MINISTRY IN THE ELCA SEEMED TO HAVE arrived at a crossroads. Up to that point, I had been the lone voice (later joined by a few others) to raise initial questions regarding the adequacy of Lutheran seminary studies for Asian ministry in North America. The issue now became a wider concern among Asian leadership. I had argued on numerous occasions that preparing women and men for ministry required taking seriously their historical and contemporary contexts and the particularities of those whom they will serve. To do otherwise is to do a disservice to these students and discounts the importance and the needs of the communities to which they would return.

In the early 1990s, James Moy and Bill Wong were working in tandem to provide theological education for Southeast Asians. Churchwide staff responsible for such education also appeared to be more open to considering various options. In addition, Asian Lutherans were beginning to wonder about possible linkage with individual Lutherans and Lutheran churches in Asia, and to wrestle with the idea of whether or not a paradigm shift was necessary in directing the development of Asian ministry.

This chapter addresses the issues raised above and examines the development of an Asian studies program, the first Asian Lutheran International Conference, the planning for the second, and the establishment of the Center for Chinese Ministry. The period covered is from 1994 to 2000.

ASIAN OR CHINESE STUDIES

The program pioneered by James Moy and Bill Wong for Southeast Asian Lutherans at LS was a success. It took Southeast Asian context into account and prepared a cadre of leaders. However, this program was not connected with any regular seminary curriculum. Something needed to be done.

Simon Lee was the catalyst for starting a process of formal deliberation on this issue. In a December 1, 1994, letter to Dr. Henry F. French, dean of academic affairs, LS, Lee stated that he was following up the conversation he had with French in October regarding "the possibility of expanding the curriculum offer[ed] at...Luther Seminary to include studies in Chinese ministry," and asked French "to seriously consider such a proposition."[1]

By October 1995, the idea of a Chinese study program had found its way into DM. In consultation with Wong, the grant writer Moy secured funding from Lutheran Brotherhood to bring a group of key leaders together to deliberate on this issue.

The First Meeting

The first meeting of the planning team[2] was held on January 10-11, 1997, at PLTS, facilitated by Rev. Arnold R. Mickelson. The group felt that the program should go beyond Chinese and should be Asian ministry studies. The team then drafted a philosophical statement to guide the development of such a program.

The group defined Asian ministry studies "as a program whose primary focus is preparing ELCA candidates for ministry with and to Asian people. This [would] be done by providing theological studies shaped by global and contextual awareness and the knowledge of the religious, cultural, political, and philosophical background of the Asian communities."[3] The planners also felt that "continuing education for rostered leaders and for lay leadership development in Asian congregations"[4] should be part of this program.

The planners further laid out a tentative curriculum and assigned the task of implementing the program to the Western Mission Cluster (WMC).[5] The group recommended that the following eight points be considered: That there be "an advisory committee...consultation with the Theological Education Coordinating Committee (TECC) and other seminary clusters,...cooperative programs with theological institutions in Asia,...integration of an overseas component,...an M.Div. program,...Asian supervisors and mentors for the contextual component,...allowance of multiple sites to meet the Lutheran residency requirement,...and continuing education."[6]

The discussion about the eligibility to enter the program required lengthy consideration. The planners finally arrived at an agreement that the following population was targeted for this program "(in order of priority)":

1. Asians whose primary language is one of the Asian languages...
2. Asians whose primary language is English...
3. Asians and others interested in Asian studies.[7]

The planning team also voiced the need for a program coordinator.

During the course of the two-day meeting, one of the LS representatives surfaced an undated document entitled "Asian Studies Project." [8] The purpose of this document was "to respond to the Asian Studies Planning Group, in preparation for the participation of Luther Seminary in the meeting planned for January 10-11, 1997, at PLTS." [9] This document listed four academic programs: "(I) Master of Divinity Program; (II) Master of Arts and Certificate Program; (III) Administration; (IV) Funding." [10] Under the "Master of Divinity Program," the document outlined the "Targeted Audience," "Program for Chinese Focus," and " Program for East Asia Focus." [11] The program for Chinese focus detailed two academic components and one practical. The two academic components were assigned to LS and the LTSHK and were to be taught by "a local Chinese teacher, Drs. Paul Martinson, Craig Moran,…Dr. Andrew Hsiao, Ms. Mabel Wu (alternate liturgics) and Dr. Ted Zimmerman or other faculty." [12] The practical component consisted of a "workshop with leading Chinese pastors in North America,… [a] workshop on Chinese identity on Internet, or as a component of 2, 3, 4 above, [13] in which one computer project would be required, [and] internship" [14] which was assigned to PLTS. This component was to be "directed by Dr. Edmond Yee." [15]

When I realized that my name was attached to this component, without prior consultation and agreement, I became furious and exploded. To me, this document showed a typical "missionary mind" at work—arrogant and hegemonic.

This document further outlined the "program for East Asia focus" and the "master of arts and certificate programs" without giving any assignment. However, the document stated that concerning administration, "the Global Mission Institute [at LS] be asked to provide the overall coordination for this program." [16]

On the matter of funding, this document suggested that "each institution [would provide] in-house resources.…For components that [involve] additional costs…that funding come from outside sources" [17] It also mentioned "one special cost might be in the area of overall administration and coordination," [18] without naming any funding source.

After my fury and explosion, one of the LS representatives indicated that this was not an official document and should not have been distributed. No further discussion followed.

The planning team further decided to survey other seminaries that offer such a program. Moy was responsible for designing a survey instrument. Moran, a professor at LS, and I were to contact the seminaries and report back to the team at its next meeting.

Approval and Implementation

The second meeting took place at the Marriott Hotel in Berkeley, May 30-31, 1997. Moran and I reported our findings to the team. The team

revised and refined the proposal drafted at the first meeting in order to sub-
mit the new document to the appropriate units for consideration.

The proposal was presented to seminary deans, the TECC, and the
DM board for discussion and consideration. The TECC approved the proposal
and directed it "to the Western Mission Cluster for their consideration and
response [by the February 1998 meeting]." [19] The DM board on October 11,
1997, also approved the proposal and directed it to the WMC for consideration,
with two additional recommendations: (1) "That the Western Mission Cluster
should attend to the geographic scope and name of the proposed Asian
Ministry Studies program" and (2) "that the Western Mission Cluster should also
keep in touch with Asian ministry opportunities in other parts of the country." [20]

Western Mission Cluster

Phyllis Anderson informed the WMC regarding the decision in a
memorandum dated October 21, 1997. After receiving the Anderson memorandum, WMC had a series of conversations involving faculty, committees,
and deans. The PLTS Academic Committee "referred the matter to Ed [Yee]
for conversation with Craig [Moran]." [21]

I corresponded with Moran via e-mail and met in person with him
in St. Paul on December 15, 1997. Stuhr, dean of PLTS, had also exchanged e-
mail with Dr. Marc Kolden, dean of LS. After further conversations with me
and others, Stuhr concluded that:

1. The Western Mission Cluster is willing to accept the assignment to
   develop an Asian Ministry Studies program.
2. As a 'specialization,' it would be a 'Joint Cluster Program,' i.e., planned
   and administered together.
3. Luther would concentrate on ministry with Chinese and Hmong. PLTS
   would provide preparation for ministry with Chinese, Korean now, with
   others to be added later.
4. Initially the program would be the offering of specialization in preparation for Asian Ministry, within the present M.Div. programs, at each of
   the schools.
   a. Each of the schools has the capacity, within existing resources... to
      offer the courses... called for in the proposal.
   b. 'Special training in the practice of ministry,' including CPE, intern-
      ship, and international contextual study would require adjunct
      faculty, and would be a cooperative effort of the two seminaries.
5. No new coordinator would be required at this time; the program
   could be handled within the present academic strutures of the two
   seminaries. [22]

In the meantime, Dr. David Tiede, president of LS, "responded orally at the Feb. TECC meeting, but not officially, pending consultation with PLTS."[23] LS's written response to the TECC was done by Moran.[24]

On June 1, 1998, Stuhr sent a revised "Asian Ministry Studies Program" to Lull, M. Aune, and me in which he refined his earlier report and listed the courses at PLTS/GTU that could be used to fulfill the program required and other matters related to the program.[25]

The response of the seminaries to TECC was arrived at after careful consultation between the officials of the two schools as well as thoughtful deliberation by each administration.

Advisory Committee

In 1998 an Asian Studies Program Advisory Committee was organized. The committee held its first meeting on November 4, 1998, in Houston, Texas.[26] LS and PLTS representatives, as well as DM staff, updated the committee on what had been transpiring at each institution. The committee laid out the scope for the program and a series of courses, and listed adjunct faculty, both domestic and international. It also outlined the following steps:

- January 11, 1999: Greg [Villalon] and Pongsak [Limthongviratn] meet with the president and dean of LS.
- February 19, 1999: Greg and Pongsak meet with the president and dean of PLTS (Issues to be addressed are: need, expectations, course, team teacher, catalogue to include Asian Studies Program, budget involved, recruitment, etc.).
- February 26, 1999: Second Meeting at PLTS.
- May 7-8, 1999: Third Meeting (Hawaii). (Dean [s] of LS and PLTS will be invited to the 2nd and 3rd meeting.)[27]

The committee further discussed ongoing input from this committee and printing the brochure to introduce the program.[28]

The second and third meetings were held as scheduled. The major items discussed were the production of a brochure, ongoing support, and program beyond the year 2000.[29]

Visits to Seminaries

On January 15, 1999, Limthongviratn paid a visit to LS to meet with Tiede and Moran. At this meeting it was decided that "the term 'Asian Studies Program' sounds complicated. A change to 'Leadership Development for Chinese Ministries' is suggested."[30] It was agreed that LS would focus "on [a] Chinese program for 2-3 years."[31] The participants further stated that "Luther is committed to support this project and will work with PLTS, CMM, DM and other churchwide related units."[32] The Chinese program would be a pilot project that could be used as a model for a Hmong program later.

The program at LS would begin in the fall of 1999. "Simon Lee's name is mentioned [as] a possible adjunct faculty to coteach with Paul Martinson and/or Craig Moran for a period of one month.... Pongsak will work on the budget for the implementation of this plan." [33]

The Limthongviratn and Villalon visit to PLTS, however, did not materialize. In the meantime, both seminaries launched the program in the fall of 1999. Martinson offered a course at LS on "Reading Asian Scriptures" and I offered a course at PLTS called "Christianity and Chinese Culture." A bilingual brochure announcing the commencing of the program was also produced.

ASIAN LUTHERAN INTERNATIONAL CONFERENCE

"The first Asian Lutheran International Conference brought 80 participants and 10 stewards... from 22 countries [34] on Jan. 22-26, 1999, to the Lutheran Theological Seminary in Hong Kong. Participants explored and reflected on the theme 'Asian Lutheranism—Which Way?' through a series of presentations, responses and discussion," announced a March 3, 1999, ELCA news release.

This section focuses on the development of this conference [35] and the planning for the second in Bangkok, Thailand, in 2001.

Genesis

The genesis of this conference can be traced to Bill Wong's resignation from CMM in 1996. Before Wong left the office, he called me to say that he had some year-end funds left over that he would like me to put to good use. During the conversation it was decided that I would use the money to bring Asian seminary faculty [36] and students together for discussion and fellowship at the next Association of Asian Lutherans—ELCA assembly.

The association held its biennial assembly on July 26-27, 1997, in Los Angeles. During the time set aside for faculty-student discussion and fellowship, I surfaced the idea of having an international conference in order to make connection between North American Asian Lutherans and the Lutheran churches and Lutherans in Asia. I had long believed that for Asian ministries in North America to flourish, this connection was essential. Both J. Paul Rajashekar and Stacy Kitahata, who have a wide range of international experiences, endorsed the idea. The students also expressed consent.

The idea of an international conference was presented to the executive committee of the association for consideration. The executive committee endorsed the idea in principle and instructed Limthongviratn, who provided staff support to the association, to explore the possibility and feasibility of an international conference. Limthongviratn and Fred Rajan were enthusiastic because they had discussed the very same idea in May 1997.

Limthongviratn soon organized a planning team to work on the conference theme and agenda.

Planning Process

The planning team members consisted of individuals from India, Hong Kong, Indonesia, and the United States, plus staff from DGM and CMM.[37] The first meeting was held April 5-7, 1998, at PLTS. At this meeting the team members decided the name of the conference would be Asian Lutheran International Conference (ALIC). They chose the theme "Asian Lutheranism—Which Way?" and three sub-themes: (1) "Asian Ministries in a Religio-Socio Pluralistic Context: Mapping the Way," (2) "Asian Leadership in a Context of Pluralism: Leading/Following the Way," (3) "Theological Education in Asia and North America: On the Way."

Moreover, the team agreed that a speaker from North America and one from Asia would address each of the subthemes. Each subtheme also would have a respondent either from North America or Asia. In addition Ms. Regina Samuel of Malaysia was asked to give an overview on the topic "Lutheran Churches in Asia Today: A Reflection," and Dr. Choong Chee Pang of Singapore was asked to speak on "Lutheran Identity in a Pluralistic Context" with Wi Jo Kang as the respondent.[38]

Emerging Issues

A total of 88 persons attended the conference. They were from the following 17 countries: China (Hong Kong and Taiwan), Malaysia, Singapore, Thailand, Japan, Korea, Laos, Philippines, India, Indonesia, Papua New Guinea, USA, Canada, Germany, the United Kingdom, Cambodia, and Myanmar.

The following issues surfaced from presentations, discussions, and responses as areas for further discussion: Asian theology and Asian hermeneutic; relationships between North American and Asian churches; the dynamics of cultures and traditions within the Asian and Asian-American contexts; Asian leadership style; being an Asian Lutheran in a pluralistic context; Asian ecumenical and interreligious dialogues; responsive theological education for Asians; the role of women and female church leaders; issues of justice, service, mission, proclamation, and so forth; and congregation as centers for mission and transformation.[39]

The conferees also accepted the proposal to establish a network, as laid out by the planning team at the April 1998 meeting, and adopted ALIC as the name for the conference. In this document the planning team articulated five objectives, laid out a structure, and established function and membership of the steering committee, frequency of the conference, financial support, affiliation, and accountability.

Planning for the Second Conference

After the first conference a steering committee was constituted. [40] The first meeting was in Oakland, California, June 7-8, 1999, with three DGM staff present as advisors. [41] The steering committee "reaffirmed the plan to have the Second Asian Lutheran International Conference in 2001" with the theme "Asian Ministries: Challenges and Opportunities." [42]

Rev. Ginda Harahap, LWF-DMD (Department for Mission and Development) Asia Secretary, joined the discussion by telephone and invited David Chen, chair of the steering committee and Limthongviratn "to present the proposal for the Second Asian Lutheran International Conference at the Asian Church Leadership Conference (ACLC) in November 1999, in Chennai, India."[43] Prior to the November 1999 meeting, Limthongviratn discussed the matter of funding ($15,000) from LWF with Harahap, who responded positively.

In the meantime two Asian organizations [44] related to the LWF in Asia had met and endorsed the proposal. The ACLC endorsed the proposed conference, including the request for funding from LWF. Following the Chennai meeting, Limthongviratn once again wrote to Harahap regarding funding from LWF. Again Harahap was positive. However, when Limthongviratn approached DMD with a request, it was turned down. This funding problem prevented some of the members of ACTEA (Advisory Committee for Theological Education in Asia) and ARCC (Asia Regional Coordinating Committee) from attending the 2001 conference.

The second meeting of the steering committee was held on May 12-13, 2000, in Bangkok, Thailand, to work out the details for the conference. The conference was to be held March 30-April 3, 2001, at the Royal Princess Hotel, Bangkok. While the planners were moving ahead, a knotty problem surfaced in Chicago. At the center of the difficulty were issues of money and power. These issues directly affected the Asian Lutheran community's right to make decisions for itself, including the planning of the second conference. When the leadership of the Asian Lutheran community was informed of the problem, they requested that churchwide staff convey to all parties involved the community's resolute desire for self-determination. The issue, as of December 2000, had not been resolved.

CENTER FOR CHINESE MINISTRY

The idea of having a Chinese person direct Chinese ministry development is not new either for the ELCA or for one of its predecessor bodies. In the early 1980s, when I was employed by DMNA to serve as resource developer-consultant for Asian ministry, some of the immigrant Chinese pastors already voiced their desire for such a person. When Bill Wong became the CMM director for Asian ministry, the issue surfaced again, culminating with a discussion with Wong and Robert Hoyt, DO staff, at the May 24-27, 1994, Chinese Ministry Mission Strategy Consultation in Alhambra, California.

Nearly 11 months later, Hoyt and Wong sent a memorandum to the Chinese pastors, informing them that DO "has no money to add a staff person for Chinese ministry. What the Division is considering is identifying a Chinese pastor of a Chinese ministry where the Division is providing subsidy. Rather than consider it support so that the pastor can be full time with that ministry, the Division would use its support to buy the pastor's time to be such a spokesperson." [45] "This," the memorandum continues, "is only in the idea stage and is not approved yet." [46] Apparently the idea was never approved.

Conscious of an Hispanic model in the ELCA and DO's willingness to provide some support, Rajan wrote a concept paper entitled "Center for Chinese Ministry" and presented it to the CMM steering committee for consideration at its October 1999 meeting.

In this paper Rajan outlined three elements that seemed to be missing in the previous discussions: structure, function, and accountability. [47] The steering committee endorsed the concept paper. Shortly afterwards, Limthongvirtn went to work, consulting with the Chinese community on how to establish such a center.

By November 21, 1999, everything seemed to be in place. On that day, Limthongvirtan wrote to four Chinese pastors and two laypersons stating, "after consultation with the Rev. Fred Rajan, Executive Director of the Commission for Multicultural Ministries and the Rev. David Chen, the president of the Association of Asians and Pacific Islanders, it is my honor to appoint you as board member of the Center for Chinese Ministry from December 1999 to April 2002." [48] Limthongvirtan went on to say that he hoped and prayed for "an [installation] service during [the] 2000 Asian Leadership Conference scheduled for March 30-April 2, 2000." [49]

The board was installed during the 2000 Asian Leadership Conference and David Chen was appointed half-time director. The center has a three-year commitment of support from DO and DM. The first year budget was $50,000. The current year budget is $35,000. Chinese congregations also provide budgetary support. Thus far the center has produced a directory of Chinese congregations, pastors, and leaders of the ELCA.

15

MISSION BLUEPRINT

IN 1988 DR. RALPH A. BOHLMANN, THE NEWLY ELECTED PRESIDENT OF THE LCMS, "asked that a Mission Task Force be formed 'to carry out a broad review of the Synod's mission activity and to recommend strategies and actions for the future.'" [1]

A 13-member Mission Task Force was formed in 1988. In 1990 the task force published "Mission Blueprint for the Nineties (MBN)," after its members had "studies reports, observations, experiences, and recommendations from missionaries, mission executives, denominational leaders, district personnel, and others committed to Christ's Great Commission." [2] MBN contains detailed background information and a set of 15 goals for mission.

In 1992 The LCMS in convention adopted MBN. The second goal is related to the subject of this book. Discussion in this chapter focuses on this goal and how it is being actualized in relationship to Asian ministries in America. [3] The period covered in this chapter spans from 1988 to 2000.

A WORLD MISSION FIELD

The second goal simply states: "To view the United States as a World Mission Field: the 'Centripetal Model: A Window of Opportunity.'" [4] The document explains, "in the 'Centripetal Model,' the Lord reverses the flow, pulling hundreds of thousands of people toward the United States." [5] As to why the mission task force viewed the United States as a world mission field, the same document further states, "Though millions are unchurched, the United States is on the cutting edge of international mission opportunity." [6] By sharing the gospel with these unchurched immigrants, the gospel eventually will centrifugally reach their homelands.

The document further points out the various resources that are at the church's disposal for ministry and concludes with the following recommendations:

1. Districts strong in membership and fiscal resources, but without burgeoning ethnic concentrations explore ways to join with districts overwhelmed by ethnic challenges.
2. The Board for Mission Services structure itself to assist districts and congregations in culture-specific mission.
3. The Board for Mission Services, cooperating with district mission boards, call and support evangelistic missionaries to serve in ethnic minority population centers.
4. A variety of new partnerships be formed between the Synod and auxiliary agencies or existing partnerships be strengthened to consolidate resources. [7]

In order to bring these recommendations to fruition, the Board for Mission Services (BMS) in 1992 called Rev. Robert J. Scudieri, to serve as area secretary for North America.

THE MAN AND HIS TASK

Scudieri was born and reared in the New York City area where he attended public schools. At an early age he felt the call to ministry. Thus, after high school he began preparation for ministry, first at Concordia College in Bronxville from which he received his A.A. degree in 1964. From there he went to Concordia College in Fort Wayne, Indiana. He was awarded a B.A. degree in 1966. Following the path that many LCMS seminarians have trod, he entered CS, St. Louis. He served two parishes in New Jersey. In 1984 Scudieri became a mission counselor for the English District.

"In 1976... Scudieri received an S.T.M. degree in pastoral counseling from New York Theological Seminary, in conjunction with the Postgraduate Center for Mental Health." [8] Five years later on May 17, 1981, he was awarded a D.Min. degree from the same institution. "From January to June 1991, he was a research fellow at Yale Divinity School." [9]

Scudieri's interest in mission led him to be "one of the founders of the Lutheran Society for Missiology." [10] He has been serving as the society's chairman since its inception in 1992. The book he authored, *Apostolic Church: One, Holy, Catholic and Missionary*, further reflects his interest in mission and missiology.

Under his leadership, The LCMS structured the region of North America, within the context of the second goal, into 15 mission fields, ranging from African immigrant ministry to campus ministry to Vietnamese ministry. For these mission fields, he devised a strategy for North America, [11] which includes setting up 15 task forces for the 15 mission fields. "Each task force exists to strategize for the expansion of the mission field it represents in the United States. Each of the task forces has... a strategy for its field." [12] As for

Asians, there are five fields: Asian Indian, Chinese, Hmong, Korean, and Vietnamese. In addition, conversations have begun with the Lutheran church in Japan about missionary work in America. These Asian mission fields are the focus of the next section.

CONFERENCE, FIELD COUNSELOR, AND MISSION SOCIETY

Beginning in the mid-1980s, Asian leaders in The LCMS met biennially as a caucus to discuss mission and ministry, as well as to share fellowship and support. [13] However, these gatherings produced few results due to language difficulties, cultural differences, and diverse ministerial needs. In the early 1990s, it was decided to dissolve the caucus and to form a conference for each group.

When Scudieri became the area secretary for North America, BMS appointed a field counselor from each ethnic group and each conference formed a task force to work with the field counselor. In addition to field counselor, there are also North America counselors. "Each year the North America task forces meet in St. Louis for their annual fall meeting. During that time the leaders (counsels and field counselors of the North America mission fields) review the existing North America strategy statement and suggest changes." [14] In a sense the strategy for each Asian group continues to evolve.

Chinese Ministry

The first Asian ministry in The LCMS was Chinese, beginning in 1936 (see chapter 2). By 1997, there were 15 established Chinese congregations and seven missions throughout the synod. The next group for which there were ministry efforts was the Koreans, followed by the Southeast Asians and South Asians. With this background and the current context in mind, each field is organized into conference, task force, and mission society. Some fields are further along in organization than others. The structure and function of each component and how they are interrelated are described in what follows.

Chinese Ministry Conference

The conference was organized in 1992 at the request of the Chinese pastors. The purpose of the conference is for "sharing the Gospel of Jesus Christ with people of Chinese origin in North America and other parts of the world." [15] The role of CMC is to "serve the congregations, their issues, and disputes," while the "field counselor and his committee serve the Synod." [16]

The first meeting was held on May 18, 1992, in Millbrae, California. At this conference the participants were divided into groups for the purpose of discussing components of planning, namely purpose statement, situation analysis, environment analysis, and strategy plan. [17] This later became the basis for the formulation of the ministry strategy.

The conference elected the following officers: Rev. Terrence Chan, chairman; Rev. Daniel Lee, vice chairman; Rev. Henry Lai, secretary; Rev. David Tin, treasurer. [18]

At the same conference, Scudieri "announced [that] the Rev. Terrence Chan [was] appointed as the field counselor for Chinese Ministry by the Board of Mission Services." [19] At this point, the conference accepted Chan's dual role. Four years later his dual capacity was questioned by the Chinese Ministry Conference Task Force (CMCTF), forcing Chan to give up his chairperson role.

The Chinese Colloquy program was a major issue that surfaced at this conference. The participants felt that the "requirement of hours and courses is inadequate." [20] The conferees passed a motion to the effect that "CMC shall communicate this feeling to the Synodical President Dr. Ralph Bohlmann, regarding the future admission of the colloquy students into the pastoral ministry." [21] At a subsequent teleconference, Chan was designated as the person to draft a letter to Bohlmann. The conference also dealt with the matter of constitutional amendments.

The conference further authorized Lee, the vice-chair, to spearhead the production of an English-Chinese edition of Luther's Small Catechism. [22] Along with Luther's Small Catechism, the CMC as of this writing has published eight tracts in Chinese on topics about stewardship and what Lutherans believe, and for evangelism purposes.

Four years later, Lee was elected chair of the CMC when Chan stepped down. Lee was born and grew up in Hong Kong, where he obtained two B.A. degrees, one from Zhuhai College and the other from Concordia Seminary. Later he came to the United States to attend Concordia Teachers' College, from which he obtained an M.A. degree in education. He further received another M.A. degree in education from the Chinese University of Hong Kong. For eighteen years he served as principal of LCHKS's elementary and junior high schools. Lee was also active in the synod, having served as its second vice president. After his retirement from being an educator, Lee immigrated to America and became pastor of a congregation in Seattle, Washington. Concurrently he serves as the editor of Good News, a quarterly Chinese magazine.

Lee is aware that Chinese ministries in North America cannot be done in isolation. Thus in setting goals for 1996-1997, he suggested that CMC consider networking "with Chinese Lutheran churches in Asia, and the Northwest District China Connection Committee, LCMS Districts and the Campus Ministry for mutual support." [23] His fellow officers approved his suggestion and pledged to work on networking with the entities that Lee identified.

On May 6-8, 1999, the CMC met in Bellevue, Washington. The organization appeared to be having some financial difficulties. Subsidies from the synod would be decreased incrementally. Much time was spent discussing how to assess CMC annual dues. It was decided that each ministry should contribute $200 per year to CMC. "In addition, extra dues (which turned out to be two dollars) will be assessed from each ministry on the basis of confirmed membership." [24] But this seemed to be a temporary solution. For the long term "CMC has to find ways to raise funds or reduce expenses." [25]

Another unsettling matter seemed to disturb the conferees. The Chinese Book of Worship, which was supposed to have been published by this time, was still not done. In answering a question regarding the book, chair Lee responded, "The Chinese Book of Worship should be published in about two years, God willing." [26] Lee did not seem to be too optimistic.

CMC meets annually. Funding for the conference comes from different sources, including some funds from BMS, membership fees, and individuals. CMC spearheads mission among the Chinese in North America for The LCMS.

Chinese Ministry Task Force

The Chinese Ministry Task Force (CMTF) was formed early on to work with the field counselor in new mission development. The membership consists of officers of CMC and other elected individuals. Its members meet once a year. At other times CMTF holds teleconferences as the need arises.

As previously mentioned, Chan was appointed field counselor in 1992. He still holds this position as well as that of pastor of New Life Chinese Lutheran Church in San Francisco, a congregation belonging to the English District. Chan was born in August 1958 in Hong Kong and moved to San Francisco with his parents when he was a young child. On June 6, 1976, at age 17, he was baptized into the faith. After high school graduation he attended Concordia University in Portland, Oregon, from which he received his B.A. degree in Christian education in 1981. In 1986 he received his M.Div. degree from CTS, Fort Wayne, Indiana. In addition Chan did graduate studies in counseling at California State University, Hayward, California, and theology at PLTS. Moreover, Chan holds certificates in many other areas of professional training.

Before becoming the founding pastor of New Life Chinese Lutheran Church on August 1, 1994, Chan had served the church in other professional capacities. For example, he served as a director of Christian education at St. Philip Lutheran Church, Dublin, California, from July 1981 to July 1985, and as a vicar at True Light Lutheran Church, New York City. From October 1987 to July 1994, he served as pastor of Lutheran Church of the Holy Spirit, San Francisco. He has served as member and chair of numerous committees and boards in The LCMS.

Chan is also a contributing author to various synodical publications and is currently writing a book, *Harvest Waiting*. This book is about how to reach the Chinese in North America.

In consultation with members of the task force, Chan, as field counselor, has devised a strategy for Chinese ministry in North America. The latest version is dated November 15, 1998. In the version, Chan provides a historical overview of Chinese ministry development in The LCMS, articulates a vision for ministry, and sets priorities and goals for 1998-1999 and for the next five years beyond 1999. The goals he articulates include new ministry development, expansion of established mission fields, identification of new fields, recruitment of missionaries and candidates for ministry, and campus ministry. One of his long-term goals is to have a full-time Chinese counselor within five years. It is also his plan to develop two funding sources for new mission. Finally he lays out a strategy to achieve the goals. The salient features of his strategy include an emphasis on "Church Extension through Leadership Development (CELD)…'fishing pools' (initial contact with the unchurched),…innovative tele-missioning campaigns,…and cell groups." [27]

Chinese Lutheran Mission Society

The Chinese Lutheran Mission Society was established by CMC. The purpose is to raise funds to subsidize existing missions. [28] A board governs the society and its members are elected by CMC. Funds for the society's activities come from Chan's field counselor budget.

In theory the society is an intrinsic part of the structure and operation of CMC and the task force. The three entities function in a circular way to support one another. In reality at present, the society, due to the lack of budgetary support and leadership, does not function the way it is supposed to. At this writing, the future of the society remains in doubt.

The three entities mentioned above—Chinese Ministry Conference, Chinese Ministry Task Force, and Chinese Lutheran Mission Society—are recognized and supported to a certain extent by BMS. In addition there are two other organizations working with Chinese and Asian Americans in North America that deserve to be mentioned.

Midwest Chinese Ministries

On October 17, 1997, the officers of CMC sounded an alarm during their telephone conference. Chan, the field counselor and an adviser to CMC, reported that "Edmund Lim has established an independent mission society in the mid-west to carry out mission work in the districts in the mid-west. This might cause confusion since there is already a Mission Society in existence." [29] Discussion ensued. The participants of this teleconference "suggested that Edmund Lim contact Rev. David Tin (president of CLMS) to discuss the details." [30] The task of bringing the two parties together was given to Chan, who agreed "to initiate contacts." [31]

In actuality Midwest Chinese Ministries (MCM) "was formed early in 1996 by a group of pastors and lay people from the Fort Wayne area to help in promoting the outreach among the Chinese." [32] Lim was not the founder of MCM. His presence in the Midwest no doubt contributed to its establishment.

In a brochure, produced by MCM, the purpose of the organization is stated thus: "The mission of the MCM is to proclaim the gospel of Jesus Christ to Chinese people and to train them for Christian discipleship." [33] The same brochure mentions that Chinese ministries were already going on in four cities in Indiana and in two in Ohio.

Moreover, according to the information provided in the brochure, Lim "was called by the Indiana District as Missionary-at-Large to the Chinese on November 3rd, 1996." [34] Lim, a Lutheran pastor from Singapore, was born December 20, 1954, in Singapore. He received his primary and secondary education in public schools. In 1982 he obtained a B.Th. degree from the Singapore Bible College and became the first native clergy to take over a congregation from an American missionary. He furthered his theological education at CTS, Fort Wayne, Indiana. He was awarded the S.T.M. degree in 1988. Presently he is a candidate for the doctor of missiology degree at the same seminary.

MCM provides two means for outreach: (1) Bible study and out-reach activities and (2) Chinese worship services and Sunday school. Worship is conducted in Chinese and English.

Center for Asian-American Evangelism

The Center for Asian-American Evangelism (CAME), located in Alexandria, Virginia, "is a ministry agency organized in 1999 and is recognized by The LCMS Board for Mission Services as a mission society-agency with a statement of partnership. CAME is an independently operated, non-profit organization of The LCMS. It is funded by grants and private donations." [35] During its first year of existence, "CAME was able to help 23 new Asian churches begin on the East Coast." [36]

CAME's existence is justified on theological and demographic grounds. Thus, its mission is "to equip Lutheran congregations to reach out to the 97 percent of Asian-Americans who are unchurched."

Its goals are (1) to educate Lutheran congregations of the need to reach out to Asian-Americans and about the cultures of the Asian ethnic groups, (2) to support districts and congregations in initiating Asian-American ministries, (3) to identify and recruit leaders from Asian communities and to "provide the leaders of Asian communities mentoring, support, and networking opportunities," (4) to conduct needs assessment in Asian communities, (5) to raise funds for Asian outreach, and (6) to encourage multiethnic and multigenerational ministries.

This is a membership-based organization with a budget of $184,122 for the year 2000. LCMS World Mission, Lutheran Brotherhood, Aid Association for Lutherans, congregational benevolences, free-will offerings from congregations, as well as three districts are its main funding sources.

This agency does not have any connection with CMC or MCM. Its major objective for the year 2000 is "to assist in educating East Coast congregations of the need to reach the rapidly growing Asian American communities on the East Coast with the Good News." [37]

Korean Ministry

In 1971 The LCMS entered its first ministry with the Korean-Americans in Los Angeles. As of June 1998, 37 ministries are associated with the Korean Ministry Conference (KMC). [38]

From 1985 to 1992, Korean clergy in The LCMS had been meeting jointly with, as well as separately from, other Asian groups. The group adopted a constitution sometime before 1990. When it was actually adopted is not clear, although the first time the constitution was amended was on June 13, 1990. The record of this conference is at best confusing. For example, on the back page of the English version of the constitution, it is stated that both the sixth and seventh conferences occurred in different months in 1993. [39] The minutes of the seventh conference show that it was held in 1992.

In 1992 10 regular members and four associate members attended the seventh conference, held in Garden Grove, California. The main agenda items included reports from each ministry, election of officers, and appointment of a field counselor.

The following individuals were elected officers: Rev. Younghwan Hong, [40] president, and Rev. Chunho Song, vice president. Rev. Younchul Kim was appointed secretary by the president. The conferees further unanimously elected Hong to be the field counselor. As the field counselor, Hong would receive reimbursement for travel and telephone expenses from BMS.

The purpose of KMC "is [aiming] to get fellowship that communicate[s] effectively the works of God's salvation toward Korean immigrants who [reside in] North America." [41] This purpose statement was amended by the 1998 conference to read, "To spread the gospel of God's salvation in an effective way to both Koreans in the United States and also Koreans in other countries. To pursue fellowship between the churches and pastors." [42]

By 1995 the Korean Ministry Church Planning Task Force came up with a strategy statement, a two-page document. The purpose of this strategy statement is "to encourage, envision, and support The Lutheran Church-Missouri Synod's districts, circuits, and local congregations to proclaim the Gospel to the Korean people in North America." [43] The strategy statement contains six priorities for mission, three goals, six strategies, and a budget.

The first of the three goals is to "establish a national Korean Mission Society by 1997 to support the planting of new Korean churches in North America." [44] However, as of this writing, the mission society has not been established. The second goal calls for the developing of "five mission stations by tentmaking ministry [in] New York, Colorado Springs, Las Vegas, Los Angeles, [and] Richmond." [45] The third goal calls for planting five new Korean churches in the next five years.

Along with amending the constitution, the conferees at the 1998 gathering made three major decisions. They decided that there was a need to study clergy salaries and benefits, to study Lutheran theological vocabularies so that they may know how to translate them appropriately into Korean, and to organize a task force to work with the field counselor. The job of selecting a task force was given to the officers of KMC.

As to why the group decided to study clergy salaries and benefits, the minutes do not indicate. Private conversations, however, revealed an awareness among the Korean clergy about how low their salaries are.

Asian Indian Ministry

In 1895 the first missionary from The LCMS arrived in India and others soon followed, resulting in the founding of India Evangelical Lutheran Church. This church continues to maintain a close relationship with The LCMS. On September 11, 1994, at Trinity Lutheran Church, St. Louis, Missouri, The LCMS commissioned Rev. Jaya P. Bijjia, a clergyperson from India, as a missionary-at-large for Asian Indian ministries in North America. On the same day, Asian Indian Ministries of North America (AIMNA) was organized. AIMNA set the following mission goals:

1. To establish AIMNA—LCMS…in all Districts…with trained Asian Indian pastors.
2. To help immigrants…to settle in their foreign land.
3. To help people to worship the Lord in their own culture.
4. To help children and youth to grow in their own culture….
5. To help immigrant Christians to reach their own people….[46]

To reach the goals, AIMNA articulated the following strategies:

1. Survey North America and identify the Asian Indian people.
2. Inform the Districts about open doors for the Gospel among Asian Indians.
3. Identify the local church, which can sponsor this mission.
4. Arrange cultural gatherings for local Indians to hear the Gospel.
5. Identify a leader and train him to be their local pastor. [47]

The strategies seem to be working. By October 13, 2000, there are "18 'centers' [for ministry] all over the U.S." [48] With the help of a few others, Bijjia "travels to most of these places reasonably regularly." [49]

Presently Professor Victor Raj, CS, St. Louis, serves as field counselor of AIMNA. His responsibilities include planning meetings and coordinating the mission endeavors.

Raj was born and grew up in India, where he received his basic theological training. In 1981 he obtained his graduate degree from CS, St. Louis. From 1971 to 1990, he served India Evangelical Lutheran Church "as pastor and in various other positions." [50] In 1990 he became the chairperson of the Division of Theology of Concordia University in Wisconsin. In 1995 he joined the CS faculty as a mission professor of exegetical theology.

In late July 2000, the Asian Indian group of The LCMS "registered a society with the name AIMNA." [51] The purpose of this society is to assist the group in mission and ministry with Asian Indians in North America.

Vietnamese Ministry

The first Lutheran church in North America to organize a Vietnamese congregation was The LCMS. By 1996 The LCMS had four ministries with the Vietnamese. In the same year, a task force was organized to assist the synod and districts in initiating ministry with the persons of Vietnamese heritage.

The task force developed a strategy statement, the purpose of which is to "reach out and minister to the Vietnamese people in the United States with Word and Sacraments." [52] The document lists four critical targets, gives the current status of Vietnamese ministry, sets the goals and lists five objectives, one of which is "to establish and found VLMS on April 18-21, 1997," and another objective is to "organize [a] Vietnamese Ministry General Conference." [53] The document further identifies sites for future ministries.

The Vietnamese Ministry General Conference was established. It roughly parallels a task force. Rev. Minh Chau Vo, pastor of the Vietnamese ministry, St. Louis, Missouri, was appointed field counselor to give advice and counsel to the district and the synod.

Japanese Ministry

On September 21-22, 1999, 51 years after the first missionary from The LCMS arrived in Japan, a group of 25 people including Rev. Masahiro Ando, secretary of missions of the Japan Lutheran Church (JLC), gathered together in St. Louis, Missouri, to discuss ministry with the Japanese in America. There were four purposes for this gathering:
   1. Networking among those engaged in ministries to Japanese.
   2. Formalizing an official channel for these ministries.

3. Sharing resources for ministry with each other.

4. Encouraging expansion of ministries throughout the U.S. [54]

Presently some congregations are engaged in a variety of ministries with the Japanese nationals working temporarily in the United States. At this meeting, Scudieri had hoped the group would agree to establish a task force for Japanese ministry. The group, however, felt that it was premature to establish such a task force but would welcome the forming of the Japanese Ministry Association (JMA). Having failed to achieve his hope, Scudieri then expressed the willingness "to provide some funding to an interim Japanese Ministry Association," [55] with the understanding that most of the support would come from local sources.

On May 1, 2000, Rev. David R. McClean, president of the Japanese Mission Society sent out an invitation to those who were interested in Japanese ministries to come to St. Louis June 20-21, 2000, for "the constituting meeting of the Japanese Ministry Association." [56] Thus, on this day the JMA was born.

Prior to founding JMA, The LCMS had received a missionary, Dr. Chizuo Shibata of the Japan Lutheran Church, to work among Japanese nationals in New Jersey. Shibata worked with a group of persons who had organized the Megumi Church. On April 1, 2000, Rev. Shozo Osawa took over his work. By this time the Megumi Church services had been discontinued. Osawa was called to the New Jersey District as a Japanese missionary to Japanese for a two-year term.

In the meantime, the International Lutheran Laymen's League also expressed an interest in Japanese ministry in the United States. Scudieri has been in conversation with Japanese Lutheran officials regarding the possibility of a lay missionary to work among the Japanese in Manhattan, New York.

On June 20, 2000, JMA came up with a "Working Agreement," including a mission statement and five objectives on mission and ministry with the Japanese in America. [57]

PARADIGM SHIFT

The LCMS's approach to ethnic ministry apparently represents a significant paradigm shift. In the past, ethnic ministries were directed and carried out by white congregations and mission societies. But now they are being directed and implemented "by indigenous people to their own people through a synod level task force." [58] Even though the second goal of MBN does not explicitly call for the creation of synod level task forces and ethnic mission societies to carry out mission and ministry, apparently the mission executives feel that this is the way to accomplish this goal. Observers agree that in the short term, this shift has generated excitement and enthusiasm among the ethnic groups.

EPILOGUE

A NEW HORIZON

THE DEVELOPMENT OF ASIAN LUTHERAN MINISTRIES IN NORTH AMERICA, beginning in 1936, was a gradual process. But with the increasing numbers and constant arrival of new immigrants, the sudden presence of refugees, together with the availability of clergy from Asia and North America, the pace accelerated. Asian Lutherans themselves, with determination and courage, surely played a key role in such acceleration. Today there are Asian Lutheran congregations and missions scattered all over North America, like isolated drops of tea flowing in a bucket of milk, unable to penetrate the depth or to spread across the breadth of the bucket. The isolation sometimes is by institutional design and at other times by a group's own desire.

Such isolation, when viewed from a distance, appears to give different ethnic groups a sense of cohesion, solidarity, power, self-determination, comfort, and security. But when the isolation is looked at and examined within the contexts of ecclesiastical polity and policy and the history of North American racism, such a sense becomes illusory. Asian Lutheran ethnic groups have no power either to impact the institution or the opportunity to share in a meaningful way their own cultures and spiritual heritages, even if they so desire, with the wider church. The Lutheran denominations in North America are cultural churches on both institutional and congregational levels. That is, they are the embodiment, not without justification, however, of Eurocentric cultures, which to a large extent excludes other cultural traditions in North America.

Even if Asian Lutherans could puncture the cultural boundary, there remains a question of theology to be answered. Western theologians and biblical scholars have interpreted Christian Scriptures throughout the centuries to meet their own needs and to justify their own actions or inactions within their historical and contemporary contexts. Can Asian Lutherans, who come from a variety of contexts—indeed some of those contexts have an intimate relationship with Western colonialism and imperialism—accept and apply the theology or theologies of these theologians and scholars into their own contexts? This author thinks not. And yet from my own perspective, most Asian Lutheran clergy live and preach this very theology, which has been used in so many ways as a tool of oppression, stripping the dignity, respect, and self-knowledge of people of color in North America and elsewhere.

If Asian Lutheran ministries are to flourish and soar like the supple, graceful, and beautiful crane, gaining new angles of vision as it surges higher and higher, Asian Lutheran professionals must assume a greater responsibility. We must develop suitable hermeneutic tools so that a theology responsive and responsible to an Asian-American context might result and with which we may meet our own people's needs, spiritual and mundane. Admittedly this is a call to action for the Asian Lutheran community. Should the response to this call be positive, then I would like to offer a caveat here. In the course of developing a responsive and responsible theology, we must pay attention to the various traditions. They must not be indiscriminately discarded or retained, but first, as I argue elsewhere, "we must ask, what role could and/or should the traditions play in our ascending the mountaintop to view a new horizon?" [1]

NOTES

INTRODUCTION: CASTING A BRICK

1. Donald S. Lopez (ed.), *Asian Religions in Practice: An Introduction*, 113.

CHAPTER 1: THE OTHER SHORE

1. Luo Manhua (ed.), *Huaren jiaohui shouce (Handbook on Chinese Churches)*, 367.
2. Kenneth Scott Latourette, *The Chinese: Their History and Culture*, 183.
3. For chronology and facts on early Chinese immigration see William L. Tung, *The Chinese in America, 1820-1973*.
4. For ministry with early Chinese immigrants see Horace R. Cayton and Anne O. Lively, *The Chinese in the United States and the Chinese Christian Churches*. This work also briefly mentions Roman Catholic efforts with the Chinese.
5. For chronology and facts on early Japanese immigration see Masako Herman (comp.), *The Japanese in America, 1843-1973*.
6. *Ibid.*, 4.
7. *Ibid.*, 7.
8. For information on Protestant work among the Japanese see Sumio Koga (comp.), *A Centennial Legacy: History of the Japanese Christian Missions in North America, 1877-1977*, vol. 1.
9. For detail see Carey McWilliam, *Prejudice—Japanese Americans: Symbol of Racial Intolerance*; Morton Grodzins, *Americans Betrayed: Politics and the Japanese Evacuation*. For documents on the decision to intern the Japanese, see Roger Daniels, *The Decision to Relocate the Japanese Americans*, 61-132.
10. For detail see Roger Daniels, *The Decision to Relocate the Japanese Americans*, 3-58.
11. For chronology and facts on Korean immigration see Hyung-chan Kim and Wayne Patterson (comps. and eds.), *The Koreans in America, 1882-1974*.
12. This program was sponsored by the government scholarship. The aim was to send young and bright Filipinos and Filipinas to the United States to study. By 1912 209 people benefited from this program.
13. For chronology and facts on early Filipino immigration see Hyung-chan Kim and Cynthia C. Mejia (comps. and eds.), *The Filipinos in America, 1898-1974*.
14. *Ibid.*, 12.
15. For detail on early Asian Indian immigration and the formation of a biethnic community see Karen Isaksen Leonard, chapter 2 in *The South Asian Americans*.
16. Rabindra N. Kanungo, *South Asians in the Canadian Mosaic*, 35.

17. Jean Chesneaux, *The Vietnamese Nation: Contribution to a History*, (trans. by Malcolm Salmon), 194.
18. *Ibid.*, 206.

CHAPTER 2: SEEKING THE WAY

1. Abdel Ross Wentz, *A Basic History of Lutheranism in America*, 181.
2. *Ibid.*
3. *Ibid.*, 183.
4. In the "Report on Asian Ministry, June 1995," produced by the Asian Ministries Program, Commission for Multicultural Ministries, ELCA, it is stated on page 9 that True Light Lutheran Church "began in 1946 with support of The LCMS." The source of this information was attributed to my article in *The Lutheran* (April 16, 1986), 11. This is wrong. In my article I simply stated, "The Lutheran Church—Missouri Synod began work in New York City's Chinatown in the 1930s. As a result, True Light Lutheran Church came into being." 1936 was the actual date for the beginning of this congregation, not 1946.
5. *True Light Lutheran Church 40th Anniversary* 1936-1976, 5.
6. Caroline C. Young, "Mary E. Banta: Condensed from True Light News 1950," in Wing Jean (ed.), *The Biography of Our Mary E. Banta*. [Hereafter cited as *The Biography*.]
7. *Ibid.*
8. See Chinese introduction to *The Biography*, written by Wing Jean. [Hereafter cited as Chinese Introduction.]
9. See "Miss Mary E. Banta with Church of All Nations," (condensed from "The Christian Advocate," 1935, in *The Biography*, n.p. [Hereafter cited as "Miss Mary E. Banta."]
10. See Chinese Introduction.
11. Caroline C. Young. *The Biography*, n.p.
12. Wing Jean in *The Biography* attributed this verse to Exodus 3:14.
13. See *The Biography*, n.p.
14. *Ibid.*
15. *Ibid.*
16. See "Miss Mary E. Banta," in *The Biography*, n.p.
17. *Ibid.*
18. *Ibid.*
19. *Ibid.*
20. *True Light Lutheran Church, 25th Anniversary*, 16. [Hereafter cited as 25th Anniversary.]
21. *True Light Lutheran Church, 40th Anniversary*, 5. [Hereafter cited as 40th Anniversary.] Marion Klaus was an English Sunday school teacher in the Chinese Department of CAN.
22. *Ibid.*
23. 25th Anniversary, 5. A copy of this resolution is also found in the Atlantic District Archive.
24. This figure is highly questionable. Traditionally the Chinese lived in the San Francisco Bay area. Cayton and Lively maintained in their book, *The Chinese in the United States and the Chinese Christian Churches*, published in 1955, that the Chinese population of New York City at the time was 18,327.
25. Proceedings of the Twentieth Convention of the Atlantic District of the Ev. Luth Synod of Missouri, Ohio, and Other States, June 22-25, 1936, 40.

26. *Ibid.*

27. 40th Anniversary, 6.

28. The name of the seminary was not mentioned in his clerical biography. It suggested that Chang completed his training in 1949.

29. *The Biography*, n.p.

30. Bruce Edward Hall, *Tea That Burns*, 231.

31. "Ban jiaoshi yu huafu ertong zhi ganquing" (Love between Miss Banta and the Children of Chinatown), in *The Biography*, n.p.

32. Kwong later married Joseph Wong, a Lutheran clergyman.

33. See Ruth Kwong, "She Is a Faith Child of God," in *The Biography*, n.p.

34. Moy became a state official at the age of 23, and as a journalist he spent time in China where he became dean of the Customs College. During World War II he was commissioned a Major General in the Chinese National Army. After the war, he returned to the United States and "was instrumental in the creation of the committee known as 'Aid Refugee Chinese Intellectuals, Inc.'" See "A Tribute to a Trusting Friend," in *The Biography*, n.p.

35. *Ibid.*

36. See Ernest J. Kunssch, "What Can I Say," in *The Biography*, n.p.

37. See *The Biography*, n.p.

38. See Martha E. Hoffman, "The Magic Name—Miss Banta," in *The Biography*, n.p.

39. Wonnor Yee letter to author, January 20, 2000.

40. *Ibid.*

41. True Light Lutheran Church, 50th Anniversary. 36.

42. 40th Anniversary, 17.

43. *Ibid.*

44. *Ibid.*

45. Cayton, Horace R. and Anne O. Lively, *The Chinese in the United States and the Chinese Christian Churches*, 55.

46. James Moy's e-mail to author, April 11, 1999, 1.

47. Norman J. Threinen, *Like a Leaven: A History of the Alberta-British Columbia District of the Lutheran Church-Canada*, 116.

48. *Ibid.*, 116, 117.

49. *Ibid.*, 117.

50. *Ibid.*, 138.

51. *Ibid.*, 179.

52. *Ibid.*

53. *Ibid.*

54. Rev. Holt gave the figure 16 in "Brief History of Our Speaker—Rev. Wilbert Holt." This figure is questionable even if Holt included St. Mary's Catholic Church.

55. James Chuck, *An Exploratory Study of the Growth of Protestant Chinese Churches in San Francisco*, 1950-1992, 15-21.

56. See *Lutheran Church of the Holy Spirit, 10th Anniversary 1964-1974*, n.p.

57. For information on the congregation's programs and stories about other staff members, see the Lutheran Church of the Holy Spirit Twentieth Anniversary, 1964-1984.

58. *Ibid.*, 4.

59. Herman, 30. The 442nd combat team was the most decorated regiment during World War II.

60. Toshio Okamoto, private notes to author, September 13, 1999. [Unless indicated otherwise, all quotes for this section are from private notes to author.]

61. For this section I rely heavily on the information provided me by Rev. Toshio Okamoto.
62. The 1965 Lutheran Annual listed Los Angeles as its location; the 1966 Annual listed Gardena.

CHAPTER 3: MISSIONARIES AT HOME

1. James Reed, *The Missionary Mind and American East Asia Policy, 1911-1915*, 12.
2. *Ibid.*
3. Yearbook—45th Annual Convention of the United Danish Evangelical Lutheran Church, June 10-15, 1941, 9.
4. *Ibid.*
5. Report of the Thirty-Eighth Annual Convention of the Pacific District, October 21-25, 1942, 37.
6. Yearbook of the United Evangelical Lutheran Church, 1947, 51.
7. *Ibid.*
8. *Ibid.*
9. *Ibid.*
10. *Ibid.*
11. Forty-Fourth Annual Convention of the Pacific District of the United Evangelical Lutheran Church, October 31, 1948, 17.
12. *Ibid.*
13. Minutes of the Eighth Annual Meeting of the Board of Home Missions of the United Evangelical Lutheran Church, February 14-16, 1950, 45.
14. Minutes of the Board of Home Missions of the United Evangelical Lutheran Church, February 26-March 1, 1951, 52.
15. Yearbook to the 56th Annual Convention of the United Evangelical Lutheran Church, June 17-22, 1952, 28.
16. Report of the Forty-Eighth Annual Convention of the Pacific District of the United Evangelical Lutheran Church, November 6-9, 1952, 8.
17. Minutes of the Board of Home Missions of the United Evangelical Lutheran Church, February 25-26, 1952, 48.
18. *Ibid.*, 46.
19. *Ibid.*, 47.
20. *Ibid.*, 46, 47.
21. Yearbook to the 58th Annual Convention of the United Evangelical Lutheran Church, June 15-20, 1954, 59.
22. Yearbook to the 59th Annual Convention of the United Evangelical Lutheran Church, June 21-26, 1955, 16.
23. Minutes of the 12th Meeting of the Board of Home Missions of the UELC, February 17-18, 1954, 72.
24. See National Lutheran Council resolution of March 22-23, 1955, for detail.
25. Minutes of the BHM of UELC, February 24, 1959, 92.
26. Dr. Swenson was born in Nebraska in 1886 and died in Pasadena, California, in 1965. In 1913 he and his wife set sail for China as missionaries, serving in Henan Province from 1913 to 1946, then in Hankou prior to the establishment of the People's Republic of China in 1949. Then they served in Taipei, Taiwan, from 1952 to 1957. While they were in China, Swenson served the mission field in a various capacities, including serving as a bishop of the Chinese Lutheran Church of the Augustana Mission; as a vice-archbishop of the Lutheran Church of China. For further information see Minutes of the Fifth Annual Convention of

the Pacific Southwest Synod of the Lutheran Church in America, May 16-19, 1966, 74.

CHAPTER 4: ANOTHER BEGINNING

1. Minutes of the Tenth Biennial Convention of the United Lutheran Church in America, October 14-21, 1936, 167.

2. Proceedings of the Forty-Sixth Annual Convention of the Evangelical Lutheran Synod of California, 1937, 31.

3. Minutes of the Eleventh Biennial Convention of the United Lutheran Church in America, October 5-12, 1938, 201.

4. *Ibid.*

5. *Ibid.*

6. Minutes of the Twelfth Biennial Convention of the United Lutheran Church in America, October 9-16, 1940, 226.

7. Actually, as early as 1935 there were already four second-generation Japanese-American clergymen ministering among the Nisei. Sumio Koga (comp.), *A Centennial Legacy: History of the Japanese Christian Mission in North America, 1877-1977*, vol. 1, 18.

8. Minutes of the Thirteenth Biennial Convention of the United Lutheran Church in America, October 14-21, 1942, 168.

9. *Ibid.* It was possible that Knudten was permitted to visit Manzanar, the camp closest to Gardena. However, Lester E. Suzuki in his comprehensive work, *Ministry in the Assembly and Relocation Centers of World War II*, made no mention of any Lutheran ministry in any camp.

10. Minutes of the Fourteenth Biennial Convention of the United Lutheran Church in America, October 11-17, 1944, 151. [Hereafter cited as 1944 Report.]

11. *Ibid.*

12. BAM purchased a house located at 127 Clifton Avenue, Minneapolis, and converted it into a hostel. The War Relocation Board and the pastors of the Twin Cities endorsed the ministry.

13. This missionary was Miss Martha B. Akard.

14. 1944 Report, 152.

15. The Rev. J. Ernest Messer was the pastor of this congregation.

16. Proceedings of the Forty-Sixth Annual Convention of the Evangelical Synod of California, May 11-13, 1937, 31.

17. The 1944 Home Mission Committee report seems to support my last observation. It reported that the building had been repaired and attendance went up 100 percent and that the congregation was now able to pay its share of benevolence in full.

18. Lewis Samuel Godfrey Miller letter to Paul T. Nakamura, May 18, 1953.

19. Minutes of the Sixteenth Biennial Convention of the United Lutheran Church in America, October 6-14, 1948.

20. Minutes of the Eighteenth Biennial Convention of the United Lutheran Church in America, October 8-15, 1952, 661.

21. *Ibid.*, 696.

22. *Ibid.*

23. Minutes of the Nineteenth Biennial Convention of the United Lutheran Church in America, October 6-13, 1954, 308.

24. *Ibid.*

25. *Ibid.*, 308, 309.
26. *Ibid.*, 309.
27. *Ibid.*
28. *Ibid.*
29. *Ibid.*, 310.
30. *Ibid.*
31. *Ibid.*, 313.
32. *Ibid.*
33. *Ibid.*
34. *Ibid.*
35. *Ibid.*, 823.
36. *Ibid.*
37. Paul T. Nakamura, "Kikuno Miyagi Nakamura," n.d., 1.
38. The *News Service* of the United Lutheran Church in America maintained that the grade awarded to Miller was a "Fourth" instead of "Third," as other sources indicated.
39. *News Service* of the United Lutheran Church in America, August 14, no year.
40. Paul T. Nakamura, "Beginning I," n.d., 1.
41. *Ibid.*
42. Paul T. Nakamura, "Report on Japanese Christian Work of the United Lutheran Church in America," June 1953, 1.
43. *Ibid.*, 3.
44. *Ibid.*
45. *Ibid.*
46. *Ibid.*, 4.
47. Minutes of The United Lutheran Church in America, Twentieth Biennial Convention—October 10-17, 1956, 938.
48. This quote is from Ujiie's tape to the author.
49. *Ibid.*
50. *Ibid.*
51. *Ibid.*

CHAPTER 5: MOVING AHEAD

1. John H. Tietjen, *Memoirs in Exile: Confessional Hope and Institutional Conflict*, 6.
2. The dispute between the two camps is well documented by others. For an insider's view, see John H. Tietjen, *Memoirs in Exile*.
3. See document called "Goals for this Conference."
4. *Ibid.*
5. See "Declaration."
6. *Ibid.*
7. *Ibid.*
8. Both Zion Lutheran Church, San Francisco, and the Lutheran Church of Our Savior, San Jose, extended their ministries into the Chinese community.
9. Moon was born in Korea. In 1955 he came to the United States for higher education. He attended St. John College in Kansas and received his B.A. degree from Fort Wayne Senior College in Indiana in 1957. Two years later he obtained the M.Div. degree from Concordia Seminary, St. Louis. He did graduate studies at Washington University, St. Louis, from which he received an M.A. degree in 1962. In 1968 he obtained the Ph.D. degree from St. Louis University, St. Louis. Moon is presently chief vice president of Concordia University in Irvine, California.

10. Moon and his colleagues organized Concordia College, now Concordia University, in Irvine, California, in 1976.

11. This seminary was founded by LCMS missionaries in 1983. Previous to the founding of the seminary, pastors were trained at the Lutheran Theological Academy founded in 1965. For detail see Won Yong Ji, *A History of Lutheranism in Korea, A Personal Account,* 122.

12. "Philippine Lutheran Mission in Hawaii—18-Month Evaluation," 1. [Hereafter cited as "18-Month Evaluation."]

13. The Pacific Missionary Newsletter, vol. I, no. 1 (January/February 1978), 1.

14. *Ibid.* 2.

15. 18-Month Evaluation, 2.

16. *Ibid.*

17. *Ibid.* The supporting bodies consisted of "the District, Synod, and congregation that have selected the Lutheran Philippine Ministry as part of the personalized giving programs."

18. Stienbeck letter, dated June 6, 1978, 1.

19. *Ibid.*

20. Actually, Dennis Kastens first wrote to Bugtong inviting him to come to Hawaii in 1973, but Bugtong declined. He had just been installed at St. Peter's Lutheran Church in New Hamburg and at St. Paul's Lutheran Church in Tavistock, Ontario, Canada, as pastor of this dual parish. Kastens kept sending letters and church bulletins to Bugtong to inform him about the development of this ministry.

21. *Ibid.,* 2.

22. *Ibid.*

23. The 18-month Evaluation stated that Bugtong arrived in September 1975. I think this is a mistake. The year should be 1978.

24. Iverson letter, March 28, 1979, 2.

25. Bugtong letter, February 14, 1980, 2.

26. Notes from Bugtong to author, June 6, 2000.

27. *Ibid.*

28. Iverson letter to Robert Meyer, June 21, 1982.

29. Bugtong letter, August 15, 1982.

30. *Ibid.*

31. *Ibid.*

32. *Ibid.*

33. Meyer letter to Roger Leenerts, February 2, 1983.

34. Louis Y. Nau letter, April 27, 1983, to Theo. A. Iverson.

35. *Ibid.*

36. See "Field Visitation—Honolulu, Hawaii," April 2-5, 1983.

37. "Racism in the Church," A Statement of the Seventh General Convention of The American Lutheran Church, adopted October 14, 1974, 1.

38. *Ibid.* 2.

39. Chao Weijan, "Zizhuan" (Autobiography), 1962, 2. This is an autobiography written in Chinese by David Chao.

40. *Ibid.,* 2.

41. *Ibid.,* 3.

42. Kairos was formally established in February 1986 by Sigurd Aske, a former Norwegian missionary to China. The aim is to broadcast the gospel to mainland China.

43. See Service of Installation for Simon Wing-Shing Lee, pastor of Chinese Lutheran Church of Honolulu, July 16, 1981.
44. Rev. Lee Wing-Shing, "Chinese Lutheran Church of Honolulu," February 1999, 2. This is an unpublished article written in Chinese.
45. Social Statements, The Lutheran Church in America, "Race Relations," adopted by the Second Biennial Convention, July 2-9, 1964, 1.
46. *Ibid.*, 3.
47. "History of the Consulting Committee for Minority Group Interests," 1. (Accession #1987-427; Files, 1969-1985; Box 4 Folder 8, ELCA Archives.)
48. *Ibid.*
49. *Ibid.*
50. *Ibid.*
51. Robert J. Marshall, memorandum to "Members of the Consulting Committee on Minority Group Interests," February 6, 1973, 1.
52. *Ibid.*
53. "History of the Consulting Committee for Minority Group Interests," 2.
54. Western Canada Synod Annual Convention, April 19-21, 1974, 10.
55. Western Canada Synod Annual Convention, June 19-22, 1975, 16.
56. *Ibid.*
57. *Western Canada Lutheran* (August-September 1974), 1.
58. *Ibid.*
59. *Ibid.*
60. *Ibid.*
61. Paul T. Nakamura, "LOC Members—Dr. Edmond Yee Project," n.d., 2.
62. *Ibid.*
63. *Ibid.*
64. Paul T. Nakamura, "Lutheran Oriental Church," n.d., 1.
65. *Ibid.*
66. *Ibid.*

CHAPTER 6: SNAPSHOTS, GENERATION ONE
1. Diane Mei Lin Mark, *Seasons of Light: The History of Chinese Christian Churches in Hawaii*, 2.
2. "Report on Asian Ministry," CMM, ELCA, June 1993, 12.
3. Chu's correspondence with author, 3. [Hereafter cited as Chu.]
4. *The 1988 Directory of the ELCA Pastors* indicates that he graduated from Hamma in 1950. But the *Life Sketches of Lutheran Ministers of North Carolina and Tennessee Synods, 1773-1965* states that he received his B.D. degree in 1951. According to Hamma's own record, Chu received his degree in 1951.
5. Chu, 5.
6. Minutes of the United Lutheran Church in America: Nineteenth Biennial Convention, October 6-13, 1954, 790.
7. Chu, 5.
8. Edwin O. Reischauer, *The Japanese*, 72.
9. "The Reverend Eiichi Matsushita, 1930–1984." A bulletin announcing his death in 1984.
10. *Ibid.*

11. The "point-of-breaks" theory was developed by Charles H. Cooley, a sociologist. The "point-of-breaks" refers to "a junction point or a breaking point." Matsushita applied "it to the life of the church, especially as it relates to church extension and church development." For further information see Eiichi Matsushita, "Division for Mission in North America, Department for Church Extension, Lutheran Church in America," March 1975. (Unpublished paper.)

12. Matsushita offered the "balloon" theory in conjunction with his discussion on congregational spot study and membership characteristics. For further information see Eiichi Matsushita, "Church and Community Research Handbook," vols. 2 and 3. New York: Division for Mission in North America, Lutheran Church in America, 1983 and 1984. (Unpublished papers.)

13. Mabel Moy, e-mail to author, October 3, 2000, 4. [Unless otherwise indicated, all quotes for this section are derived from Mabel Moy's e-mail to author.]

14. Japan annexed Korea in 1910.

15. Lewis M. Holm, "From Buddhist Village to Wartburg Seminary: An Interview with Wi Jo Kang," *ALC World Mission Review* (1981-1982), 33.

16. Kang's e-mail to author, February 29, 2000.

17. *Ibid.*

18. Tsan's correspondence with author.

19. "Cell 55," Christmas 1991, 1.

20. *Ibid.*

21. *Ibid.*

22. "Biographical Sketch," Lutheran Council in the USA, 1982, 1.

23. *Ibid.*, 1, 2.

24. *Ibid.*, 2.

25. *Ibid.*

CHAPTER 7: SNAPSHOTS, GENERATION TWO

1. "Acts of Conscience: Some Followed Orders; Feng Shan Ho Worked to Save Jews," *San Francisco Chronicle*, March 23, 2000, A13.

2. Lily R. Wu, "Asian—and American," *Lutheran Woman's Quarterly*, Fall 1991, 5.

3. *Ibid.*

4. *Ibid.*

5. Hall, *Tea that Burns*, 230, 231.

6. Lily R. Wu, paper to author, n.d., 1.

7. *Ibid.*

8. *Ibid.*

9. *Ibid.*, 2.

10. *Ibid.*

11. Lily R. Wu, resume, n.d., 1.

12. *Ibid.*

13. *Ibid.*, 2.

14. This church continues to have strong relationship with The LCMS. It also has a working relationship with other Lutheran churches in India.

15. Curriculum Vitae of J. Paul Rajashekar (1999), p. 8.

16. Fern Lee Hagedorn, resume, n.d., 1.

17. Hagedorn, Autobiography, July 29, 1999, 1.

18. *Ibid.*

19. *Ibid.*, 2.

20. Hagedorn, resume, n.d., 1.

21. *Ibid.* This documentary won the Angel award by Religion in Media.
22. *Ibid.*
23. *Ibid.*
24. *Ibid.*
25. News Release, April 22, 2000, 1.
26. *Ibid.*, 1, Both can be viewed on the Internet at: http://www.newmediabible.org.
27. Hagedorn, Autobiography, 4.
28. *Ibid.*
29. *Ibid.*
30. *Ibid.*
31. See chapter 10 for detail.
32. Charles Matsumoto, e-mail to author, February 23, 2000, 1. Ault, Colorado, was not an internment camp.
33. *Ibid.*
34. *Ibid.*
35. *Ibid.*
36. See chapter 10 for detail on the evolution of this organization and the role Matsumoto played in it.
37. Corazon Gutierrez Aguilar, Autobiography, n.d., 2.
38. *Ibid.*, 4.
39. Donna Osteraas, "Mission: Possible—Lutheran Brotherhood Supports Evangelism and Outreach," *Lutheran Brotherhood Bond*, January/February, 1999, 28.
40. *Ibid.*
41. *Ibid.*
42. *Ibid.*
43. George Tan, "My Journey," unpublished paper to author, June 2, 1999.
44. Cherian C. Puthiyottil, resume, n.d., 3.
45. *Ibid.*

CHAPTER 8: A GIANT STEP
1. The name of the committee was the Inter-Lutheran Coordination Committee on Theological Education and Leadership Development for Minority Ministries.
2. In this volume Hawaii is considered to be part of North America.
3. Edmond Yee, memorandum to Howell S. Foster, January 23, 1978.
4. The original note was addressed to "Resident of 1617 South Monterey Road, Alhambra, California 91803.
5. Edmond Yee, memorandum to Minnick, August 2, 1979, 1.
6. *Ibid.*
7. *Ibid.*, 2.
8. Trudy Wei, "My Story of Becoming a Lutheran," n.d., 1.
9. *Ibid.*
10. *Ibid.*
11. *Ibid.*
12. *Ibid.*, 2.
13. This document was produced on May 31, 1979, and amended on November 2, 1979.
14. "Immigrating Pastors and the Lutheran Church in America," 1.
15. Edmond Yee, memorandum to Rev. M. L. Minnick Jr., August 24, 1982, 1.
16. *Ibid.*
17. M. L. Minnick Jr., letter to Ed Yee, March 14, 1983.

18. See Stanley Olson's March 23, 1984, letter for detail.
19. *Ibid.*, 1.
20. *Ibid.*
21. Walter Wagner, letter to Stanley E. Olson, April 2, 1984, 1.
22. M. L. Minnick, letter to Edmond Yee, June 8, 1984.
23. There were indeed a large number of Asian clergy desirous to become members of the Lutheran ministerium, but not many were qualified.
24. The ELCHK also entered into conversation with the ALC regarding the possibility of sending a pastor to the United States to work with the Chinese. For further information, see "Partnership in Mission: The Evangelical Lutheran Church of Hong Kong and The American Lutheran Church," June 17, 1981. However this conversation did not result in the ELCHK sending a pastor to the United States through the ALC.
25. M. L. Minnick, letter to Rev. John Tse, October 9, 1981.
26. "Review of JELC Cooperative Ministry with ALC and LCA in the U.S.A.," n.d., 3. [Hereafter cited as "Review."]
27. *Ibid.*, 1.
28. *Ibid.*
29. See Review, 2.
30. See "Description of DMNA/LCA Experience in the JELC/LCA Missionary Program," February 18, 1986. [Hereafter cited as "Description."]
31. *Ibid.*
32. *Ibid.*
33. *Ibid.*
34. See Review, 2.
35. See Description.
36. *Ibid.*
37. For detail see Warren A. Sorteberg, "Consultation between Japan Evangelical Lutheran Church (JELC), The Lutheran Church in America (LCA), The American Lutheran Church (ALC), March 5-7, 1986. [Hereafter cited as Consultation.]
38. *Ibid.*, 1.
39. See Consultation, 1.
40. The Princeton and Honolulu sites did not materialize.
41. See M. L. Minnick's letter to "Japan Evangelical Lutheran Church," February 4, 1988, 1.
42. *Ibid.*, 2.
43. *Ibid.*
44. See "The Western Regional Lutheranism Consultation," a document from PLTS, February 7, 1979, 2. [Hereafter cited as "PLTS document."]
45. John Nasstrom, memorandum to "Members, Inter-Lutheran Coordinating Committee," October 9, 1978.
46. See PLTS document.

CHAPTER 9: RIGHT DIRECTION

1. Official Report and Minutes: Nineteenth Annual Convention, The American Lutheran Church South Pacific District, May 31-June 2, 1979, 67.
2. This is the official title in the district's annual report. However, there is a variant on this title. The commission's minutes give the name as "Bishop's Commission on Asian Ministries."
3. Official Report and Minutes: Twenty-First Annual Convention, The American Lutheran Church South Pacific District, April 30-May 2, 1981.

4. Minutes of Bishop's Commission on Asian Ministries, March 9, 1982, 3. [Hereafter cited as "Minutes, March 9, 1982."]

5. *Ibid.*

6. Minutes of Bishop's Commission on Asian Ministries, July 20, 1982, 2.

7. *Ibid.*, 3.

8. Minutes of Bishop's Commission on Asian Ministries, December 1, 1982, 3.

9. Minutes, March 9, 1982, 3.

10. For further detail see Minutes of Bishop's Commission on Asian Ministries, December 1, 1983, 2.

11. *Ibid.*

12. *Ibid.*

13. Official Reports and Minutes: Twenty-Third Annual Convention, The American Lutheran Church South Pacific District, June 16-18, 1983, 15.

14. This was the only orientation ever held in the South Pacific District throughout the life of the commission.

15. Official Reports and Minutes: Twenty-Fifth Annual Convention, The American Lutheran Church South Pacific District, April 26-28, 1985, 83.

16. Official Reports and Minutes: Twenty-Sixth Annual Convention, The American Lutheran Church South Pacific District, April 25-27, 1986, 99.

17. Delbert E. Anderson, letter to Bishop Paul E. Erickson, September 9, 1983, 2.

18. Paul E. Erickson, letter to Rev. Delbert E. Anderson, September 1, 1983.

19. Edmond Yee, memorandum to Rev. M. L. Minnick Jr., January 16, 1984, 1 [Hereafter cited as "Yee, Memorandum."]

20. Julie Williams, e-mail to author, December 1, 1999, 1. [Hereafter cited as "Williams, e-mail."]

21. Yee, Memorandum.

22. *Ibid.*

23. Williams, e-mail, 1.

CHAPTER 10: COMMUNITY IN ACTION

1. Mencius, *The Mencius*, Book I, chapter 1.

2. Edmond Yee, memorandum to Rev. M. L. Minnick Jr., January 24, 1980.

3. *Ibid.*

4. James Moy, letter to Dr. Massie Kennard, July 7, 1980.

5. The bylaws were proposed at the meeting, but the person who was responsible for putting them together did not seem to do anything about them afterwards.

6. Around the time of the executive committee meeting in August 1982, no one outside the "association" knew anything about the organizational structure or anything else. I, however, later received a copy of the Chu-Chow letter of November 2, 1982, sent to me by someone outside of the group with the following comment: "This might help you to understand what is going on among these people."

7. By now, the organization was in transition from Asian Pastors and Professional Workers Conference to Asian American Caucus. And the Caucus's executive committee was supposed to be called Advisory Committee. Hence the confusion in the August 5-6, 1982, minutes.

8. Nakamura was not a member of the committee.

9. Notes of Meeting of Asian Pastors and Professional Workers' Executive Committee, August 5-6, 1982, 2.

10. *Ibid.*

11. *Ibid.*, 3.

12. The Chinese Rhenish Church by then had already established a mission in North America.

13. Minutes of the Asian American Caucus Conference, September 20-23, 1983, 6.

14. Minutes of the Joint-Asian Conference of The American Lutheran Church and the Lutheran Church in America, November 4-6, 1985, 5.

15. Asian Caucus Newsletter, November 1985, 1.

16. *Ibid.*

17. See Minutes of the Asian Caucus Executive Committee meeting, May 15-16, 1985, 1.

18. Minutes of the Asian American Caucus Conference, September 20-22, 1983, 1, 2.

19. These recommendations were sent to DMNA and DSMA.

20. Lily Wu, Fred Rajan, and Edmond Yee, *Eternal River: An Asian Cultural Awareness Resource*, page before the dedication page.

21. For detail see Lily Wu (ed.), *Catching a Star: Transcultural Reflections on a Church for All People*, 48-116. [Hereafter cited as *Catching a Star.*]

22. The LCMS decided not to participate after its officials had a chance to review the initial proposal.

23. For Asian participants list see *Catching a Star*, 124, 349.

24. For the Asian Caucus's contributions see *Catching a Star*, 125-129; 353-355.

25. "The ALC-LCA-AELC Consultation on Theological Education was begun in 1973 by the ALC and LCA. ... The AELC jointed in 1981. The consultation [was then] engaged in planning for theological education in the new Lutheran church." See Lloyd E. Sheneman, "Theological Education and The New Lutheran Church," Southeastern Synod: Professional Leaders Convocation, September 24-25, 1985, 1. I was a member of the consultation from 1983-1986.

26. KCRA-TV, "Perceptions-Yellow Peril," December 23, 1984. [Hereafter cited as "KCRA-TV."]

27. *Ibid.*

28. Edmond Yee, letter to Edwin Meese, September 22, 1986, 1.

29. This might have something to do with fact that Meese is a Lutheran and good friend of this author's boss, Walter M. Stuhr.

30. Linda K. Davis, letter to Edmond Yee, October 10, 1986, 1. "The Federal trial came to a close in September 1984 when Ronald Ebens, the admitted killer of Vincent Chin, was sentenced to 25 years in prison. Michael Nitz was acquitted," KCRA-TV.

31. *The Japanese American Incarceration: A Case for Redress.* Fourth Edition, June 1981, 24. This work provides a quick summary of the cause leading up to the internment.

32. "Against All Odds: The Japanese Americans' Campaign for Redress," C16-90-1006.0, Case Program, John F. Kennedy School of Government, Harvard University, 1990, 1. This work gives an excellent summary of the Redress Movement by the Japanese community and others.

33. Minutes of the Tenth Biennial Convention of the Lutheran Church in America, June 25-July 2, 1980, 97.

34. *Ibid.*, 318.

35. *Ibid.*, 318, 319.

36. *Ibid.*, 324.

37. Minutes of the Twenty-First Annual Convention of the Pacific Southwest Synod of the Lutheran Church in America, April 22-25, 1982, 46, 47.

38. *Ibid.*, 47.

39. Charles Matsumoto, e-mail to author, February 28, 2000, 2.

40. Minutes of the Twelfth Biennial Convention of the Lutheran Church in America, June 28-July 5, 1984, 691.
41. Manzanar was one of the 10 internment sites.
42. *West County Times*, Saturday, July 22, 2000, A7.

CHAPTER 11: A DIFFERENT LANDSCAPE

1. For details on the organization see Richard W. Solberg, *Open Doors: The Story of Lutherans Resettling Refugees*.
2. Lanai Michelle Byg, e-mail to author, August 21, 2000, 1.
3. In all probability these four ministries were the first or among the earliest ministries initiated with the refugees by the Lutheran churches.
4. I am deeply indebted to Donald Rudrud and Donald Moorman, who provided me with written information on ministries in Minnesota and California, respectively, with Southeast Asians. Without their generous assistance, this chapter could not have been written.
5. Donald Moorman, correspondence to author, February 28, 2000, 1. [Unless otherwise indicated, all quotes in this section are derived from Moorman's correspondence with author.]
6. The man was officially designated a vicar.
7. Concordia Publishing House, 1993.
8. Sunthi Paul Chookiatsirichai, resume, n.d., 1.
9. Minutes of the Concerned Group for East Asian Ministries, February 5, 1985, 1.
10. Edmond Yee, memorandum to Rev. M. L. Minnick Jr., April 9, 1985, 1.
11. *Ibid.*
12. *Ibid.* In Philadelphia African-Americans tried to run Asians, the Hmong in particular, out of town.
13. *Ibid.*, 2.
14. Hang Chay and John R. Cochran, "A New Community in Philadelphia, A New Ministry in the Church," (unpublished article) 1.
15. *Ibid.*, 1, 2.
16. The other two were David Sasaki and Jimmy Castro who served in Hawaii.
17. Donald Rudrud, "Southeast Asian Ministry in Minneapolis 1980-1998," (an unpublished paper to the author), n.d., 1. [Unless otherwise indicated, all quotes for this section are derived from the Rudrud paper.]

CHAPTER 12: SOMETHING NEW

1. For detail see Edgar R. Trexler, *Anatomy of a Merger: People, Dynamics, and Decisions that Shaped the ELCA*.
2. "Report of Executive Director," CMM, October 18-20, 1991, 915.
3. The Constitution of the Evangelical Lutheran Church in America, 16.41.E87a.
4. *Ibid.*, 16.41.E87f.
5. "Report of Director for Asian Ministries," CMM, October 11-12, 1996, 201.
6. Interview with William E. Wong, December 17, 1998. [Hereafter cited as "Interview."]
7. *Ibid.*
8. *Ibid.*
9. *Ibid.*
10. *Ibid.*
11. "Report of Director for Asian Ministries," CMM, October 1-3, 1988, 100.
12. Minutes of Subcommittee on Evangelism, Cooperative Parish Projects

Committee, January 31, 1989, 1.

13. Rev. Len Harms of The LCMS was the other project manager.

14. Interview.

15. Notes on 1996 ELCA Korean Ministries Gathering, January 18-20, 1996, 1.

16. "Report of Director for Asian Ministries," CMM, October 1-3, 1988, 101.

17. Interview.

18. This newsletter was edited by Rev. Yin Ying, but the project itself was short-lived due to ELCA's budget cuts and Wong's move to a different position.

19. "Report of Director of Asian Ministries," CMM, October 19-21, 1990, 103.

20. Minutes of the Steering Committee, CMM, January 11-12, 1992, 1.

21. *Ibid.*

22. "Report of Director for Asian Ministries," CMM, March 12-14, 1993, 100-101.

23. Taosheng is a Lutheran publishing house associated with the Evangelical Lutheran Church of Hong Kong and the Taiwan Lutheran Church in Taiwan.

24. The first consultation was held on June 27-28, 1991, at Faith Lutheran Church, Monterey Park, California.

25. "Report of Director for Asian Ministries," CMM, October 8-10, 1993, 100.

26. *Ibid.*

27. "Report of Director for Asian Ministries," CMM, October 6-7, 1995, 100.

28. *Ibid.*

29. Rhonda Goldman for Fred Rajan to ELCA, August 9, 1996, 1.

30. Author's interview with Limthongviratn, March 28, 2000.

31. "Report of the Executive Director," CMM, Part II, October 8-9, 1999, 741.

32. Bachmann, 205.

33. A seminary organized and supported by a group of conservative individuals who were dissatisfied with the ALC.

34. "Report on Multicultural Mission Strategy," CMM, ELCA, 1991, 1. [Hereafter cited as "MMS."]

35. I was the Asian representative on this task force.

36. MMS, 1.

37. "Report of Executive Director," CMM, October 19-21, 1990, 915.

38. *Ibid.*

39. *Ibid.*

40. *Ibid.*

41. *Ibid.*, 915, 916.

42. *Ibid.*, 917.

43. *Ibid.*, 916.

44. "Report of Executive Director," CMM, March 20-22, 1992, 905.

45. *Ibid.*, 907.

46. "Report of Executive Director," CMM, September 25-27, 1992, 701.

47. *Ibid.*

48. *Ibid.*

49. Minutes of the Steering Committee of the CMM, March 11-12, 1994, 5.

50. *Ibid.*, 703.

51. "Report of Executive Director," March 12-14, 1993, 721.

52. *Ibid.*

53. For detail see "Major Program Directions for 1995-1997," October 8-9, 1993, 707, 708.

54. See "Concept Paper: Ethnic Ministry Programs, CMM," October 8-9, 1993, 700-702.

55. They were Duane Addison, Cal Holloway, Jennie Lightfoot, and Pablo Jose Quinones.

56. Minutes of the Executive Committee, CMM, March 15, 1994, 1.

57. Minutes of the Executive Committee, CMM, March 28, 1994, 1.

58. The consultants were Jerome Dorsey, Paul Nakamura, Gordon Straw, and Maria Valenzuela.

59. The Asian community remained silent.

60. Minutes of the Executive Committee, CMM, May 9, 1994, 1.

61. *Ibid.*

62. "Report of Executive Director," CMM, March 11-12, 1994, 719.

63. *Ibid.*

64. "Report of Executive Director," CMM, October 11-12, 1996, 545.

65. *Ibid.*, 545, 546.

66. Minutes of the Steering Committee, CMM, October 11-12, 1996, 7.

67. *Ibid.*, 8.

68. See chapter 14 for detail.

69. For detail see "Report of Executive Director," Part II, CMM, October 8-9, 1999, 741-747.

70. *Ibid.*, 743.

71 "Report of Executive Director," CMM, March 3-4, 2000, 728.

CHAPTER 13: ON THE MOVE

1. Bruce Edward Hall, *Tea That Burns*, 189.

2. Unless otherwise indicated, all quotes in the Moy section are derived from the author's interview with him, June 9, 2000.

3. Unless specified all quotes in this section are from Kitahata's communication with the author.

4. Delene Costanted, "DGM appoints new Director for International Scholarships and Communications," 1.

5. *Ibid.*

6. *Ibid.*

7. *Ibid.*

8. *Ibid.*

9. Announcement, n.d., 1.

10. *Ibid.*

11. *Ibid.*

12. Job S. Ebenezer, resume, n.d., 1.

13. Job S. Ebenezer, letter to author, June 23, 1999, 1. [Unless otherwise indicated, all quotes in this section are derived from Ebenezer's letter.]

14. Quote is from George-Guiser's e-mail to author, February 22, 2000. [Unless indicated otherwise, all subsequent quotes for this section are from the same source.]

15. Peter Yung-ming Lai, vita, n.d., 3.

16. M. L. Minnick Jr., memorandum to Michael Cooper-White, 1.

17. *Ibid.*

18. Eardley Mendis, "A Short Story of Eardley Mendis," n.d., 1.

19. *Ibid.*

20. *Ibid.*

CHAPTER 14: ASIAN LUTHERANISM—WHICH WAY?

1. Simon Lee, letter to Henry F. French, 1.
2. Members of the planning team were David Chen, Robert Hoyt, Simon W. S. Lee, Pongsak Limthongviratn, Paul V. Martinson, Craig J. Moran, James Y. K. Moy, A. Craig Settlage, Walter M. Stuhr, William Wong, and I.
3. Division for Ministry, Board Meeting Agenda, October 10-12, 1997, 211. [Hereafter cited as "Agenda."]
4. *Ibid.*
5. The Western Mission Cluster comprises LS and PLTS.
6. Agenda, 212.
7. *Ibid.*
8. See "Asian Studies Project" for detail. [Hereafter cited as "Project."]
9. *Ibid.*, 1.
10. *Ibid.*, 1, 2.
11. *Ibid.*, 1.
12. *Ibid.*
13. This refers to "Chinese History, Philosophy, Religions, … the Chinese Experience in North America, … Great China," as stated in "Asian Studies Project" distributed by one or both LS representative(s) at the meeting.
14. Project, 1.
15. *Ibid.*
16. *Ibid.*
17. *Ibid.*, 2.
18. *Ibid.*
19. Agenda, 209-211.
20. Phyllis Anderson, memorandum to President Timothy Lull, Dean Walter Stuhr, President David Tiede, and Dean Marc Kolden, October 21, 1997, 1.
21. W. Stuhr, memorandum to T. Lull, E. Yee, January 22, 1998, 1.
22. *Ibid.*
23. W. Stuhr, memorandum to T. Lull (Administrative Council), E. Yee, M. Aune (Academic Committee), June 1, 1998, 1. [Hereafter cited as "Memorandum to T. Lull."]
24. See Craig Moran, "Asian Studies Program Report," n.d.
25. See "Memorandum to T. Lull."
26. The following people were present: David Chen, Simon Lee, Pongsak Limthongviratn, Hansel Lo, Craig Moran, Fred Rajan (partial), Gregory Villalon, and I.
27. Asian Studies Program Advisory Committee Meeting, November 4, 1998, 3.
28. See Minutes of the November 4, 1998, meeting for detail.
29. See agendas for February 26-27 and May 7-8, 1999, for detail.
30. "A Summary from the Meeting with President David [Tiede], Luther Seminary," January 15, 1999, 1.
31. *Ibid.*
32. *Ibid.*
33. *Ibid.*
34. This figure is questionable. Different documents give a different figure. Most likely the actual number of countries represented at the conference was 17, including countries of origin of staff and stewards.
35. The LCMS was not part of this conference.
36. Stacy Kitahata, Paul Rajashekar, and I were present at the association assembly.
37. LWF staff was unable to attend this meeting.

38. For detail see Paul Rajashekar, Lily R. Wu, and Pongsak Limthongvirtn, eds. *Asian Lutheranism—Which Way?*

39. "First Asian Lutheran Conference: Summary and Recommendations," (first draft), January 25, 1999, 2.

40. Members were Naohiro Kiyoshihe, Lam Tak Ho, Harlen Simangunsong, Prasanna Kumari, David Chen, Cora Aguilar, Paul Rajashekar, Lily Wu, and Timothy Fong.

41. They were Will Herzfeld, Thomas Schafer, and Margrethe Kleiber.

42. Pongsak Limthongviratn, "The Progress of Asian Lutheran International. Conference (ALIC): A report submitted to ACTEA and ARC," October 16, 2000, 3.

43. *Ibid.*

44. The organizations are ACTEA and ARCC.

45. Robert Hoyt and Bill Wong, memorandum to Chinese Pastors, April 11, 1995, 1.

46. *Ibid.*

47. See Fred Rajan, "Center for Chinese Ministry," October 1999.

48. Pongsak Limthongvirtan, memorandum to Thomas Chen, Hansel Lo, Peter Wang, Simon Lee, Joy Pan, and Trudy Wei.

49. *Ibid.*

CHAPTER 15: MISSION BLUEPRINT

1. Introduction in "Mission Blueprint for the Nineties: Summary," St. Louis: Concordia Publishing House, n.d., [Hereafter cited as "MBN."]

2. *Ibid.*

3. I am deeply indebted to Robert J. Scudieri and others who so graciously provided the information for this chapter.

4. MBN, 2.

5. *Ibid.*

6. *Ibid.*

7. *Ibid.*

8. Scudieri's communication with author, n.d.

9. *Ibid.*

10. *Ibid.*

11. Robert J. Scudieri, "Strategy for North America Mission Fields," unpublished paper, October 1, 1998. [Hereafter cited as "Strategy."]

12. *Ibid.*

13. Author's interview with Rev. Terrence Chan, March 19, 1999. [Hereafter cited as "Interview."]

14. Strategy, 1. For further information see "North America Mission Task Forces," unpublished paper, April 1, 1997.

15. Constitution of the Chinese Ministry Conference (Revised and Adopted April, 1998), 1.

16. Minutes and Notes of the CMC Task Force and North America Mission Leaders' Conference (St. Louis, Missouri, January 18-20, 1996), 3.

17. For detail see Minutes from the Chinese Ministry Conference of North America, May 18, 1992, 1.

18. *Ibid.*, 2.

19. *Ibid.*

20. *Ibid.*, 3.

21. *Ibid.*, 3, 4.

22. Lee translated Martin Luther's Small Catechism with Explanation based on a 1986 edition published by Concordia Publishing House, USA. The Literature

Department, LCHKS, published this translation in 1999.

23. Notes and Minutes of the Chinese Ministry Conference, Officer Telephone Conference, November 8, 1996, 2.

24. Minutes of the Chinese Ministry Conference Annual Meeting, May 6-8, 1999, 1, 2.

25. *Ibid.*, 2.

26. *Ibid.*

27. Strategy, 4.

28. Interview.

29. Notes and Minutes of the Chinese Ministry Conference, Officer Telephone Conference, October 17, 1997, 2.

30. *Ibid.*

31. *Ibid.*

32. This information is from a brochure called, "Midwest Chinese Ministries, (MCM). However, Lim in an e-mail to author, October 13, 2000, states "The Midwest Chinese Ministries ... LCMS, Indiana District, was formed in 1995 to assist me [Lim] in my [Lim's] pioneering work of mission starts among Chinese people in smaller Midwestern cities."

33. *Ibid.*

34. *Ibid.*

35. Unless specified, all information and quotes for this section come from the organization's brochure.

36. Robert J. Scudieri, letter to author, December 14, 2000, 1.

37. "Year 2000 Objectives," 1.

38. The official name for the conference is supposed to be the Korean Lutheran Ministry Conference in North America, but in actual usage, it varies from Korean Ministry Conference to North America Korean Minister's Conference. For the sake of consistency I will use the name "Korean Ministry Conference" throughout this chapter.

39. Constitution of the Korean Ministry Conference, 6.

40. For Hong's biography, see chapter 5.

41. *Ibid.*, 1.

42. Minutes [in Korean] of the KMC, June 26-27, 1998, 8.

43. "Korean Ministry Church Planning Task Force Strategy Statement," 1.

44. *Ibid.*

45. *Ibid.*

46. Jaya P. Bijjia, "Asian Indian Ministries of North America," 1.

47. *Ibid.*

48. Raj Victor, e-mail to author, October 13, 2000, 1.

49. *Ibid.*

50. *Ibid.*

51. *Ibid.*

52. "Vietnamese Lutheran Task Force Strategy Statement," October 11, 1996, 1.

53. *Ibid.*, 1, 2.

54. "Gathering of Japanese Ministry Leaders," September 21-22, 1999, 1.

55. *Ibid.*, 3.

56. David R. McClean, letter, May 1, 2000.

57. I am indebted to Carol Christianson who provided me with a copy of the working agreement.

58. Paul Moldenhauer, "Notes from the first meeting of those doing ministry with Japanese in the United States," September 21-22, 2000, 1.

EPILOGUE: A NEW HORIZON

1. Edmond Yee, "Ministry in a Pluralistic Context: Mapping the Way," in *Asian Lutheranism—Which Way,* Paul Rajashekar, Lily Wu, and Pongsak Limthongviratn, eds., 58.

BIBLIOGRAPHY

BOOKS

Ali, K. *A New History of Indo-Pakistan, Since 1526.* Lahore: Aziz Publishers, 1977.

Andracki, Stanislaw. *Immigration of Orientals into Canada with Special Reference to Chinese.* New York: Arno Press, 1978.

Bachmann, E. Theodore, and Mercia Brenne Bachmann. *Lutheran Churches in the World.* Minneapolis: Augsburg, 1989.

Buchignani, Norman, and Doreen M. Indra with Ram Srivastiva. *Continuous Journey: A Social History of South Asians in Canada.* Toronto: McClelland and Steward Limited, 1985.

Cayton, Horace R., and Anne O. Lively. *The Chinese in the United States and the Chinese Christian Church.* Abridged version. 1955.

Chan, Wing-tsit, Isma'il Ragi Al Faruqui, Joseph M. Kitagawa, and P.T. Raju, eds. *The Great Asian Religions: An Anthology.* New York: The MacMillan Company, 1969.

Chandler, David P. *A History of Cambodia.* Boulder: Westview Press, 1983.

Chandra, Bipan, Mriduala Mukherjee, Aditya Mukherjee, K. N. Panikkar, and Sucheta Mahajan. *India's Struggle for Independence.* New York: Penguin Books Ltd., 1989.

Chapman, Graham P. and Kathleen M. Baker, eds. *The Changing Geography of Asia.* London: Routledge, 1992.

Chesneaux, Jean. *The Vietnamese Nation: Contribution to a History.* Sydney: Current Book Distributors PTY. LTD., 1966.

Daniels, Roger and Harry H. L. Kitano. *American Racism: Exploration of the Nature of Prejudice.* Englewood Cliffs: Prentice-Hall, Inc., 1970.

Daniels, Roger. *The Decision to Relocate the Japanese Americans.* Philadelphia: J.B. Lippincott Company, 1975.

Hall, Bruce Edward. *Tea That Burns.* New York: The Free Press, 1998.

Herman, Masako, comp. *The Japanese in America, 1843-1973.* Dobbs Ferry: Oceana Publications, Inc., 1974.

Ide Anak Agung Gde Agung. *From the Formation of the State of East Indonesia Towards the Establishment of the United States of Indonesia.* Trans. Linda Owens. Jakarta: Yayasan Obor Indonesia, 1996.

John F. Kennedy School of Government. *Against All Odds: The Japanese Americans'
    Campaign for Redress.* C16-90-1006.0. Cambridge: John F. Kennedy School
    of Government, Harvard University, 1990.
Kalbach, Warren E. *The Impact of Immigration on Canada's Population.* Ottawa:
    Dominion Bureau of Statistics, 1970.
Kanungo, Rabindra N. *South Asians in the Canadian Mosaic.* Montreal: The Kala
    Bharati Foundation, 1984.
Kim, Hyung-chan and Cynthia C. Mejia, comps. *The Filipinos in America, 1898-1974.*
    Dobbs Ferry: Oceana Publications, Inc., 1976.
Kim, Hyung-chan and Wayne Patterson, comps. *The Koreans in America, 1882-1974.*
    Dobbs Ferry: Oceana Publications, Inc., 1974.
Koga, Sumio, comp. *A Centennial Legacy: History of the Japanese Christian Missions
    in North America, 1877-1977.* Vol. 1. Chicago: Nabart, Inc., 1977.
Latourette, Kenneth Scott. *A History of Christian Missions in China.* New York: The
    MacMillan Company, 1929.
Leonard, Karen Isaksen. *The South Asian Americans.* Westport: Greenwood Press, 1997.
Lopez, Donald S. Jr. *Asian Religions in Practice.* Princeton: Princeton University Press,
    1999.
Luo Man-hua, ed. *Huaren jiaohui shouce (Chinese Churches Handbook).* Hong Kong:
    Chinese Coordination Centre of World Evangelism, 1981.
Manich, M.L. *History of Laos: (including the history of Lannathal, Chiengmai).*
    Bangkok: Chalermnit, 1967.
Mark, Diane Mei Lin. *Seasons of Light: The History of Chinese Christian Churches in
    Hawaii.* Honolulu: Chinese Christian Association of Hawaii, 1989.
Mencius. *The Mencius.* Translated by D. C. Lau. Baltimore: Penguin Books Ltd., 1976.
Minamiki, George, S.J. *The Chinese Rites: From Its Beginning to Modern Times.*
    Chicago: Loyola University Press, 1985.
Myer, Milton W. *Asia: A Concise History.* Blue Ridge Summit: Rowman and Littlefield
    Publishers, Inc., 1997.
The National Committee for Redress and Japanese American Citizens League. *The
    Japanese America Incarceration: A Case for Redress.* Fourth Edition. San
    Francisco: The National Committee for Redress and Japanese American
    Citizens League, 1981.
Neill, Stephen. *Colonialism and Christian Missions.* London: Lutterworth Press, 1996.
Nielsin, Niels C., Norvin Hein, Frank E. Reynolds, Alan L. Miller, Samuel E. Karff, Alice
    C. Cochran, and Paul McLean. *Religions of the World.* New York: St. Martin's
    Press, 1983.
Reed, James. *The Missionary Mind and American East Asia Policy, 1911-1915.*
    Cambridge: Council on East Asian Studies, Harvard University, 1983.
Reischauer, Edwin O. *The Japanese.* Cambridge: Harvard University Press, 1978.
Shankar, Lavina Dhingra and Rajini Shrikanth, eds. *A Part Yet Apart: South Asians in
    Asian America.* Philadelphia: Temple University Press, 1998.
Sokyo Ono. Shinto. *The Kami Way.* Rutland: Charles E. Tuttle Company, 1962.
Solberg, Richard W. *Open Doors: The Story of Lutherans Resettling Refugees.* St. Louis:
    Condordia Publishing House, 1992.
Suzuki, Lester E. *Ministry in the Assembly and Relocation Centers of World War II.*
    Berkeley: Yardbird Publishing Co., 1979.
Swenson, Victor E. *Parents of Many: Forty-five Years as Missionaries in Old, New, and
    Divided China.* Rock Island: Augustana Press, 1959.

Terweil, B. J. *A History of Modern Thailand, 1767-1942*. St. Lucia: University of
    Queensland Press, 1983.
Threinen, Norman J. *Like a Leaven: A History of the Alberta-British Columbia District of
    Lutheran Church—Canada*. Edmonton: Alberta-British Columbia District,
    1994.
Tietjen, John H. *Memoirs in Exile: Confessional Hope and Institutional Conflict*.
    Minneapolis: Fortress Press, 1990.
Trexler, Edgar R. *Anatomy of a Merger: People, Dynamics, and Decisions that Shaped
    the ELCA*. Minneapolis: Augsburg Fortress, 1991.
Tu Wei-Ming. *Confucian Thought: Selfhood as Creative Transformation*. Albany: State
    University of New York Press, 1985.
Tung, William L. *The Chinese in America, 1820-1973*, Dobbs Ferry: Oceana
    Publications, Inc., 1974.
Tweed, Thomas A., and Stephen Prothero, eds. *Asian Religions in America: A
    Documentary History*. New York: Oxford University Press, 1999.
Wentz, Abdel Ross. *A Basic History of Lutheranism in America*. Philadelphia:
    Muhlenberg Press, 1955.
Wu, Lily R., Fred Rajan, and Edmond Yee. *Eternal River: An Asian Cultural Awareness
    Resource*. Minneapolis: Augsburg Publishing House/Fortress Press, 1988.

ARTICLES

"A Canadian Lutheran First: Chinese Pastor Ordained." *Western Canada Lutheran*
    (August-September 1974).
"Acts of Conscience: Some Followed Orders; Feng Shan Ho Worked to Save Jews."
    San Francisco Chronicle (March 23, 2000).
"Funds OK'd for Recreation of WWII Internment Camp." *West County Times* (July 22,
    2000).
Holm, Lewis M. "From Buddhist Village to Wartburg Seminary: An Interview with Wi
    Jo Kang." *ALC World Mission Review* (1981-1982): 32-25.
Lee Wing-Shing. "Chinese Lutheran Church of Honolulu" (February 1999).
Osteraas, Donna. "Mission: Possible—Lutheran Brotherhood Supports Evangelism
    and Outreach." *Lutheran Brotherhood Bond* (January-February 1999).
Wu, Lily R. "Asian—and American." *Lutheran Woman's Quarterly* (Fall 1991):4-7.
Yee, Edmond. "Asian Americans: A Variety of Gifts." *The Lutheran* (May 21, 1986):11.
————— "Asian Americans: An Intentional Ministry." *The Lutheran* (May 7,
    1986):11.
————— "Asian Americans: Toward Mutual Ministry." *The Lutheran* (June 4,
    1986):11.
————— "Asian Americans: Becoming Lutheran." *The Lutheran* (April 16,
    1986):11.
————— "Yellow Chrysanthemums: Asians in America." *The Lutheran* (April 2,
    1986):13.

DISSERTATIONS AND THESES

Cho, Grace Young Hie. "Organization and Program Development for the Korean
    Central Church of Berkeley." D.Min. project, Pacific School of Religion,
    Berkeley, 1986.

Hovley, John Evangelist, C.S.J. "The Development of the Christian Religion Among the Chinese People of San Francisco." Unpublished M.A. diss., Catholic University of America, Washington, D.C., 1944.

Hung, Chen-Huei. "A Historical Survey of the Confrontation between the Charismatic Movement and the Social Liberation Movement in the Presbyterian Church in Taiwan." D.Min. diss., San Francisco Theological Seminary, 1996.

Kleiber, Margrethe S.C. "A Statistical Information on Asian/Pacific Communities in the Evangelical Lutheran Church in America." M.Div. thesis, Pacific Lutheran Theological Seminary, Berkeley, 1993.

MINUTES, REPORTS, PROCEEDINGS, AND MISCELLANEOUS DOCUMENTS

ALC. 1976 Reports and Actions (Part 1)—Eighth General Convention of The American Lutheran Church, October 6-12, 1976.

ALC. 1978 Reports and Actions (Part 1)—Ninth General Convention of The American Lutheran Church, October 18-24, 1978.

ALC. 1982 Reports and Actions (Part 1)—Eleventh General Convention of The American Lutheran Church, September 6-12, 1982.

The Atlantic District. Proceedings of the Twentieth Convention of the Atlantic District of the Evangelical Lutheran Synod of Missouri, Ohio, and Other States, June 22 to 25, 1936.

Bishop's Commission on Asian Ministries. Minutes of Bishop's Commission on Asian Ministries, South Pacific District, The American Lutheran Church, 1979-1984.

The Board of Home Missions. Annual Report of the Board of Home Missions of the United Evangelical Lutheran Church, February 24-25, 1959.

The Board of Home Missions. Minutes of the Eighth Annual Meeting of the Board of Home Missions of the United Evangelical Lutheran Church, February 14-16, 1950.

————. Minutes of the Board of Home Missions of the United Evangelical Lutheran Church, February 26-March 1, 1951.

————. Minutes of the Board of Home Missions of the United Evangelical Lutheran Church, February 25-26, 1952.

————. Minutes of the 11th Annual Meeting of the Board of Home Missions of the United Evangelical Lutheran Church, February 25-26, 1953.

————. Minutes of the 12th Meeting of the Board of Home Missions of the United Evangelical Lutheran Church, February 17-18, 1954.

————. Minutes of the 12th Annual Meeting of the Board of Home Missions of the United Evangelical Lutheran Church, February 17-18, 1954.

————. Minutes of the 13th Annual Meeting of the Board of Home Missions of the United Evangelical Lutheran Church, February 9-10, 1955.

————. Minutes of the 14th Annual Meeting of the Board of Home Missions of the United Evangelical Lutheran Church, February 22-23, 1956.

————. Minutes of the 15th Annual Meeting of the Board of Home Missions of the United Evangelical Lutheran Church, April 8-9, 1957.

————. Minutes of 16th Annual Meeting of the Board of Home Missions of the United Evangelical Lutheran Church, February 25-26, 1958.

————. Minutes of the Board of Home Missions of the United Evangelical Lutheran Church, February 24, 1959.

————. Minutes of the 17th Annual Meeting of the Board of Home Missions of the United Evangelical Lutheran Church, February 24-25, 1959.

The Board of Home Missions, Executive Committee. Minutes of the Executive Committee of the Board of Home Missions of the United Evangelical Lutheran Church, March 15, 1955.

————. Minutes of the Executive Committee of the Board of Home Missions of the United Evangelical Lutheran Church, October 26, 1956.

————. Minutes of the Executive Committee of the Board of Home Missions of the United Evangelical Lutheran Church, January 10, 1957.

————. Minutes of the Executive Committee of the Board of Home Missions of the United Evangelical Lutheran Church, February 24, 1959.

Chinese Ministry Conference. Constitution of the Chinese Ministry Conference of the Lutheran Church—Missouri Synod, April 1998.

————. Minutes from the Chinese Ministry Conference of North America. May 18, 1992. LCMS.

————. Minutes of the Chinese Ministry Conference Annual Meeting. May 6-8, 1999. LCMS.

————. Notes and Minutes of the Chinese Ministry Conference, Officer Telephone Conference. LCMS, October 17, 1997.

Chuck, James. *An Exploratory Study of the Growth of Protestant Chinese Churches in San Francisco, 1950-1992.* 1992.

Clergy of The American Lutheran Church Biographical Record, Code No. B-0208.

Commission for Multicultural Ministries. Report on Asian Ministry, Chicago: Commission for Multicultural Ministries, ELCA, June 1993.

Division of American Missions. Minutes of the Division of American Missions, National Lutheran Council, 1954 and 1955.

ELCA. *1988 Directory of the Evangelical Lutheran Church of America Pastors.* Minneapolis: Augsburg Fortress, 1988.

The Evangelical Lutheran Synod of California. Proceedings of the Forty-Sixth Annual Convention of the Evangelical Lutheran Synod of California, May 11-13, 1937. [*Note: the Evangelical Lutheran Synod of California, The Evangelical Lutheran Synod of the Pacific Southwest, and the Evangelical Synod of the Pacific Southwest are one and the same synod. Later these names were changed to Pacific Southwest Synod.*]

————. Proceedings of the Forty-Ninth Annual Convention of the Evangelical Lutheran Synod of California, April 23-25, 1940.

————. Proceedings of the Fiftieth Annual Convention of the Evangelical Lutheran Synod of California, May 8-12, 1941.

————. Proceedings of the Fifty-First Annual Convention of the Evangelical Lutheran Synod of California, April 28-30, 1942.

————. Proceedings of the Fifty-Second Annual Convention of the Evangelical Lutheran Synod of California, May 10-13, 1943.

————. Proceedings of the Fifty-Third Annual Convention of the Evangelical Lutheran Synod of California, May 1-4, 1944.

————. Proceedings of the Fifty-Seventh Annual Convention of the Evangelical Lutheran Synod of California, January 26-29, 1948.

The Evangelical Lutheran Synod of the Pacific Southwest. Proceedings of the Sixty-Third Annual Convention of the Evangelical Lutheran Synod of the Pacific Southwest, February 1–4, 1954.

The Evangelical Synod of the Pacific Southwest. Proceedings of the Sixty-Fourth Annual Convention of the Evangelical Lutheran Synod of the Pacific Southwest, January 24-27, 1955.

The Evangelical Lutheran Synod of the Pacific Southwest. Proceedings of the Sixty-fifth Annual Convention of the Evangelical Lutheran Synod of the Pacific Southwest, May 7-10, 1956.

The Evangelical Lutheran Synod of the Pacific Southwest. Proceedings of the Sixty-sixth Annual Convention of the Evangelical Lutheran Synod of the Pacific Southwest, May 13-16, 1957.

The Evangelical Lutheran Synod of the Pacific Southwest. Proceedings of the Sixty-seventh Annual Convention of the Evangelical Lutheran Synod of the Pacific Southwest, May 13-15, 1958.

The Evangelical Synod of the Pacific Southwest. Proceedings of the Sixty-eighth Annual Convention of the Evangelical Synod of the Pacific Southwest, May 19-21, 1959.

The Evangelical Synod of the Pacific Southwest. Proceedings of the Sixty-ninth Annual Convention of the Evangelical Synod of the Pacific Southwest, May 9-12, 1960.

"Gathering of Japanese Ministry Leaders." The Lutheran Church—Missouri Synod. September 21-22, 1999.

Holt, Wilbert. "Brief History of Our Speaker—Rev. Wilbert Holt." An unpublished paper.

"An Inventory of the Lutheran Church in America: Race Relations." New York: LCA, DMNA, 1976.

Korean Ministry Conference. Constitution of the Korean Ministry Conference of The Lutheran Church—Missouri Synod. n.d.

Lutheran Church of the Holy Spirit, 10th Anniversary 1964-1974. San Francisco.

LCMS. Minutes of the Korean Ministry Conference. June 26-27, 1998. LCMS.

LCMS. Minutes and Notes of the Chinese Ministry Conference Task Force and North America Mission Leaders' Conference. January 10-20, 1996. LCMS.

LCMS. "Mission Blueprint for the Nineties: Summary." St. Louis: Concordia Publishing House, n.d.

Lutheran Hour Ministry. "LHM—Japanese Ministry in the USA: Congregational Evangelism Project Approach—June 2000." Lutheran Hour Ministry.

Moldenhauer, Paul. "Notes from the First Meeting of Those Doing Ministry with Japanese in the United States." September 21-22, 2000. LCMS.

National Coalition for Redress and Reparation. The Japanese American Incarceration: A Case for Redress. Fourth edition. National Coalition for Redress and Reparation, June 1981.

North Carolina and Tennessee Synods. Life Sketches of Lutheran Ministers of North Carolina and Tennessee Synods, 1773-1965. n.d.

Osawa, Shozo. "Greetings and My Profile." n.d.

The Pacific District. Report of the Thirty-Seventh Annual Convention of the Pacific District of the United Danish Evangelical Lutheran Church in America, October 22-26, 1941.

————. Report of the Thirty-Eighth Annual Convention of the Pacific District of the United Danish Lutheran Church in America, October 21-15, 1942.

————. Report of the Forty-Third Annual Convention of the Pacific District of the United Evangelical Lutheran Church, October 22-29, 1947.

————. Report of the Forty-Eighth Annual Convention of the Pacific District of the United Evangelical Lutheran Church, November 6-9, 1952.

————. Report of the Fifty-Third Annual Convention of the Pacific District of the United Evangelical Lutheran Church, October 17-20, 1957.

The Pacific Missionary Newsletter. Vol. 1, No. 1, (January-February 1978). LCMS.

The Pacific Southwest Synod. Minutes of the Fourth Annual Convention of the Pacific Southwest Synod of the Lutheran Church in America, June 1-4, 1965.

————. Minutes of the Fifth Annual Convention of the Pacific Southwest Synod of the Lutheran Church in America, May 16-19, 1966.

"Partnership in Mission: The Evangelical Lutheran Church of Hong Kong and The American Lutheran Church." June 17, 1981.

"Pastor Osawa's Report: Japanese Mission Society Meeting, St. Louis, MO." June 20-21, 2000. LCMS.

"Race Relations." The Lutheran Church in America, July 1964.

"Racism in the Church," A Statement of the Seventh General Convention of The America Lutheran Church, October 14, 1974.

Rajashekar, Paul, Lily R. Wu, and Pongsak Limthongvirtn, eds. *Asian Lutheranism—Which Way?* Bangkok: Prachoomthong Printing Group Co., Lit., 2000.

South Pacific District. Official Report and Minutes, Fourteenth Annual Convention, South Pacific District, The American Lutheran Church, May 16-18, 1974.

————. Official Report and Minutes, Seventeenth Annual Convention, The American Lutheran Church, South Pacific District, May 12-14, 1977.

————. Official Report and Minutes, Eighteenth Annual Convention, The American Lutheran Church, South Pacific District, April 27-29, 1978.

————. Official Report and Minutes, Nineteenth Annual Convention, The American Lutheran Church, South Pacific District, May 31-June 2, 1979.

————. Official Reports and Minutes, Twentieth Annual Convention, The American Lutheran Church, South Pacific District, May 8-10, 1980.

————. Official Reports and Minutes, Twenty-First Annual Convention, The American Lutheran Church, South Pacific District, April 30-May 2, 1981.

————. Official Reports and Minutes, Twenty-Second Annual Convention, The American Lutheran Church, South Pacific District, May 20-22, 1982.

————. Official Reports and Minutes, Twenty-Third Annual Convention, The American Lutheran Church, South Pacific District, June 16-18, 1983.

————. Official Reports and Minutes, Twenty-Fourth Annual Convention, The American Lutheran Church, South Pacific District, May 3-6, 1984.

————. Official Reports and Minutes, Twenty-Fifth Annual Convention, The American Lutheran Church, South Pacific District, April 26-28, 1985.

————. Official Reports and Minutes, Twenty-Sixth Annual Convention, The American Lutheran Church, South Pacific District, April 25-27, 1986.

True Light Lutheran Church, 25th Anniversary, 1936-1961. New York.

True Light Lutheran Church, 40th Anniversary, 1936-1976. New York.

True Light Lutheran Church, 50th Anniversary, 1936-1986. New York.

ULCA. Minutes of the Tenth Biennial Convention of The United Lutheran Church in America, October 14-21, 1936. Philadelphia: The United Lutheran Church Publication House, n.d.

————. Minutes of the Eleventh Biennial Convention of The United Lutheran Church in America, October 5-12, 1938. Philadelphia: The United Lutheran Church Publication House, n.d.

————. Minutes of the Twelfth Biennial Convention of The United Lutheran Church in America, October 9-16, 1940. Philadelphia: The United Lutheran Church Publication House, n.d.

————. Minutes of the Thirteenth Biennial Convention of The United Lutheran Church in America, October 14-21, 1942. Philadelphia: The United Lutheran Publication House, n.d.

————. Minutes of the Fourteenth Biennial Convention of The United Lutheran Church in America, October 11-17, 1944. Philadelphia: The United Lutheran Church Publication House, n.d.

————. Minutes of the Sixteenth Biennial Convention of The United Lutheran Church in America, October 6-14, 1948. Philadelphia: The United Lutheran Church Publication, n.d.

————. Minutes of the Eighteenth Biennial Convention, October 8-15, 1952, The United Lutheran Church in America. Philadelphia: The United Lutheran Church Publication House, n.d.

————. Minutes of The United Lutheran Church in America, Nineteenth Biennial Convention, October 6-13, 1954. Philadelphia: The United Lutheran Church Publication House, n.d.

————. Minutes of The United Lutheran Church in America, Twentieth Biennial Convention, October 10-17, 1956. Philadelphia: The United Lutheran Church Publication House, n.d.

————. "News Service." The United Lutheran Church in America, August 14; n.y.

The Vietnamese Lutheran Task Force. Vietnamese Lutheran Task Force Strategy Statement, October 11, 1996. LCMS.

The Western Canada Synod. The Western Canada Lutheran (August-September 1974).

Wing Jean, ed. The Biography of Our Miss Mary E. Banta. New York: True Light Lutheran Church, 1954.

Wu, Lily R., ed. Catching a Star: Transcultural Reflections on a Church for All People. Unpublished proceedings of the Transcultural Seminar, LCA, 1981.

LETTERS, PAPERS, AND DOCUMENTS

Letters of Charles Matsumoto. 2000.
Letters of Ditlev Cotthard Monrad Bach. 1955-1957.
Letters of Donald Moorman. 2000.
Letters of Pongsak Limthongviratn. 1992, 1993, 1998-2000.
Letters of S. Samuel Ujiie. 1954-1956, 1959, 1960, 1963, 1964.
Letters of Wonnor Yee. 2000.
Letters, documents, and papers of Edmond Yee. 1977-1989, 1991-2000.
Letters and papers of Fern Lee Hagedorn. 1982, 1986, 1995, 1996, 1999, 2000.
Letters and papers of Fred Rajan. 1992-1996, 1998-2000.
Letters and papers of James Moy. 1980, 1998-2000.
Letters and papers of Lily Wu. 1985, 1987, 1990, 1992, 1994-2000.
Letters and papers of Paul T. Nakamura. 1953-1955, 1957, 1992, 1998-2000.
Letters and papers of Robert J. Scudieri. 1989, 1991, 1992, 1996-2000.
Letters and papers of Theodore Iverson. 1977-1980, 1982, 1999.
Letters and papers of Toshio Okamoto. 1991, 1999.
Papers of William E. Wong. 1990-1996.

YEARBOOKS

The 1965 Lutheran Annual. St. Louis: Concordia Publishing House, 1964.
The 1966 Lutheran Annual. St. Louis: Concordia Publishing House, 1965.
1972 Immigration Statistics Canada. Ottawa: Information Canada, 1974.
1973 Immigration Statistics Canada. Ottawa: Information Canada, 1975.
1974 Immigration Statistics Canada. Ottawa: Information Canada, 1975.
1975 Immigration Statistics Canada. Ottawa: Information Canada, 1976.
1976 Immigration Statistics Canada. Ottawa: Information Canada, 1977.
Immigration Policy Branch. *Immigration to British Columbia: Facts and Figures, May1991.* Victoria, BC: Immigration Policy Branch, Ministry of Provincial Secretary and Ministry Responsible for Multiculturalism and Immigration.
Yearbook—44th Annual Convention of the United Evangelical Lutheran Church, June 19-24, 1940. Blair: Lutheran Publishing House, n.d.
Yearbook—45th Annual Convention of the United Evangelical Lutheran Church, June 10-15, 1941. Blair: Lutheran Publishing House, n.d.
Yearbook—46th Annual Convention of the United Evangelical Lutheran Church, June 9-14, 1942. Blair: Lutheran Publishing House, n.d.
Yearbook—47th Annual Convention of the United Evangelical Lutheran Church, June 1-6, 1943. Blair: Lutheran Publishing House, n.d.
Yearbook—48th Annual Convention of the United Evangelical Lutheran Church, June 6-11, 1944. Blair: Lutheran Publishing House, n.d.
Yearbook—49th Annual Convention of the United Evangelical Lutheran Church, June 19-24, 1945. Blair: Lutheran Publishing House, n.d.
Yearbook—50th Annual Convention of the United Evangelical Lutheran Church, June 18-23, 1946. Blair: Lutheran Publishing House, n.d.
Yearbook—51st Annual Convention of the United Evangelical Lutheran Church, June 24-29, 1947. Blair: Lutheran Publishing House, n.d.
Yearbook—52nd Annual Convention of the United Evangelical Lutheran Church, June 15-20, 1948. Blair: Lutheran Publishing House, n.d.
Yearbook—53rd Annual Convention of the United Evangelical Lutheran Church, June 21-26, 1949. Blair: Lutheran Publishing House, n.d.
Yearbook—54th Annual Convention of the United Evangelical Lutheran Church, June 13-18, 1950. Blair: Lutheran Publishing House, n.d.
Yearbook—55th Annual Convention of the United Evangelical Lutheran Church, June 19-24, 1951. Blair: Lutheran Publishing House, n.d.
Yearbook—56th Annual Convention of the United Evangelical Lutheran Church, June 17-22, 1952. Blair: Lutheran Publishing House, n.d.
Yearbook—57th Annual Convention of the United Evangelical Lutheran Church, June 16-21, 1953. Blair: Lutheran Publishing House, n.d.
Yearbook—58th Annual Convention of the United Evangelical Lutheran Church, June 15-20, 1954. Blair: Lutheran Publishing House, n.d.
Yearbook—59th Annual Convention of the United Evangelical Lutheran Church, June 21-26, 1955. Blair: Lutheran Publishing House, n.d.
Yearbook—60th Annual Convention of the United Evangelical Lutheran Church, June 19-24, 1956. Blair: Lutheran Publishing House, n.d.
Yearbook—61st Annual Convention of the United Evangelical Lutheran Church, June 13-18, 1957. Blair: Lutheran Publishing House, n.d.
Yearbook—62nd Annual Convention of the United Evangelical Lutheran Church, June 19-24, 1958. Blair: Lutheran Publishing House, n.d.
Yearbook—63rd Annual Convention of the United Evangelical Lutheran Church, June 18-23, 1959. Blair: Lutheran Publishing House, n.d.

INDEX

ABOUT THE AUTHOR

Edmond Yee was born on January 11, 1938, in Taishan District, Guangdong Province, China, into a well-to-do family. His father immigrated to the United States as a teenager and served in the U.S. Army during World War I. Like many immigrants from China, his father left his family behind in the old country. By the time Yee was born, his father had already returned to America to avoid the impending spread of war into Southern China. His mother and extended family raised him.

World War II deprived Yee an opportunity to attend school, but his mother taught him at home. His elder brother impressed upon him the significance of the Confucian scriptures and transmitted rudimentary understanding of the same. After the war, Yee was enrolled at the village elementary school where he accumulated an impressive record of truancy. Nevertheless, he also had shown a measure of intellectual curiosity and capacity.

In 1950 at the age of 13, Yee left China with his elder brother for Hong Kong where they stayed until 1958. A change in family fortune deprived Yee an opportunity to attend school, but his thirst for knowledge led him to spend time reading in bookstores and occasionally attending night school as often as his income allowed. By the time Yee arrived in Hong Kong most Lutheran missionaries had left China. A few remained in Hong Kong and eventually gave birth to the Evangelical Lutheran Church of Hong Kong. One of the mission stations was not far from where Yee lived. A friend introduced him to the mission so that he could read the books there. Before long Yee became involved with the youth group, choir, and more. He was baptized at age 18 and became a member of the North Point Lutheran Church (now Grace Lutheran Church).

Two years after his baptism, Yee arrived in Salt Lake City, Utah, to be united with his father. In the summer of 1958 he began working at the Canton Café, a restaurant owned by his uncle, in Ogden. That fall he enrolled in a business college in the city. The Asian community in Ogden was small and voiceless, and the majority worked in the service sector. Yee was deeply impacted by the situation.

During that year Yee felt the call to ministry. He entered Midland

Lutheran College, Fremont, Nebraska, in the fall of 1959 as an "adult special." This category of admission was reserved for persons without a high
school diploma or with little formal education. Yee received the B.A. degree
from Midland; the M.Div. degree from Pacific Lutheran Theological
Seminary (PLTS), Berkeley; the M.A. degree from San Francisco State
University; and the C.Phil. and   Ph.D. degrees from the University of
California at Berkeley in the field of traditional Chinese literature and intellectual history.

In the ELCA today, as well as among its predecessor church bodies,
Yee plays an active role in ethnic ministries, cross-cultural awareness, multicultural mission efforts, Asian and Pacific Islander theology, and theological education. Dr. Yee was a charter member of Our Savior's Lutheran
Church, Salt Lake City, and has served as pastor of a two-point parish in
Evansberg and Wildwood, Alberta, Canada. In January 1978, Yee began service to the wider church as DMNA resource developer-consultant for Asian
ministry and as adjunct professor at PLTS.

Dr. Yee currently serves as director of Theological Education for
Emerging Ministries, since 1989, and as Professor of Asian Studies at PLTS.
He teaches classical Chinese, Confucian thought, East Asian religions, and
multicultural studies. He is a member of the core doctoral faculty for the
Graduate Theological Union, a Berkeley-based consortium, and has served
as chair of the Asia/Pacific Working Group. A recognized academic and
church leader, he is a four-time recipient of the GTU's Newhall Fellowship
and the 1992 recipient of the PLTS Outstanding Alumnus in Specialized
Ministry Award. In 1994, Yee was a visiting scholar at the Chinese University
of Hong Kong, and in 1997 he was an ELCA delegate to the Ninth Assembly
of the Lutheran World Federation, held in Hong Kong.